Wisdom With
Understanding
is Better
Than Rubies

Lurine Karon Greenberg
Fine Arts Collection

Yale Broadway Masters

GEORGE GERSHWIN

LARRY STARR

With a Foreword by Geoffrey Block, General Editor

Yale UNIVERSITY PRESS NEW HAVEN & LONDON

Yale University Press books may be purchased in quantity for educational, business, or
promotional use. For information, please e-mail sales.press@yale.edu (U.S. office)
or sales@yaleup.co.uk (U.K. office).

Set in Electra Roman type by Tseng Information Systems, Inc.
Printed in the United States of America.

Library of Congress Cataloging-in-Publication Data
Starr, Larry.
George Gershwin / Larry Starr.
p. cm. — (Yale Broadway masters)
Includes bibliographical references and index.
ISBN 978-0-300-11184-2 (hardcover : alk. paper)
1. Gershwin, George, 1898–1937. 2. Composers—
United States—Biography. I. Title.
ML410.G288S73 2011
780.92—dc22
[B]
2010018384

A catalogue record for this book is available from the British Library.

This paper meets the requirements of ANSI/NISO Z39.48-1992 (Permanence of Paper).

10 9 8 7 6 5 4 3 2 1

This book is dedicated to my father,
and to the memory of my mother.

Contents

Foreword

FOR MORE THAN THREE DECADES, IN PROVOCATIVE AND PERCEP-
tive books and essays, Larry Starr has been enlightening readers about
American composers as diverse as Charles Ives, Aaron Copland, and
George Gershwin. He has also written an acclaimed text on American popular
music. In *George Gershwin*, Starr surveys the genre on which Gershwin, one
of our most revered composers, spent most of his time and attention during
the less than two decades of a meteoric career that vanished like a comet in
1937, when the young composer died of a brain tumor. In an early chapter
Starr discusses the quality and diversity of Gershwin's musical language and
the consequent critical difficulties in isolating a particular "Gershwin style."
Gershwin's compositional versatility was so fecund that he could compose a
show like *Primrose* for British audiences in a style (or more accurately styles)
vastly different from the same year's jazzy Broadway hit, *Lady, Be Good!*
Readers will learn the context as well as the musical substance of Gershwin's
show tunes, how they fit into the plot when they do (and what is gained as
well as lost when they do not). They will hear old songs anew, by learning how
Gershwin used songs to capture musically the wit and emotional range of
his characters, as well as the droll snap of the lyrics by his equally individual
brother, Ira. Starr enriches our appreciation of Gershwin's stunning, seemingly showstopping songs by explaining how music can convey satire (especially pronounced in *Of Thee I Sing*), and how music can sustain a psycho-
logical trajectory over an evening, while still offering truly memorable tunes
full of grace and joy.

Starr has been in the forefront of Gershwin studies, and in this book he offers new approaches to a central but comparatively little-known aspect of the composer's career, the Broadway musicals. His conclusions depart significantly from the ideas of an earlier Gershwin advocate, Leonard Bernstein, who was fundamentally unsympathetic to the 1920s versions of this genre. In his 1956 televised lecture on American musical comedy (published in *The Joy of Music* in 1959), for example, Bernstein shared with his national audience his "sneaky feeling" that George and Ira Gershwin's "lovely song called 'Someone to Watch Over Me'" from their 1926 hit *Oh, Kay!* "was written *before* the book was written, instead of having evolved logically out of the book, because it doesn't *quite* fit the situation in which it was sung." After offering a plausible argument concerning the incongruities between the lyrics of the song and its dramatic situation, Bernstein concludes that, since "the lyrics are so distinguished and fresh, and the tune is a knockout," it doesn't matter that the character played by Gertrude Lawrence seems to have forgotten that she has already met (onstage, that is) the person she imagines meeting someday, according to the song's lyrics. Given that Bernstein regarded the "mad, gay 1920s" as "the adolescence of our musical comedy," the question of whether a great popular song such as "Someone to Watch Over Me" perfectly fit the show's story could be flippantly answered with "What's the diff?" (the '20s equivalent of "So what?").

Bernstein did not know that, in its original first-act position in the show, the lyrics of this song did evolve logically out of its book, and that the infelicity occurred when the song was moved during the Philadelphia tryouts to act 2 but with the lyrics unchanged. He was correct in pointing out that the perceived quality of the song made it seem unnecessary for Ira to adjust his lyrics for the song's new dramatic situation. And although Bernstein may not have known that many musicals of the 1920s, the decade in which Gershwin composed most of his shows, contain many examples of careful integration of story with songs, he was aware of some songs that fell outside this category, such as the "mammy song," "Clap Yo' Hands," also from *Oh, Kay!* — Bernstein's "favorite example of nonintegration," in which the characters significantly demonstrate their awareness of this song as a dramatic non sequitur (if not its racial condescension).

The truth of the matter is that most of us still don't really know how Gershwin's many song hits were used in shows such as *Lady, Be Good! Girl Crazy, Oh, Kay!* and *Of Thee I Sing*, four shows engagingly explored in this volume, much less how the less well-known and less autonomous songs were intricately entwined with their plots. By the time readers finish Starr's chapter on *Lady, Be Good!* for example, Gershwin's Broadway debut with Ira, they will have their suspicions confirmed that the show's still-familiar title song "gloriously flaunts its irrelevance." More surprisingly, readers will also learn that the show's other seemingly gratuitous hit, "Fascinating Rhythm," which enters as a specialty number for Ukulele Ike (Cliff Edwards), perhaps best remembered today as the voice of Walt Disney's Jiminy Cricket in the animated film *Pinocchio*, gradually evolves into an integral component of the show and in the end succeeds in "conveying information essential to the resolution of the plot."

In an imaginary conversation titled "Why Don't You Run Upstairs and Write a Nice Gershwin Tune?" also published in *The Joy of Music*, Bernstein espoused the then prevailing view that Gershwin's concert works were as nonintegrated as the shows. *Rhapsody in Blue*, for example, was "a string of separate paragraphs [i.e., tunes] stuck together—with a thin paste of flour and water" and "not a composition at all." Starr's essay, "Musings on 'Nice Gershwin Tunes'" published in *The Gershwin Style* (1999), alludes to Bernstein's conversation in its title and in the course of the essay persuasively shows striking differences between what the composer himself considered a nice Gershwin tune and the substantially different melodies he created for his concert works. In the present volume Starr further develops his compelling brief on behalf of Gershwin as a free-ranging and technically mature composer, rather than a genius songsmith laying autonomous golden song eggs in a cubicle.

After an interlude on the concert music, in which he suggests ways these works benefited from the composer's immersion in show music, Starr revisits *Of Thee I Sing*, the greatest hit book musical of the 1930s and the first musical to win the Pulitzer Prize. He argues passionately and persuasively that its recent neglect is unjustified. The final chapters offer a fresh look at Gershwin's final work for Broadway, the much-studied *Porgy and Bess*, and Gershwin's fleeting but important grand finale in Hollywood, in particular the Fred Astaire and Ginger Rogers classic, *Shall We Dance*. Just as he succeeds in putting the songs back where they started on the Broadway stage, Starr places the canonic opera *Porgy and Bess* and the film scores, as well as the more familiar and increasingly respected concert works, within the larger context of Gershwin's astonishingly productive but relatively little explored career as a Broadway composer.

Starr's careful but bold reevaluations fundamentally revise our understanding and appreciation of Gershwin's popular music for the stage (and of the works as a whole). Given the limelight Gershwin now justly, if posthumously, draws as a doyen of twentieth-century concert music and opera, this book is as timely as it is important. I think Bernstein would have enjoyed this book, and I think you will too.

GEOFFREY BLOCK
General Editor

Preface

M Y PERSONAL EXPERIENCE WITH GERSHWIN'S MUSIC BEGAN so early in my childhood that I cannot recall a time when I was unaware of it. Among the 78 rpm records owned by my parents were the two albums of original cast recordings of *Porgy and Bess*. Although I knew nothing about the story of the opera, the music and even the words (although I couldn't understand a good many of them at the time) must have been utterly compelling to my inchoate musical consciousness. I played the records over and over, to the extent that I can still clearly remember—nearly six decades after all the records got either broken or lost—the colors of the labels and the physiognomy of the grooves on every side of every disc.

My first "professional" experience with Gershwin's music, at age sixteen, was of a decisively different nature. Incoming freshmen wishing to major in music at Queens College, CUNY, were required to demonstrate their keyboard skills in auditions before a faculty member. Listening at the door, I was able to hear the student who preceded me perform the second of Gershwin's preludes. When he was finished, the professor said "Well, that's very nice. Now, can you play something serious?" Thus was I introduced, right at the outset of my college career, to the academic establishment's disdain for Gershwin—an all-too-typical attitude at the time. (Fortunately for me, I had prepared a "serious" twentieth-century piano work, by Bartók! Evidently the Hungarian master's high-spirited tribute to European folk styles in his "Six Dances in Bulgarian Rhythm" was presumed a more rarefied aesthetic achievement than Gershwin's eloquent tribute to the American blues song.) I kept my cherished memories of *Porgy and Bess* tightly closeted for many years thereafter. So reluctant was I to have those memories disturbed that I resisted attending a performance of the Houston Grand Opera's epoch-making revival of *Porgy and Bess* (1976) in New York until its unprecedented six-month run on Broadway was nearly over. I feared that the received wisdom—that *Porgy* was an overblown musical with an embarrassing libretto, stereotyped characters, clumsy recitative, and uninspired orchestration—would prove correct.

The received wisdom proved anything but correct, and the revelatory experience of Gershwin's opera on the stage kindled my desire, as a teacher and a scholar, to play a role in challenging the erroneous and uninformed attitudes and impressions that still prevailed among academics and other intellectuals. Not surprisingly, given my background and profession, this campaign took the form of courses and articles that made the case for Gershwin as an "art music" composer. I started with a defense of *Porgy and Bess* as a brilliant and successful opera. Then I turned to the composer's concert music, arguing that it was innovative and well-crafted, finally embracing Gershwin's classic songs as excellent examples of American art song—an approach that works well for much of the "great American songbook" from Gershwin's era. With the obvious exception of *Porgy and Bess*, the shows for which Gershwin's songs were originally written played no part in my study of this repertoire. Those shows were long forgotten, and the songs had long since assumed a vigorous life totally independent of their origins.

When Geoffrey Block, general editor for the Yale Broadway Masters series, approached me to write the volume on Gershwin, I was naturally flattered and tempted. At the same time, I was presented with a problem. My own study of Gershwin's music had assumed a context totally divorced from the Great White Way. What would happen if Gershwin's oeuvre were to be conceptually and practically resituated with Broadway squarely at the center? Could such an approach yield any fresh insights into a body of work so widely known and, happily, now so widely celebrated?

My discovery, embodied in the present volume, is that returning Gershwin to Broadway, far from proving anachronistic from a twenty-first-century standpoint, actually opens new avenues of approach to his entire musical output. Repositioning Gershwin as a "Broadway master" offers novel and provocative perspectives. First of all, it prompts a reconsideration of his songs in terms of the shows for which they were intended and the performers for whom they were conceived. This in turn refreshes and even revises our understanding of those songs, in terms of both composition and performance. Turning to Gershwin's concert music, a Broadway perspective invites recognition of the composer's telling and virtuosic fusion of American popular idioms with the forms and stylistic elements of European art music. Rather than simply ignoring the obvious elements of Broadway style clearly present in works such as *Rhapsody in Blue* or *An American in Paris*—or worse, feeling that these elements should occasion excuses or embarrassment—the Broadway perspective encourages us to celebrate the remarkable way in which Gershwin brought the American vernacular into the concert hall. Viewed in this light, the concert works become themselves the productions of a masterful showman, who was developing through his Broadway musicals an increasingly sophisticated sense of how to hold an audience's attention successfully over an extended time span.

Finally, *Porgy and Bess* itself was originally, and with Gershwin's own blessing, a "Broadway opera," and much about the work is illuminated by acknowledging its pedigree. *Porgy and Bess* synthesized everything Gershwin had learned about music theater during his years as a Broadway composer with the mastery of orchestration and large-scale forms he had developed through his experience with concert music, and the work has ended up enriching both Broadway and the opera house. The culminating insight yielded by a Broadway perspective is a realization of the extent to which Gershwin's oeuvre, for all its wondrous diversity, may be understood as the expression of an integrated creative consciousness.

My book follows the general principles and organizational strategies that have guided the Yale Broadway Masters series. It has been written with general readers, as well as students and scholars, in mind, and my hope is that it will appeal to the nonspecialist, while also having something to offer highly trained musicians and music theater aficionados. An opening chapter of biographical import is followed by one on Gershwin's musical style. A close look at three representative shows forms the core of the book: *Lady, Be Good!* (1924), *Of Thee I Sing* (1931), and of course *Porgy and Bess* (1935). These shows provide ample points of reference to facilitate understanding the development of Gershwin's approach to music theater and to enhance appreciation of his accomplishments. The detailed discussions of the three shows offer case studies of how scripts, lyrics, and music function—sometimes independently, but most often interdependently—to achieve particular theatrical results. Analyses of the songs place the music within the context of the shows, with the intent of shedding fresh light on both. Gershwin wrote his songs to fill specific theatrical needs, and an awareness of this contributes a perspective that otherwise would remain unperceived, a perspective that surely encourages further understanding and appreciation of these songs.

A succinct chapter is devoted to shining a Broadway spotlight on Gershwin's concert music, with the goal of illuminating that which Gershwin brought from the Great White Way to Carnegie Hall (and beyond). Since Gershwin concluded his all-too-brief career in Hollywood, a final chapter considers a representative film musical (*Shall We Dance*, 1937) in the light of Gershwin's Broadway years, along with aspects of the composer's remarkable legacy.

It should be apparent that this book is a highly selective critical study and does not attempt a comprehensive survey of any kind; this is in keeping with the scope and intent of most volumes in the Yale Broadway Masters series. I hope that my treatment of individual songs and shows will suggest productive avenues of approach to Gershwin works not discussed here, and that the Broadway perspective provides a stimulus to further productive thought about Gershwin's career and legacy that will venture well beyond what is specifically addressed in these pages.

Gershwin himself, like all of his American contemporaries working in music theater, assumed that Broadway shows were transient phenomena of little likely enduring interest. This assumption reflected not the quality of effort that Gershwin (and the best of his Broadway colleagues) invested in these shows, merely the commercial and cultural realities of the time. While Gershwin staked his permanent reputation on his concert works and his opera, he lived just long enough to discover that his theater songs were outlasting his expectations of their ephemerality. Arguably his publication of *George Gershwin's Song-book* in 1932, presenting eighteen songs written between 1919 and 1931 both in original sheet music versions and in elaborate settings for piano solo, constituted the composer's acknowledgment of the emerging "classic" status of these works. It follows then that perhaps Gershwin would not have been too surprised to learn that later admirers of his music might eventually return to his shows in an effort to enrich and deepen their understanding of his complete oeuvre.

Acknowledgments

ANY PEOPLE HAVE ASSISTED ME INVALUABLY IN THE CONCEP-
tion and preparation of this book. I must begin by thanking my
parents, who introduced me at an early age to the joys of music
and specifically to the marvels of Gershwin. In many respects this volume
represents the fruit of the encouragement they gave their young child to in-
dulge his obvious fascination with the records they brought into the family
home, selflessly tolerating his obsessive replaying of them long after they
were permanently etched in his memory. Like all such gifts, this one from
my parents was given unstintingly, without any thought of reward. The re-
wards have all been mine, and all I have to offer in return to my parents is my
eternal gratitude.

Next I must acknowledge Geoffrey Block, whom I am proud to call my
friend, an individual who gives renewed vitality to that old and now infrequently heard characterization "a gentleman and a scholar." It was Geoffrey,
the series editor for Yale Broadway Masters, who first proposed to me the
undertaking of this project, and who patiently and silently held it in reserve
for me until I finally felt able to say yes. Throughout the period of my work
on this book he has been a remarkably generous source of advice, encouragement, and constructive criticism. Thanks also to Judith Tick for prodding me
gently but convincingly at a well-chosen time to accept Geoffrey's proposal.

I had the benefit of release time from teaching as a Royalty Research
Fund Scholar at the University of Washington to assist me for a period during
the writing of this book, and my institutional home has been supportive of me
in numerous other ways. Graduate students in music history at the University

of Washington have given of their time and efforts in exemplary service as my research assistants; my thanks to Ryan Banagale, Aimee Mell, Vilde Aaslid, Shelley Lawson, and especially to Elizabeth Knighton (who read the entire manuscript in draft and offered numerous helpful suggestions) and to Jacob Cohen (who prepared the musical examples for publication).

Among the scholars who have generously shared their knowledge by responding to numerous queries that arose in the course of my work are Richard Crawford, Howard Pollack, Wayne Shirley, and the late William G. Hyland, who sent me a large box of valuable research material he had acquired in the course of his own work on Gershwin. George J. Ferencz provided helpful information about the orchestrations of Gershwin's shows, and of the recent restorations of those shows. Robert Kimball, artistic advisor for the Ira and Leonore Gershwin Trusts, has assisted me in ways possible only for a person with his connections to the Gershwin family and the Gershwin heritage, and I thank him profoundly for that. Michael Owen, archivist for the Ira and Leonore Gershwin Trusts, lent me his expertise in the process of selecting photographs for the book and was a model of professionalism, friendliness, and thoroughness. Marty Jacobs and Chris Murtha at the Museum of the City of New York also provided much-needed assistance with the illustrations.

At Yale University Press, Jack Borrebach, Keith Condon, Joseph Calamia, and William Frucht were all exceptionally supportive of this project and most generous with practical assistance. Finally, Duke Johns proved the ideal copyeditor for the manuscript by offering appropriate emendations and suggestions for improvement, while always respecting the substance and style of my work, and I remain deeply grateful to him for this.

CHAPTER 1

In Lieu of Biography

Concepts and Images from a Short but Full Life

IT IS CUSTOMARY TO BEGIN A BOOK OF THIS NATURE WITH A BIO-
graphical sketch of its subject. In the case of George Gershwin (1898–
1937), such an enterprise might seem unnecessary, since he has become
an iconic figure to the extent that the pivotal facts and the important works
are well known to most people with even a passing interest in American
culture. I suspect many readers would find it redundant, for example, to
have presented to them yet again the story of the unprecedented and tri-
umphant debut of *Rhapsody in Blue* at Paul Whiteman's famous "Experiment in Modern Music" concert in 1924. Gershwin's creation of the unique
"American folk opera" *Porgy and Bess* in the mid-1930s and its later conquest
of opera houses around the world forms the stuff of another oft-repeated nar-
rative. And is there anyone who needs to be reminded about Gershwin's out-
pouring of great Broadway songs that have long since become established
standards for everyone—from nightclub singers to jazz instrumentalists to
aging rock stars? A new Gershwin biography seems to appear every four or
five years with remarkable regularity, and the majority of these books often
do little more than spin individual variations on what are by now well-worn
themes.

The basic facts about Gershwin's life—the facts that are constantly repeated in all accounts of any substance—stem from a handful of sources, beginning naturally enough with Isaac Goldberg's vivid 1931 biography *George
Gershwin: A Study in American Music*, written with the composer's active
participation. Next was the commemorative volume *George Gershwin*,
edited and designed by Merle Armitage and published in 1938, the year fol-

lowing Gershwin's untimely death at age thirty-eight from a brain tumor. Goldberg planned to complete his biography, but died himself in 1938. Eventually in 1958 a new edition of Goldberg's book was published, supplemented by Edith Garson. The same year brought to light an important dual biography of George and Ira Gershwin, *The Gershwin Years* by Edward Jablonski and Lawrence D. Stewart. Meanwhile, Oscar Levant's *A Smattering of Ignorance*, with its sizable section on "My Life: Or the Story of George Gershwin," had appeared in 1940 and added considerably to the body of Gershwin lore. Other important reminiscences by those who knew Gershwin, along with excerpts from the composer's correspondence and other primary documents, were eventually collected in *The Gershwins* by Robert Kimball and Alfred Simon, which was published in 1973 on the seventy-fifth anniversary of George Gershwin's birth. Although it seems inconceivable, the handful of short but essential articles Gershwin wrote and published about himself and his music have never been collected in a single book. Gregory R. Suriano's *Gershwin in His Time: A Biographical Scrapbook, 1919–1937*, published in 1998, reprints most of them.[1]

The story that emerges from these basic sources may be summarized in a series of brief phrases, each suggestive of a rich phase in a fast-moving, all-too-brief lifetime: the active childhood on the streets of New York City; the piano lessons beginning about age twelve; the departure from high school to become a "piano pounder" at Jerome H. Remick's in Tin Pan Alley; the years of apprenticeship, quickly achieving an initial culmination in the first Broadway musical (*La-La-Lucille!*) and the first hit song ("Swanee"), both from 1919; the remarkable series of successful Broadway shows throughout the 1920s, culminating in Gershwin's biggest success, *Of Thee I Sing*, in 1931; the parallel career as a composer for the concert hall beginning with *Rhapsody in Blue*; the premiere of *Porgy and Bess* in 1935; the departure for Hollywood in 1936 and the work as a film composer cut short by early death. It seems truly a breathless sprint of a career, marked by unprecedented and breathtaking accomplishments, and it comes as no surprise that Gershwin became a legendary figure in American music.

The dominating, persistent presence of Gershwin in American musical culture stands in the starkest contrast, however, to the long-term neglect of Gershwin by American scholars. An anomaly emerges readily from an examination of the abundant Gershwin literature. Not until well over a century after his birth in 1898 was this essential American musician and cultural icon finally honored with a thorough and satisfactory scholarly biography, Howard

Pollack's *George Gershwin: His Life and Work*.[2] Pollack offers an intelligent and remarkably comprehensive summary and synthesis of the available material on Gershwin—old and recent, published and unpublished, celebrated and obscure, reliable and less than reliable. The situation suggests that, far from being simply redundant, attempts to produce significant biographies of Gershwin for the twenty-first century represent contributions to a new, large-scale work in progress. And this inevitably raises an important question: apart from the familiar stories and anecdotes that provide a lively but ultimately spotty portrait, how much do we really know about this American icon? We may see here the manifestation of a paradox. And the concept of paradox itself sheds an illuminating light on central aspects of Gershwin's personality and achievement and on the history of his music's reception.

As the Brooklyn-born son of an immigrant Jewish couple from Russia, Gershwin was an aggressive assimilationist.[3] He desired above all to become a quintessential American and to be regarded, nationally and internationally, as a musical spokesman for his country. Lacking traditional academic training in music and having cut his professional teeth in the commercial hustle-and-bustle of Tin Pan Alley, he sought out the elite world of the classical concert hall and yearned for the approval of its devotees and practitioners. Living in a society and at a time burdened with longstanding and painful issues centering upon race, Gershwin created music in which "white" and "black" influences coexist in evocative but reassuring harmony. It seems no mere accident that the magnum opus of this self-consciously modern, unabashedly urban, wealthy, white, northern assimilationist is a work that celebrates the story of a "backward," segregated, lower-class community of Gullah blacks in Charleston, South Carolina. Perhaps Gershwin's characterization of *Porgy and Bess* as a "folk opera" represented his own attempt to encapsulate in a single memorable phrase the many paradoxes surrounding the work and its creation. *Porgy and Bess* is many things, but in the end it is most essentially a love story. In his opera and in the vast majority of his famous songs, Gershwin set to music enduring expressions of love between men and women in its various stages and manifestations. Yet the composer himself, while linked romantically with a number of women during his lifetime, remained a bachelor who reportedly spoke often to close friends about his desire to marry.

In all of these respects, Gershwin may be viewed fruitfully as an outsider seeking entrance into a milieu or a status that was not intrinsically or readily open to him. His quests for assimilation, for acceptance, for respect and respectability, and for unhampered personal and artistic exchange among those of differing classes, races, ethnic groups, and nationalities—all of these made his journey a particularly American one, and they help account for his legendary status in a culture that lionizes its successful outsiders and individualists.

The appellation "Broadway master" certainly seems apt for Gershwin, and yet it occasions its own set of paradoxes. Broadway was unquestionably the central locus of Gershwin's activity for most of his creative life. This milieu nurtured him both as a man and as a musician, and the bulk of his output consists of musical works presented on Broadway, including nineteen complete shows and one opera. During Gershwin's early years on Tin Pan Alley, Broadway was the focus of the young songwriter's ambitions, for he was convinced that the best music of the day was being written for the musical comedy stage.[4] Yet no sooner did Gershwin become an established presence on Broadway than he started also to move beyond it. It was in 1924, a year that witnessed the Broadway openings of three successful Gershwin shows (*Sweet Little Devil* in January, *George White's Scandals of 1924* in June, and *Lady, Be Good!* in December—and this list doesn't include the successful London show *Primrose*, which opened in September of the same year), that the twenty-five-year-old composer also introduced his acclaimed *Rhapsody in Blue* to the American concert hall (in February). Restlessness is another characteristic that informed Gershwin's life and career; it is a trait that also found expression in the imaginative rhythms of his music.

While Gershwin's Broadway songs have endured spectacularly well, the shows for which they were written just as surely have not, and attempts to revive them have rarely met with any success. Occasionally a "new" Gershwin show may appear on Broadway with a new book fashioned around many of his now-standard songs, such as *Crazy for You* from 1992, but such productions are invariably far from the shows originally conceived by Gershwin and his collaborators. In effect, the music of this "Broadway master" now flourishes basically, and extensively, off Broadway: in clubs and cabarets, in concert settings, on operatic stages, and of course wherever recorded music in many styles is produced, sold, and heard.

Nevertheless, the Gershwin shows are now ripe for reevaluation. We may be sufficiently distant from them in time to see them anew: not merely as examples, among many, of the supposedly uninspired predecessors to the "mature" musicals of the 1940s and 1950s (beginning with Rodgers and Hammerstein's *Oklahoma!*); nor simply as stepping-stones in Gershwin's

own development toward opera in *Porgy and Bess*; but rather as fine representatives in their own right of a distinctive period and style in American musical
theater. And it detracts not at all from the consummate achievement of *Porgy
and Bess* to regard it as the "Broadway opera" that it literally was at the start
of its extraordinary history. Appreciating the Broadway ethos of a song such
as Sportin' Life's "There's a Boat Dat's Leavin' Soon for New York" enhances
our understanding of the broad and diverse expression Gershwin developed
in the opera for his Catfish Row community; the stylistic richness of *Porgy
and Bess* transforms a tiny and insular black neighborhood into a musical
world in microcosm. Given the racial controversies that have swirled around
Porgy and Bess, restoring the opera's Broadway context also demonstrates the
extent to which Gershwin's insistence on an African American (as opposed
to a blackface) cast—a cast drawn, again at Gershwin's insistence, from the
milieus of both Broadway and the concert hall—was significantly progressive
for his time.

Snapshots

Outlining some additional concepts that facilitate appreciation and understanding of Gershwin as a Broadway master will prove a more vivid process
if these concepts are linked to celebrated images from Gershwin's life. Re-
viewing such images will also present important aspects of biography without
necessitating another linear presentation of the familiar life story.

The Piano Comes through the Window
(Gershwin's spontaneous musicality; Gershwin as autodidact)

There are a handful of images that have endured from the recountings of
Gershwin's childhood, images that persist due to their obvious foreshadowing
of the musical career to come: six-year-old George standing outside a penny
arcade on the street, barefoot and in overalls, held spellbound by the sound
of Anton Rubinstein's "Melody in F" emerging from a player piano within;
George in public school, thrilled upon overhearing a performance by school-
mate Maxie Rosenzweig (Max Rosen) of Dvořák's Humoresque no. 7.[5] But
the sole indispensable image is that of an upright piano being hoisted into the
Gershwin family's Manhattan apartment through the window. As the composer told his first biographer, "No sooner had it come through the window
and been backed up against the wall than I was at the keys."[6]

Figure 1.1. George Gershwin at the piano, New York, mid-1920s

It is no exaggeration to characterize this crucial moment as the one when Gershwin assumed what was to be his defining posture: sitting at the piano, amazing those fortunate enough to hear him by demonstrating what seemed to be spontaneous musical gifts. It is only a slight exaggeration to quip that Gershwin rarely rose from the piano again, unless it was absolutely necessary—until, of course, his terrible illness and premature death forced him away from his beloved instrument. Shortly after Gershwin died, Rouben Mamoulian (who as the director of the first production of *Porgy and Bess* in 1935 had come to know the composer well) wrote that "George loved playing the piano for people and would do it at the slightest provocation. At any gathering of friends, if there was a piano in the room, George would play it. I am sure that most of his friends in thinking of George at his best, think of George at the piano. . . . George at the piano was George happy."[7]

The moment of the piano's arrival in the Gershwins' apartment is rich with ironies. Music had played no significant role in the life of the household before this. The piano was introduced not in the expectation that any of the four Gershwin children would have a musical career, but rather as an essential marker of middle-class respectability for this upwardly mobile Jewish family. In fact it was George's older brother, quiet, bookish Ira, for whom piano lessons had been intended, for nobody at that point held out much hope for "bad boy" George. And it is Ira Gershwin who told the story best, as part of his brief reminiscence "My Brother," published the year after George's death:

> It was when we were living on Second Avenue that my mother added a piano to our home. George was about twelve at this time. No sooner had the up-right been lifted through the window to the "front-room" floor than George sat down and played a popular tune of the day. I remember being particularly impressed by his left hand. I had had no idea he could play and found out that despite his rolling skating activities, the kid parties he attended, and the many street games he participated in (with an occasional resultant bloody nose) he had found time to experiment on a player-piano at the home of a friend on Seventh Street.

This paragraph is clinched with a simple sentence that attests both to Ira's characteristic humility and to his gift for colossal understatement: "Although our piano was purchased with my taking lessons in mind, it was decided George might prove the brighter pupil."[8]

The image of Gershwin's keyboard "debut" before his duly surprised family neatly encapsulates pivotal facts and central issues that continued to resound throughout his career and throughout the history of Gershwin reception even to the present day. Most obvious are the facts of Gershwin's seemingly innate musicality and of his abilities as an autodidact. The issues that develop from these facts are also readily apparent. In the absence of any early background in music, from where did Gershwin's musical gifts come and, more important, how far did — or could — they possibly extend? In the absence of any distinguished background as a student (Gershwin left high school before graduating), what powers of intellect did — or could — he bring to his autodidacticism? While nobody has ever questioned his abilities as a pianist, nor the success of his self-education in the rough-and-tumble "school" of popular songwriting, it has often been wondered how — or even whether — a "great" composer for the concert hall or operatic stage could emerge, in the absence of formal academic training, from a background like Gershwin's.

I have framed these issues as questions, questions that have been asked explicitly and implicitly about Gershwin since he first became a major figure on the American music scene in the mid-1920s. And more provocative perhaps than any answers that might be offered is the nature of the questions themselves, with their repetitive emphasis on absences in Gershwin's background and education. It would be equally plausible to construe these "absences" in a positive light, in terms of the possibly beneficial absence of traditional restraints and preconceptions on the development of a native American genius, and in terms of the decisively beneficial presence of the vital New York culture (musical and otherwise) in which Gershwin was immersed and in which he grew to maturity. But the story has rarely been told in this fashion, doubtless owing to the huge inferiority complex (with respect to European high culture) that haunted American intellectuals and artists—especially classical musicians—during Gershwin's lifetime, and whose effects continue to be felt, to some extent, to this day. There was simply no preexisting model for the kind of American composer that Gershwin became; he had to invent himself each step of the way, and it stands to reason that his remarkable success in doing so was met with skepticism and resentment by those personally invested in more traditional musical paths. The composer himself exclaimed to his first biographer, "I am a man without traditions!"—a statement characterized by Goldberg as "a favorite Gershwinism, at once explanation and proclamation."[9]

It seems high time for informed studies of Gershwin to slough off any shadow of defensiveness. There is evidence to substantiate the breadth and depth of Gershwin's gifts and his capabilities and assiduousness in developing them fully. It is naturally impossible to know where musical talent comes from. But it is probably not insignificant that all of George Gershwin's three siblings were also musical: younger brother Arthur tried his own hand at composition, and sister Frances, the "baby" of the family, was a capable singer and dancer, while Ira's own innate musical sense may be attested to by the artistry with which he plied his role as George's favorite lyricist— matching words beautifully to the rhythms and shapes of his brother's melodies. Clearly music was in the blood of the Gershwins. And if none of his siblings approached the heights to which George readily ascended in terms of sheer musical gifts, the question might be counterpoised: how many of George's nonsiblings did, either?

Gershwin's autodidacticism was fueled by a mind of uncommon quality, and not just in the realm of musical intelligence. He was an avid letter writer, and his many missives to friends and family are articulate and informative, qualities abundantly evident as well in the several short articles he completed for formal publication during his lifetime.[10] Gershwin was also an amateur painter of no mean ability. Those who knew him well were impressed by his wide-ranging curiosity and mental acuity. In lieu of pursuing a formal musical education, he gravitated toward private instruction with individual teachers of his own choosing, all the while demonstrating an uncanny ability to surmise who might be helpful to him at a given stage in his musical development.[11]

To suggest that Gershwin was a man of significant intellectual stature is to strongly challenge both the common Gershwin mythology and the false dichotomy so often posed between "natural" talent in the arts and achievement gained through systematic hard work on one's knowledge and craft. Yet Ira Gershwin states outright: "There was rarely a period in his [George's] life when he was not studying."[12] This lends additional heft to his brother's own assertions in the article he prepared for the *New York Sunday World Magazine* in 1930: "Many people say that too much study kills spontaneity in music, but I claim that, although study may kill a small talent, it must develop a big talent. In other words, if study kills a musical endowment, it deserves to be killed. I studied piano for four years, and then harmony. And I shall continue to study for a long time."[13] It should be underlined that Gershwin was already a thirty-one-year-old, world-renowned composer when he wrote this. His studies in composition with Joseph Schillinger still lay ahead of him.

The significance of Gershwin's autodidacticism was captured perfectly and succinctly in a statement by DuBose Heyward, the author of the novel *Porgy* and the librettist for *Porgy and Bess*, who characterized the composer as one "who possessed the faculty of seeing himself quite impersonally and realistically, and who knew exactly what he wanted and where he was going."[14] And this autodidact possessed a clear and essential understanding of the character, extent, and potential of his own gifts and capabilities. As Kay Swift, a remarkable woman who knew Gershwin as man and musician as intimately as anyone ever did, memorably put it: "I think he knew how good he was. He would have been a jackass not to, after all, wouldn't he?"[15]

On the Go
(Gershwin as athlete and dancer; Gershwin as a rhythmic being)

Unfortunately no picture exists of the piano arriving through the window in the Gershwins' apartment. Once Gershwin became famous, however, the typical posed photograph portrayed him at the keyboard. Among the many

Figure 1.2. George Gershwin with his personal trainer, beach near New York City, 1932

less formal photos that survive—apart from those that show the composer relaxing alone or with friends—are a number that portray Gershwin as an outdoorsman and as an athlete: resting or playing ball on the beach, working out with a trainer, playing tennis in Hollywood.[16] These provide important visual clues to another significant aspect of his character. The roller-skating street kid evolved into a highly active adult, always on the move. Gershwin's habitual restlessness gained an aesthetic corollary in the distinctive rhythmic profile of his music, a profile that also reflected the pulse, the energy, the exuberance, and the anxiety of the time and place in which he lived. Merle Armitage articulated this effectively: "The excitement, the nervousness and the movement of America were natural motivations in Gershwin's life and Gershwin's music."[17] Gershwin himself wrote, in a 1927 article titled "Jazz Is the Voice of the American Soul," that "If I were an Asia[n] or a European, suddenly set down by an aeroplane on this soil and listening with a fresh ear to the American chorus of sounds, I should say that American life is nervous, hurried, syncopated, ever *accelerando*, and slightly vulgar."[18] It is striking that, in choosing terms to characterize "the American chorus of sounds," the composer settled upon four words having progressively more specific relationships to musical rhythm and tempo—"nervous, hurried, syncopated, ever *accelerando*"—rather than upon words evoking melody, harmony, or other prominent aspects of musical expression.

Since Gershwin is so frequently celebrated as a melodist, it might initially seem paradoxical to define his genius primarily in rhythmic terms. Yet the composer identified with "Fascinating Rhythm" and "I Got Rhythm" also lavished equivalent rhythmic ingenuity on his famous love ballads. To offer just two examples: the endearing seductiveness of "Embraceable You" is chiefly due not to the pitch contour of its melody—which consists of simple, repetitive patterns—but to the rhythmic rests that inform those patterns at every turn, creating alternating sensations of hesitation and forward momentum; and the longing, expressive nature of the melodic line in "A Foggy Day" is dependent upon the continual syncopation characterizing that line. Gershwin was probably thinking of his tender ballads when he told S. N. Behrman that he wanted "to write for young girls sitting on fire escapes on hot summer nights in New York and dreaming of love."[19] Yet even in this remarkably poetic description, the implications of movement and restlessness are inescapable: the young girls have moved onto the fire escapes because to be indoors in New York on hot summer nights (before apartments had air conditioning) was unbearable, and, far from being simply contented with their immediate situation, these girls are "dreaming of love." In Gershwin's own life and in Gershwin's America, to have a meaningful contemporary existence was to be on the go.

The motif of constant movement was established early for Gershwin by the physical circumstances of his family, which reflected in turn the employment circumstances of his father. Ira wrote: "We were always moving. When my father sold a business and started another we would inevitably move to the new neighborhood. George and I once counted over twenty-five different flats and apartments we remembered having lived in during those days."[20] As an adult Gershwin continued to relocate and to travel, and arguably he never really settled down. His international journeys bore fruit in two works for the concert hall, the celebrated *An American in Paris* and the lesser-known *Cuban Overture*; he traversed the United States as a performer of his own music; and he ended his days as a discontented, uprooted New Yorker in Hollywood.

Given Gershwin's athletic proclivities and musical gifts, it comes as no surprise that he was known as a fine dancer. According to Fred Astaire, Gershwin even made useful suggestions to him when Astaire was choreographing his steps for the dance sequences in *Lady, Be Good!*—the first show on which he and Gershwin worked together.[21] Isaac Goldberg's description of Gershwin's conducting is also worthy of citation in this connection: "George conducts with a baton, with his cigar, with his shoulders, with his hips, with his eyes, with what not. Yet without any antics for the eyes of the audience. It is, rather, a gentle polyrhythm of his entire body—a quiet dance."[22]

All this suggests forcefully the presence of deep, underlying unities that link the character of Gershwin's inner life with the reflections of that character in his physical being and movements, and ultimately with the artistic manifestations of that character in his music. Once again it is Kay Swift who summed this up beautifully: "He and his music were all of a piece—he was exactly like his music. And he had the face, personality, and the looks, and he moved exactly the way you'd expect from his music. I never saw anyone who was more like his music."[23]

On the Cover of *Time*
(Gershwin as darling of the media; the perils of fame)

In July 1925 Gershwin became the first American-born musician to grace the cover of *Time* magazine, and this was an indication of his rapidly growing prominence.[24] His unprecedented position in the culture of his time—part "pop" personality, part "serious" composer—made him a favorite subject for media coverage, and Gershwin consequently attracted much curiosity, admiration, and even adulation from a wide public, along with a significant amount of resentment from other musicians. Gershwin had no models for this role of modern media hero that was thrust upon him; in this arena, as in so many others, he was forced to rely continually upon his own resources to invent, and sometimes to reinvent, himself. That all the media attention proved to be a double-edged sword may be illustrated briefly by tracing the convoluted fallout from an offhand remark Gershwin made to a newspaper reporter shortly after he appeared on the cover of *Time*.

A few days preceding the premiere of his Concerto in F (which took place on December 3, 1925, with the composer as soloist and the New York Symphony conducted by Walter Damrosch), Gershwin was quoted in the *New York Tribune* as saying "I started to write the concerto in London, after buying four or five books on musical structure to find out what the concerto form actually was!"[25] This statement—if we assume that Gershwin was quoted accurately to begin with—virtually drips with ironies, and leads one

Figure 1.3. *Time* magazine cover, July 20, 1925

to speculate that perhaps the composer accompanied it with a wink that remained unrecorded. By the time the concerto was commissioned by Damrosch, Gershwin was much more knowledgeable about classical music than
the statement implies, and he surely had no need to consult books on music
to learn the basics.[26] (On the other hand, Gershwin, indefatigable autodidact
that he was, might well have investigated books on musical structure for other
reasons.) Furthermore, by the time this statement was made the concerto
had been completed, and its composer obviously knew that in this work he
had deliberately played fast and loose with many of the enshrined conventions of classical concerto form and style. Why, then, would Gershwin make
such a remark to the press? Probably for no reason more profound than the

fact that it made a clever quip! For Gershwin himself and his circle of intimate friends, it provided an in-joke at the presumed expense of those who regarded him as an unschooled interloper in the world of "fine" music; at the
same time it served to position Gershwin in the general public's eye as a witty
musical "man of the people," a fine composer to be sure, but one without pre-
tensions.

The remark, however, proved too quotable for Gershwin's own good. As
is often the case with statements made to the media by popular personalities, it took on an unforeseen life of its own. Versions of it appeared in other
newspaper articles and other accounts of the concerto, fueling speculation
about Gershwin's unpreparedness to compose ambitious concert music.
Such speculation, in addition to questioning Gershwin's ability to work with
established classical forms, also cast doubt on whether he actually did his own
orchestration—since orchestration was not part of theater composers' re-
sponsibilities, and also since it was widely known and openly acknowledged
that Ferde Grofé had orchestrated *Rhapsody in Blue* for its premiere with the
Paul Whiteman ensemble in 1924 (as part of the original understanding between Whiteman and Gershwin, Grofé having served at this time as Whiteman's standard arranger). Eventually Gershwin's remark proved to have such
"legs" that an altered paraphrase of its content turned up in Goldberg's 1931
biography, now in the author's voice rather than Gershwin's: "He signed up
to write the concerto for Damrosch; . . . affixed his name to the document
. . . and then he went out to buy a book on musical form to find out how in
thunder a concerto was constructed, anyway!"[27] The sarcastic tone here is
obvious, and Goldberg knew better, but what can he have been thinking?
Could Gershwin possibly have approved this passage, more than five years
after making the original ill-fated comment? Had the "book[s] on musical
form [or structure]" assumed by this point the character of a big private joke,
shared by Gershwin and Goldberg—and if so, at whose expense was the joke
presumed to be? The answers to such questions must remain themselves the
subject of speculation, but aspersions cast on Gershwin's grasp of musical
form and of orchestration continue to be heard to this day.[28]

If being a darling of the media had its downside, it surely had its advan-
tages as well, and Gershwin learned to use them. By the 1930s he was making
increasingly savvy remarks to the press; for example, an article he wrote himself for the *New York Times* immediately following the New York opening of
Porgy and Bess reflects a careful attempt to respond to initial questions about
and criticisms of the work and to shape its reception.[29] Whatever the short-

term impact of this article might have been, it has proved valuable to later generations seeking a fuller understanding of Gershwin's artistic intentions. It should also be noted that Gershwin's great opera might never have been written in the first place had the composer not employed the medium of radio to help finance the extensive free time he required for its composition. *Music by Gershwin* proved to be a highly successful series of radio programs in 1934, thriving on the widespread familiarity of the composer's name and on the media-friendly personality he had developed and put into service as its host.

The media of his time embraced Gershwin because he was the right man in the right place at the right time — a cliché as overworked as it is, in this case, utterly true. Gershwin himself stated it directly: "My people are Americans. My time is today."[30] He was in the right place at the right time on many occasions in his career. When he was only nineteen, he had the good fortune to be introduced to the influential music publisher Max Dreyfus, who in turn had the intuition to quickly hire Gershwin as a staff composer for the firm T. B. Harms. Gershwin became friendly with Paul Whiteman in the early 1920s as a result of their mutual involvement in *George White's Scandals of 1922* on Broadway; this relationship bore ultimate fruit, of course, with Whiteman's commissioning of *Rhapsody in Blue*. Although he may not have been an assiduous follower of contemporary fiction, Gershwin was fortunate enough to have friends who gave him a copy of a popular 1925 novel by DuBose Heyward entitled *Porgy*; now all of us may consider ourselves fortunate that he read it. Many other instances of serendipity in Gershwin's life could be cited. What is important, however, is not that he was lucky. What matters is that he had the gifts and the perseverance to make the most of all his good fortune.

On Folly Island
(Gershwin in black and white)

Gershwin was a traveling man, but neither his cross-country nor his international journeys proved the richest source of Gershwin lore — notwithstanding his famous purchase of Parisian taxi horns for *An American in Paris*. It was his trip to Folly Island in South Carolina during the summer of 1934 that has yielded the principal trove of oft-repeated stories. Snapshots are not the focus here, although a couple of faded-looking black-and-white photos have been published showing Gershwin on the island.[31] Rather it is the fact that Gershwin devoted the several weeks he spent there to intensive work on *Porgy*

Figure 1.4. George Gershwin at Folly Beach, South Carolina, June 1934

and Bess, while living in close proximity to a population of Gullah blacks, whose lifestyle and culture had supplied inspiration for DuBose Heyward's original novel *Porgy* and whose particular musical culture Gershwin appreciated. The thorny complex of racial issues surrounding Gershwin's relationships to black culture — both in his life and in his music — finds an obvious focal point here. *Porgy and Bess*, an opera in which a hurricane creates a crucial dramatic turning point, has itself engendered a storm of race-centered debate, and Gershwin's sojourn on Folly Island may be located squarely in the eye of this conceptual hurricane.

The recollections by DuBose Heyward of the time he spent with

Gershwin during the Folly Island visit have provided major substance for this debate. Heyward's characterization of the composer's relationship to southern black life as being "more like a homecoming than an exploration," and his famous description of Gershwin's successful participation in Gullah "shouting," embellished with the assertion that "he is probably the only white man in America who could have done it," may have enhanced Gershwin's reputation at the time as a man qualified to write an opera on an African American subject, but they surely have done the composer and his work no favors in the context of America's recent racial climate.[32]

Porgy and Bess and the issues surrounding it will receive detailed attention in a later chapter. Passing judgments on Gershwin's interactions with African American people, and on his relationships to black culture and music specifically, will not constitute any part of this agenda. Gershwin was, as has already been emphasized, a man of his time, and he conducted himself and expressed himself verbally in accordance with the prevailing customs and mores—as did DuBose Heyward. Gershwin's music was also, for all its originality, a product of his time, was intended by the composer to be perceived as such, and consequently was fashioned to communicate directly to his contemporary audience. If in his recorded behavior and remarks, in his surviving written documents, and even in the music of *Porgy and Bess*, Gershwin expressed himself on racial matters in a manner that some might now deem essentialist, condescending, or even "racist," this does not necessarily imply anything more profound than that his time is not our time and thus, inevitably, his consciousness concerning race cannot reflect our consciousness concerning race. Lest this appear too facile a formulation, it should be remembered that racial issues in today's America are as volatile and problematic as they were in Gershwin's America, and that as a result our present commentators on these issues are arguably just as circumscribed by inherent limitations and prejudices as were past commentators. It is perilously easy to set oneself up as an "objective" observer with a purportedly enlightened perspective and proceed to render judgments on the benighted past—even while granting that someone like Gershwin may have had "good intentions." But such judgments are almost inevitably self-serving, not to mention essentialist and condescending. Hindsight of this nature is not "twenty-twenty," it is historically and culturally myopic. These documented facts remain: Gershwin moved readily and comfortably among black people, in Harlem as well as on Folly Island; he admired black music enormously; he formed and maintained meaningful and mutual friendships with black musicians.

Gershwin was perceived in his time as a "jazz composer," and much of his best-known music today clearly demonstrates influences from African American sources, most prominently heard as blue inflections in the melody and harmony and as aggressive rhythmic syncopation. Yet this is far from the whole story. Perhaps the deepest irony underlying the racial controversies that continue to swirl around Gershwin and his music lies in the simple fact that his work as a whole ranges over a substantially wider stylistic palette than is often acknowledged, and consequently is too multifaceted to be pigeon-holed in terms of any single stream of influence. Gershwin's music is as much "white" as it is "black," and is ultimately far too colorful to be restricted to those two descriptors. While there are many more snapshots, images, and concepts from Gershwin's short but full life that could arouse great interest, it is this issue of style in his music that now demands sustained attention.

CHAPTER 2

In Search of Gershwin's Style

GENERALIZATIONS THAT SUMMARIZE THE INDIVIDUAL STYLE OF A significant creator are often useful. Such statements also inevitably involve simplifications and omissions, however, to an extent that tends to increase proportionally with the significance of the creative artist in question. Obvious examples may readily be offered. To favor exclusively the "heroic" Beethoven of the Third, Fifth, and Ninth Symphonies is to reduce in importance and achievement works such as the poetic Sixth ("Pastoral") Symphony and the witty, virtually neoclassical Eighth Symphony—but may these latter two works truly be characterized as "lesser" or even as "atypical" Beethoven? Wagner's dark romanticism and progressive harmonic imagination are probably exemplified best by *Tristan und Isolde* and the music dramas of the *Ring* cycle, but does this automatically render his grand comedy *Die Meistersinger* a less characteristic and therefore less remarkable accomplishment? Turning to American composers, is Charles Ives any less himself in a small-scaled work such as *The Unanswered Question* than in the epic "Concord" Piano Sonata or the enormously ambitious Fourth Symphony? Is Copland more truly "Copland" in a celebrated, accessible, big score such as *Appalachian Spring* than in the modest, accessible *Old American Songs* or in the little-known and more arcane Quartet for Piano and Strings? Should we define Richard Rodgers's approach to the Broadway musical solely in terms of his enduring megahits with Oscar Hammerstein II, and ignore the many estimable (but now largely forgotten) shows he fashioned with Lorenz Hart?

The limitations of stylistic generalizations quickly become apparent from examples such as these. Not as apparent, perhaps, is the way in which such widely established generalizations tend to be informed and shaped by historical, cultural, and philosophical agendas. Indeed, these agendas may be embedded in individual awareness and behavior, and in cultural norms and structures, to an extent that precludes their conscious recognition by those who formulate and reiterate the generalizations. But the agendas do help account for why the generalizations endure so well. For many reasons, we tend to prize above all what we regard as originality and uniqueness, both in the creative artist and in the individual work; we tend to elevate the wide-ranging, ambitious achievement over that of more modest scope; and we tend to honor abundantly, if not exclusively, those artists and works exemplifying a concept of "progressive" evolution in the development of style—style in terms both of the broad history of an art form and in terms of an individual artist's oeuvre.

When it comes to Gershwin, it is a straightforward matter to identify the stylistic characteristics that have come to be associated most closely with his music. They are reiterated constantly in the Gershwin literature, in concert program notes, in the booklets accompanying compact discs, in public speech, and in casual conversation. That Gershwin employed blue notes (generally, flatted third and seventh scale degrees, and sometimes flatted fifth degrees as well) in his melodies and harmony, and favored syncopated rhythms, is now so well known as to constitute the musical equivalent of folk wisdom. There is also nothing mysterious or random about the selection of these particular characteristics. They are among the most prominent stylistic features of the work that first catapulted Gershwin to widespread recognition as a composer—the work that remains today his best-known, signature composition. The piece in question is, of course, *Rhapsody in Blue*, and the blue notes and syncopated rhythms are evident from the first measures (ex. 2.1).

Rhapsody in Blue functions so effectively as an exemplar of the "Gershwin style" for two reasons. The first reason is apparent and clearly justifiable: its characteristic blue notes and syncopation do permeate a significant quantity of Gershwin's other music. The other reason is less obvious and potentially more problematic: the *Rhapsody* fulfills a favored cultural role as an unprecedented and highly original piece, both in Gershwin's output and in the stylistic evolution of American music. There had been nothing like it before. Arguably there was nothing quite like it again, at least in terms of cultural impact—even for Gershwin. Still, it does not diminish the authentic achievement of the *Rhapsody* to point out that using it to represent the totality of

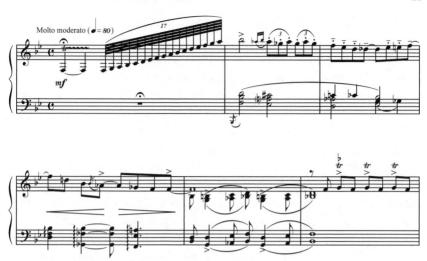

Example 2.1. *Rhapsody in Blue*, piano reduction, mm. 1–6

what is important, or even typical, in Gershwin's approach to musical style is to perpetrate a distortion.

This distortion has particularly unfortunate consequences for any attempt to provide a thorough account, and to gain a comprehensive appreciation, of Gershwin as a Broadway composer. This is because a distinctive personal style was not the single greatest asset a Broadway composer could possess in Gershwin's day. The ability to project a finely honed individual style was certainly not a handicap. The most essential asset, however, was stylistic versatility, something Gershwin learned early and mastered thoroughly. Nevertheless, a more limited view of Gershwin's musical style continues to prevail.

A strong contributing factor to the *Rhapsody*'s rapid reception as a major American work, and consequently as representative of Gershwin's style, was the fuel it added to the raging public debate at the time concerning "jazz" music. The propriety (or lack of propriety) of jazz itself, and the questions of its appropriate venues, roles, and position—if any—in American culture occasioned much contention. Nobody today would call *Rhapsody in Blue* jazz, but at a time when the label "jazz" or the adjective "jazzy" was attached to virtually any syncopated music that employed or made reference to currently popular styles, Gershwin's composition was almost universally received as an attempt to bring "jazz" into the concert hall. Thus it was the "jazzy" characteristics of Gershwin's rhythms, melodies, and harmony in the *Rhapsody* that received the most attention, that were most anticipated and discussed in his subsequent concert works, and that increasingly were regarded as the most distinctive features of his songs as well.

Gershwin himself encouraged this process, inadvertently or not, by publishing a number of short articles during the 1920s and early 1930s that addressed directly the significance of jazz to modern American music.[1] It is worth recalling that in one of these ("Jazz Is the Voice of the American Soul," published in 1927) the composer characterized American life itself as "syncopated" and "slightly vulgar"—surely "jazz" traits! Furthermore, Gershwin called attention to the blue inflections in his music, not only in the title of his most famous piece, but also in descriptions he provided of others.[2]

It is not surprising that, with the passage of time, Gershwin's style has come increasingly to be defined in terms of those enduring works that appear to be most obviously and uniquely his: *Rhapsody in Blue, Concerto in F, An American in Paris,* and *Porgy and Bess.* When this definition of style has then been applied to his songs, the obvious consequence has been that certain songs have tended to become especially favored as "classic" representations of the Gershwin style. That Gershwin may be defined—but also confined— by this process may be illustrated by a consideration of two of his best-loved and artistically remarkable songs.

Two Styles of Love: "The Man I Love" and "Love Walked In"

The famous refrain of "The Man I Love" offers a model instance of stereotypical "Gershwin style" at its most inspired. In the first measure, one hears a melodic motif that begins off the downbeat and reaches a striking flatted seventh scale degree on the rhythmically weak fourth beat (ex. 2.2). This motif proceeds to dominate the melodic and rhythmic character of the entire refrain, while its blue inflection thoroughly colors the harmony as well. It is no coincidence that this celebrated, relatively early example of the "mature" Gershwin style was composed shortly after *Rhapsody in Blue.*[3] It has often been remarked that the basic motif of "The Man I Love" resembles the one that inaugurates the piano solo in the *Rhapsody*—a motif heard frequently throughout that earlier work.[4]

The refrain of "The Man I Love" incorporates other stylistic features often cited as typical of Gershwin. In his summary of the "idiosyncratic

Example 2.2. "The Man I Love," refrain, mm. 1–8

musical characteristics" found in Gershwin's songs, Geoffrey Block observes "a predilection for repeated notes," along with a tendency to alter the harmony on each repeated note, and more generally "the use of harmony for expressive textual purposes."[5] Repeated melody notes over changing harmony are certainly evident on the words "make him stay"; the stationary melodic line with long rhythmic values musically portrays the desire for stability and permanence after the longing unease of the preceding measures, while the moving harmony sustains interest and a sense of direction. If we enlarge Block's observation to include brief repeated phrases in the melody accompanied by changing harmony, it proves to identify the underlying compositional strategy of the entire eight-measure section shown in example 2.2, which constitutes the basic strain of the song. (This A melody recurs twice in the AABA type refrain of "The Man I Love," each time with variations in the piano accompaniment that may be heard as reflections of the same general strategy, applied to the level of overall structure.) In terms of Block's "use of harmony for expressive textual purposes," this characteristic is apparent

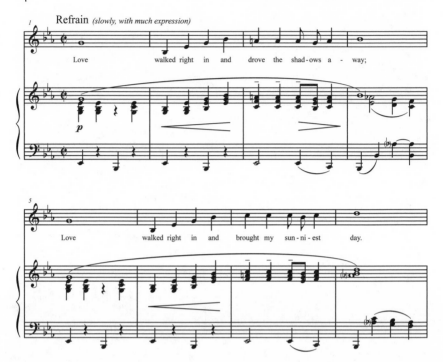

Example 2.3. "Love Walked In," refrain, mm. 1–8

throughout the refrain. Some additional details of harmony, and other aspects of "The Man I Love," will be explored shortly. But first, with the general stylistic traits of this song clearly in mind, let us take a look at "Love Walked In" (ex. 2.3).

The problem with employing "Love Walked In" as an example is that an individual who did not know the song, but who was familiar with the standard definitions of Gershwin's style, would have no reason even to suspect that Gershwin composed it. Of blue notes or syncopation there is nary a trace. The sole chromatic pitch in the first section of the refrain is an A-natural and, far from being a flatted blue fifth in disguise, this note functions obviously and classically as a leading tone to the diatonic fifth scale degree (B-flat). The opening strain shown in example 2.3 sets the pattern for the refrain as a whole in celebrating simple and conventional musical material: the notes of the tonic triad (E-flat major) and of the diatonic scale associated with it.[6] While mm. 3 and 7 do employ repeated notes (A-natural and C, respectively), the harmony underlying these notes does not alter, and there is nothing about these measures in context that attracts attention as idiosyncratically "Gersh-winesque." The note repetitions serve the unremarkable function of extending and ornamenting a specific pitch en route to the following melodic tone.

It would be easy to dismiss "Love Walked In" as an anomaly in the Gershwin canon, but there are many reasons why this approach won't do. If it were an early song, its style could neatly be characterized as "immature," and that would be that—although the quality of the song as a composition would demand attention in any case. That quality proves an indication of the truth of the matter, however; "Love Walked In" is a product of Gershwin's full maturity and in fact was one of the last songs he finished. It was published six months after his death, and introduced in the film *The Goldwyn Follies* in February 1938.[7]

The late songs that Gershwin wrote for Hollywood, including "Love Walked In," are held in particularly high esteem by connoisseurs of his music. No less an authority on American popular song than Irving Berlin told scholar Robert Kimball that "no one wrote greater songs than George and Ira did during the last year of George's life."[8] This group of songs, written for the films *Shall We Dance* and *A Damsel in Distress* (both 1937) as well as *The Goldwyn Follies*, offer other examples that could seem just as anomalous in terms of Gershwin's style, such as "I Love to Rhyme," or the refrain of "I Was Doing All Right." But any initial suspicion that Gershwin's style might have been changing at this late point in his development, moving away from what was supposedly typical of him, is quickly quashed by the presence of songs like "Slap That Bass" and "A Foggy Day" in this same group—songs as "bluesy" and syncopated as anything in the composer's earlier output.

For all of these reasons, characterizing "Love Walked In" as atypical Gershwin is simply erroneous, just as it would be mistaken to conceive of the song as immature or in any way as lesser or minor Gershwin, or to tout it as a harbinger of stylistic change. Truly there is no problem with "Love Walked In." The only problem lies with the limitations imposed by the standard definitions of Gershwin's style. Any number of "anomalous" songs, from all stages of the composer's career, could be employed equally well to demonstrate these limitations.[9] Gershwin casts his stylistic net too wide for ready reductionism, no matter how intelligently applied; there is no sine qua non that delimits the Gershwin style.[10] To illustrate this we need not even turn away from "The Man I Love." We need only enlarge our view of this song to encompass its neglected verse as well as its celebrated refrain.

Example 2.4a. "The Man I Love," verse, mm. 1–8

The verse of "The Man I Love" is infrequently performed today, and, for one who comes to it familiar only with the refrain, it seems all too easy to say why. The first eight measures of the vocal line would appear to be the work of a composer completely different from the one who wrote the refrain—and, it is tempting to add, the work of a composer apparently less than inspired (ex. 2.4a). The basic two-bar motif is simplicity itself, built on the tonic note (E-flat) and a segment of its major scale presented in purely stepwise motion and in utterly conventional marchlike rhythms, and this motif proceeds in predictable sequences up the scale. Upon reaching a single high point on the upper tonic, the melody honors traditional expectations by falling downward and concluding the first section of the verse with longer note values. One searches in vain for any hint of the expressive syncopation and blue chromaticism of the refrain; by comparison, this melody is oddly banal, almost like a nursery tune. To be sure, there are repeated notes—but too many of them, it could be argued, pounding squarely on the beat and underlined by the piano, which repeats block chords of its own.

And then there are the lyrics. Moonbeams, a little dream, and, for good measure, Prince Charming!—perhaps this is a nursery rhyme after all. Surely Ira Gershwin's lyrics for the refrain flirt with clichés, but his lyrics for the verse positively revel in them, and while George's music for the refrain pulls creatively against any tendency to hear the lyrics there in terms of mere sentimentality, his music for the verse seems to reinforce the virtually trivial character of its lyrics. Were the innovative composer and the imaginative lyricist responsible for the memorable refrain of "The Man I Love" out to lunch when the verse was created? At first blush, the verse of this song would seem to offer a good rationale for the all-too-common habit of neglecting the verses of Broadway songs when identifying what deserves to endure in the repertoire or what ought to be regarded as representative in the styles of song composers.

If the verse of "The Man I Love" appears initially far too superficial for its refrain, however, this dismissal of it is similarly far too facile. In fact the verse becomes more interesting as it goes along. And if noticing certain details of this process does not prompt reevaluation, Ira Gershwin's own account of the song's gestation should certainly bring about second thoughts: he asserts that the verse was written *after* the refrain, and therefore was created with the specific mission of adequately preparing it.[11] Whether or not one feels that the mission was accomplished, it seems only just to accord the verse a careful second look.

From the outset, both musically and lyrically, the verse offers a straightforward introduction to basic elements that will come to dominate the refrain in different and more complex manifestations. The musical elements are repeated notes, dotted rhythms, and sequences; the lyrical elements involve young girls (perhaps "sitting on fire escapes on hot summer nights in New York"?[12]) dreaming of love. These elements are first stated with an almost self-conscious simplicity, and are then developed with increasing sophistication. In the second half of the verse (mm. 9–16; see ex. 2.4b), the melody begins as if to repeat the first half but alters the anticipated sequence with the introduction of an unexpected chromatic note (A-natural) in m. 12, and in the subsequent measures abandons the sequence entirely. What follows is a new descending motif, starting off the downbeat in a manner that may be heard as anticipating the defining rhythmic character of the refrain. Meanwhile, the harmony in the piano part has been gradually incorporating instances of passing chromaticism, a process that culminates in the striking dissonance of m. 14—which Ira paradoxically provides with the word "clear," as if to suggest that this dream of love involves deeper and potentially more fraught emotions than either the listener or the protagonist of the song might initially suspect. By this point the listener is directly involved. This is because the lyrics

Example 2.4b. "The Man I Love," verse, mm. 9–16

have evolved from the inward-turned, childlike solipsism of the opening, to acknowledge the external world of other people and harsh reality and to articulate an implicit plea for attention from that world (i.e., "Although I realize as well as you . . .").

The refrain of "The Man I Love" thus represents the outcome of a developmental procedure that is presented in the verse, and it is at least arguable that the composition achieves the strongest impact when experienced as a whole. The restless syncopation, the intense melodic blue notes, and the chromatic harmonies that shift expressively with every measure in the refrain are all felt with particular intensity when preceded by the music of the verse. Syncopation and chromaticism are specifically prepared in the verse, as we have seen, while the defining new feature of the refrain—the blue notes in the melody—may be heard as growing out of the chromaticism in the piano part of the verse at the same time that they raise this chromaticism to an unforeseen level of poignancy. What has been suggested within this compressed time span may represent nothing less than the metamorphosis of childhood fantasy into adult (or at least adolescent) sexual longing.

In terms of the lyrics, the tension set up in the verse between a fairy tale–like dream world and the world of reality continues to color the refrain.

Reality intrudes most obviously in the bridge (the B section): "Maybe I shall meet him Sunday, / Maybe Monday—maybe not," and this is reflected in the music by a decisive turn to a minor key. The restless chromaticism pervading every section of the refrain suggests, however, that even the protagonist's moments of pure reverie are tinged with anxiety. The "you" first addressed in the verse is pointedly posed a question toward the conclusion of the refrain, in a particularly effective turn of phrase that thrusts the listener even more directly into the world of the song: "He'll build a little home / Just meant for two; / From which I'll never roam— / Who would? Would you?"[13]

What might be viewed as the forced simplicity that opens the verse of "The Man I Love" is obviously part of a complete conception, and it inevitably follows that the musical style of this opening—diatonic and rhythmically square as it is—must be acknowledged as an aspect of Gershwin's style. "The Man I Love" is a stylistically heterogeneous song that employs its composer's stylistic versatility to provide a richer portrayal of emotion and character than would otherwise be possible.[14] Ultimately it doesn't matter if we choose to regard the straightforward diatonic style as artificially imposed, or even as functioning with subtle irony, in this particular context. That Gershwin could embrace this style wholeheartedly to convey sincere and touching adult passion is demonstrated conclusively by "Love Walked In." Let us return to this later song to consider how this is accomplished.

The refrain of "Love Walked In" expresses fulfillment of the kind of longing so exquisitely portrayed in "The Man I Love." (Indeed, the lyrics to both songs share a significant characterization of the perfect relationship as one in which no words need be spoken for the lovers to find and recognize each other.) In "Love Walked In," Gershwin artfully manipulates his simple materials to represent a state of pure bliss; the result is at once convincing and compelling. As shown in example 2.3, the basic motif of the refrain surges upward through the notes of an E-flat major triad. The obvious goal of the first eight measures, the upper tonic E-flat, is attained immediately at the downbeat of m. 9 and is quickly reiterated in the measure succeeding (see ex. 2.5). The two high E-flats thus frame the crucial phrase "One magic moment." After the repeated surges and the dual high points, the line gracefully falls for six measures to prepare the restatement of the initial strain.

While "One magic moment" seems perfect in its immediate context, it leaves in its wake a residual tension. It is here, perhaps, that we glimpse the core of the song's artistry: the surge on "magic moment" strains toward a point of rhythmic and melodic arrival, as do the preceding surges, but the

Example 2.5. "Love Walked In," refrain, mm. 9–12

high E-flat on the fourth beat of m. 10 is left dangling. Furthermore, it could be argued that a state of true bliss should be characterized by the attainment of a single, unequivocal goal—rather than by twin E-flats. The desired arrival at a single, unequivocal goal is achieved when, in a later passage that directly parallels "One magic moment," the high E-flat is allowed to proceed upward to a lone high F on a downbeat. Significantly, this is mated with Ira's words "One look and I had *found* a world completely new." It is with the discovery of a new world, that of true love, that the protagonist fulfills a mission and that the song achieves aesthetic fulfillment.

While the refrain of "Love Walked In" reveals occasional instances of passing chromaticism, especially in the piano part, the verse is considerably more complicated harmonically. This is only appropriate, since the verse articulates the feelings of aimlessness and dissatisfaction that plagued the protagonist prior to the arrival of love. In a general sense, the strategy here is the opposite of that employed in "The Man I Love," where a deceptive simplicity in the verse gives way to the emotional complexity of the refrain. Gershwin's wide stylistic range allows for the expression of significantly contrasting states of mind and heart within the confines of a single song.

Unlike "Love Walked In," "The Man I Love" lacks a single melodic high point. The highest pitch sung in "The Man I Love" is the upper E-flat: there are two of these in the verse, and two pairs of high E-flats in the B (bridge) section of the refrain, and in none of these instances does this note function as a point of arrival. This is fitting, however, because the song remains emotionally unresolved; at the close of the refrain, the singer is still "waiting for the man I love." The blue seventh (D-flat) heard repeatedly in the refrain is always led downward rather than upward toward the diatonic seventh degree and tonic (D-natural and E-flat, respectively) of the E-flat major scale, and

Example 2.6.

this serves as another musical sign that the body of the song remains fixed in a "blues" mode and condition.[15]

The blue style that permeates the refrain of "The Man I Love" and the straightforward diatonicism that characterizes the refrain of "Love Walked In" represent but two pigments in Gershwin's multicolored stylistic palette. Depending on the requirements of a particular dramatic situation, character, lyric, or point in the musical development—or any combination of these—Gershwin could dwell extensively on a particular aspect of style, could present differing stylistic features in a deliberate sequence, or could set what seem to be opposing stylistic elements in juxtaposition to one another.[16] Another approach he employed was the unexpected synthesis of diverse elements. For example, what has come to be called the "Charleston theme" of *An American in Paris*[17] is music that combines syncopated dance rhythms, a diatonic melody, a harmonic structure derived from twelve-bar blues, and some striking modernistic dissonances in the accompanying lines.[18]

Style and (Mistaken) Identity: Gershwin among his Contemporaries

It is apparent that the typical definitions of Gershwin's style prove insufficient to the task of describing his oeuvre accurately. Such definitions can also lead, however, to erroneous preconceptions involving Gershwin's contemporaries. To illustrate this let us consider the music of example 2.6, the opening eight measures of the refrain from a 1921 song.

This music, with its prominent employment of syncopation and blue notes, would seem to offer a good early example of the "Gershwin style" as traditionally conceived. Especially striking in mm. 2 and 3 is the composer's play with the rhythmic repositioning of a repeated three-note melodic figure (the blue seventh B-flat descending to A and G); this may be heard as an an-

ticipation of the analogous, more complex employment of metric displacement found in such later Gershwin songs as "Fascinating Rhythm" (from
Lady, Be Good!, 1924) and "Fidgety Feet" (from *Oh, Kay!*, 1926). The trouble
is that example 2.6 was written not by Gershwin but by Irving Berlin. As many
readers will doubtless have recognized, this is "Everybody Step," originally
introduced in the 1921 stage show *Music Box Revue*, and made even more
familiar through its appearance in the movies *Alexander's Ragtime Band* and
Blue Skies (from 1938 and 1946, respectively).

    Should Irving Berlin then be credited with originating the "Gershwin
style," and Gershwin himself relegated to the role of imitator and disciple?
Certainly Gershwin—like everybody else involved in the popular music of
the time—knew of Berlin, and by 1919 had met the "old master."[19] Gershwin
specifically cited "Everybody Step" for "its very interesting rhythmical qualities" in a brief article he published in 1926.[20] Berlin's influence was inescapable, and this assuredly was true not only for Gershwin. It is also essential,
however, to realize a number of other things.

    First of all, neither Berlin nor any other individual should be credited
with introducing blue notes and syncopation into the stylistic repertory of
American music. By late 1920—the year before "Everybody Step" appeared—
a full-blown blues craze was gripping the popular music scene, spearheaded
by the widespread and unexpected popularity of Mamie Smith's recording
of "Crazy Blues." That same year, Marion Harris had a huge popular hit with
her version of W. C. Handy's "St. Louis Blues," a celebration of blue notes
and syncopation that had been published six years earlier, in 1914, and recorded with success by others before her. But even Handy himself, known
as "the father of the blues," acknowledged the roots of his blues style in preexisting folk sources.[21]

    The truth is that by the time Berlin wrote "Everybody Step," syncopated
figures oriented around blue notes were part of the lingua franca of Tin Pan
Alley and Broadway—and obviously of blues and early jazz—and that by the
time Gershwin employed such figures in *Rhapsody in Blue* and "The Man I
Love" (and "Fascinating Rhythm"), they were virtually clichés. What distin-
guishes a Berlin or a Gershwin work is not the presence of such material; it
is rather the artistry with which it is used. The character and design of this
artistry may vary from work to work, and from composer to composer, and
herein may lie a truly useful basis for stylistic discussion and differentiation.
Such an approach does not, however, lend itself readily to compact general-

Figure 2.1. George Gershwin with Irving Berlin (time exposure by Gershwin), Beverly Hills, 1936

izations. These observations regarding blue notes and syncopation are equally relevant to many other stylistic elements present in the musical vocabulary of a successful Broadway composer like Gershwin.

Finally, in the case of Berlin and Gershwin, evidence of influence runs both ways, and this is something that could be said about almost any pair of contemporaneous Broadway masters. If Berlin's "Everybody Step" seems distinctly to foreshadow a song such as Gershwin's "Fascinating Rhythm," it seems virtually impossible that Berlin in turn could have conceived the rhythmic tour de force of "Puttin' on the Ritz" (1928) without having heard and absorbed "Fascinating Rhythm." Fortunately, it is not necessary to ponder such a virtual impossibility; of course Berlin had heard and absorbed the Gershwin song, as Berlin was a savvy denizen of Broadway and "Fascinating Rhythm" was a hit song from a big hit show. But one need not posit a direct, linear influence here, either. The point is simply that Berlin and Gershwin (and Kern, and Rodgers, and Porter; the list could go on and on) were constantly listening to and learning from one another in an environment that was as stimulating and nurturing as it was competitive. The result was an extraordinary quantity of extraordinary music; and in this repertoire questions of precedence, influence, and personal style became inevitably tangled.

The likely influence of Gershwin on "Puttin' on the Ritz" could easily be discussed further, were this angle to be considered fruitful. For instance, the stepwise, rhythmically regular bridge section of Berlin's song demonstrates an almost uncanny resemblance to the bridge section of another song from Gershwin's *Lady, Be Good!* — "So Am I." But perhaps the most appropriate response to an observation such as this is embodied in the title of yet another, later Gershwin song (from *Of Thee I Sing*, 1931): "Who Cares?"

Among Gershwin's contemporaries, it was Jerome Kern whose early influence Gershwin most specifically acknowledged. He said of the older composer, "I followed Kern's work and studied each song that he composed. I paid him the tribute of frank imitation."[22] To illustrate both the obvious truth of this statement, and some of the complexities that erupt upon a close investigation of it, Gershwin's 1919 song "From Now On" will serve well as a focal point.

"From Now On" is a number from Gershwin's first complete score for a musical, *La-La-Lucille!* (The show achieved a modest success on Broadway in 1919, closing after 104 performances because of an actors' strike.) In seeking to fashion a convincing love song for his show, Gershwin unsurprisingly evoked tried-and-true precedents found in the work of Kern. One such precedent was Kern's enduringly popular "They Didn't Believe Me," introduced in the 1914 Broadway show *The Girl from Utah*.[23]

When considering the work of figures as imposing as Gershwin and Kern, it is most useful to look for the important constructive principles one could have learned from the other, rather than to dwell on minutiae of melodic, harmonic, or rhythmic usage. This is especially true when such minutiae tend to be elements of a widely shared musical language and not authentic markers of stylistic distinction. A comparison of examples 2.7 and 2.8 reveals how Gershwin could have absorbed from Kern a model for constructing an effective opening strain. Notice the striking similarities in basic rhythmic organization between "From Now On" and "They Didn't Believe Me": the opening of each refrain is fashioned from two-measure units that begin with pickups and arrive on long notes in the succeeding measures.[24] Even many of the specific note values are the same in these particular examples: the half notes in mm. 1 and 5; the dotted rhythms in m. 2 of each example that lead to tied whole notes; and the three quarter notes concluding each example that

Example 2.7. "From Now On," refrain, mm. 1–8

inaugurate the B sections of these refrains. Some general similarities in the details of melodic contour may also be observed readily.

There are, to be sure, important differences between the two songs as well. Kern's refrain is demonstrably more sophisticated than Gershwin's, even in its first eight measures—and proves to be immeasurably more so when the comparison is extended to include the complete songs. Example 2.7 (Gershwin) is built straightforwardly upon the sequential treatment of a basic melodic unit, but while Example 2.8 (Kern) also incorporates a sequential passage (with the sixth and seventh measures following the pattern established by the fourth and fifth measures), the sequence is inexact and constitutes only a part of the opening strain. In its overall form, the refrain of "From Now On" is based obviously on an ABAB′ formal model, whereas the refrain of "They Didn't Believe Me" is sufficiently unconventional and intricate to resist an analogous formal reduction.[25] As Gershwin matured, the more complex lessons of Kern's art came to bear increasing fruit in Gershwin's own; nevertheless, as early as "From Now On," a line of influence extending from the older composer to the younger may clearly be discerned.

Example 2.8. Kern, "They Didn't Believe Me," refrain, mm. 1–8

On the other hand, anyone purposefully seeking a characteristic Gershwin fingerprint in "From Now On" would probably seize on his employment of dotted rhythms beginning off the beat. (See ex. 2.7, mm. 2 and 6.) Dotted rhythms are indeed also present in the refrain of "They Didn't Believe Me" (ex. 2.8, m. 2), but here they seem more of a passing occurrence. Gershwin's dotted rhythms draw attention not only because of their rhythmic placement, but also owing to the melodic chromaticism accompanying them, which has no parallel in the Kern song. One might even hear an anticipation of the mature Gershwin to come, and of the characteristic motif from "The Man I Love," in these syncopated, chromatic figures. And so, even with a focus on small specific details like these, Gershwin's stylistic originality and independence assert themselves yet again.

Let us continue briefly along these lines in an attempt to give the devil his full due. Gershwin partisans familiar with another celebrated Kern song, "Whip-poor-will," might use the offbeat, chromatic, dotted-rhythm figure heard in "From Now On" as a hinge upon which to mount an assertion of Gershwin's reciprocal influence upon Kern. "Whip-poor-will" was intro-

Example 2.9. Kern, "Whip-poor-will," refrain, mm. 1–8

duced on Broadway in 1920 (in *Sally*), the year following the appearance of "From Now On" in *La-La-Lucille!* The first eight measures of Kern's refrain are shown in example 2.9, and of course mm. 2 and 6 stand out in this context.[26]

Here, however, is where the road begins to wind. Although "Whip-poor-will" was not heard in a Broadway show before 1920, it was actually written and copyrighted in 1919.[27] And Kern's publisher was the T. B. Harms Company, the very concern that was employing Gershwin at this time. Although an exact chronology cannot be traced with certainty, it seems at least possible that Gershwin—especially given his stated intense interest in following and studying all of Kern's work—could have known of "Whip-poor-will" in 1919, before it was formally copyrighted.[28] Kern aficionados could also point to the distinctive syncopated setting of the word "whip-poor-will" itself, and to the way in which the song leans on the blue seventh E-flat in the second half of the refrain (when the mode changes to the major; see ex. 2.10), to provide effective foundation for a counterassertion that Kern was still leading Gershwin stylistically at this point.[29] A discussion along these lines thus illu-

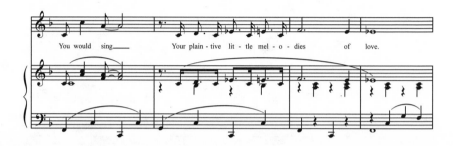

Example 2.10. Kern, "Whip-poor-will," refrain, mm. 16–24

minates the limitations inherent in focusing upon small stylistic details—
and ultimately cannot illuminate much else.

That Kern's influence on Gershwin was substantial, and made an essential contribution to the younger composer's maturation process, seems incon-
testable. That Kern's influence on Gershwin remained persistent throughout
Gershwin's career may be suggested by another look at "Love Walked In." In
the refrain of this late song, Gershwin based his melody on the notes of an
ascending major triad presented in straightforward rhythmic patterns, just as
Kern had done much earlier in "Till the Clouds Roll By" (1917)—but this is
another instance of resemblance based on stylistic details. Kern's "Look for
the Silver Lining" (1920) offered Gershwin a subtler structural lesson, however, that proved relevant to "Love Walked In": how to construct an effective
diatonic melody that makes its way more than once to the upper tonic before
achieving a single, satisfying high point on the upper second scale degree.
(The fact that "Till the Clouds Roll By," "Look for the Silver Lining," and
"Love Walked In" all were published in the same key of E-flat major facili-
tates a direct comparison among them.) Once again, it is the modeling of
effective compositional strategies that represents the significant legacy one

Figure 2.2. George Gershwin with Jerome Kern, New York,
June 1933

major creator can leave to another, not the employment of particular turns of
musical phrase readily borrowed by—and from—other composers.

Before leaving the issue of Kern's influence, the question of Gershwin's impact on the older man should be addressed seriously. That Kern admired Gershwin is widely acknowledged, and, like Irving Berlin, Kern certainly knew Gershwin's music. By 1927, when Kern achieved the pinnacle
of his own art in the music for *Show Boat*, Gershwin's work was well known
and the popular conception of the "Gershwin style" was already fairly well
established—along with that style's perceived connection to jazz, blues, and
African American musical expression, broadly conceived. So when the plot

of *Show Boat* demanded a song that would unequivocally signify "African American music," and consequently the disguised racial identity of the character singing it, Kern responded with "Can't Help Lovin' Dat Man." This song sounds nothing like a typical Kern offering, but it is replete with "Gershwin style" characteristics in the form of blue notes, syncopation, and repeated note patterns (which become virtually obsessive in the refrain). In fact the opening notes and rhythm of the verse in "Can't Help Lovin' Dat Man" directly recall the opening notes and rhythm of the refrain in "The Man I Love" (in the same key of E-flat major, as published).

It is naturally pointless to wonder whether Kern could have conceived "Can't Help Lovin' Dat Man" had he not known Gershwin's music. But the remarkable thing is this: for all of its deliberate "Gershwinisms," the song as a whole doesn't really sound like a Gershwin song. Its employment of style is too self-conscious and extreme, and for the purposes of *Show Boat* this is precisely what was required: the song had to, and does, stand out like a sore thumb. (Kern even wrote the verse in the form of a twelve-bar blues, a form Gershwin seems never to have favored in his own songs.) It is as if Kern, in "Can't Help Lovin' Dat Man," set out to write a kind of parody of a "Gershwin style" song—albeit a parody without humorous intent. That the song succeeds so well, dramatically and aesthetically, is a testament to what a master songwriter can accomplish when he deliberately filters aspects of another's sensibility through his own highly developed artistic consciousness.[30]

Those seeking a means to distinguish Gershwin unambiguously from his contemporaries working in American popular and theater music will obviously find the exploration of style, as traditionally conceived, not sufficient to the purpose. The distinction must be sought in his concert music. What makes Gershwin unique, even in this realm, is not that he attempted to compose for the concert hall—Vernon Duke (as Vladimir Dukelsky) and Alec Wilder were two others who did so extensively—but that he was so immediately and enduringly successful in his efforts. This is doubtless what Irving Berlin meant when he remarked that "George Gershwin is the only song writer I know who became a composer."[31] It should also be stressed that the reasons for Gershwin's success in the concert hall were intimately related to the reasons for his successes in Tin Pan Alley, on Broadway, and eventually in Hollywood. He had a versatile approach to musical style, he was an intelligent and empathetic collaborator, and he had an instinctive and remarkable understanding of his audience.

Style and Performance: Pop That Snaps and Cackles

Any detailed consideration of performance practice in relation to an output as extensive, as diverse, and as widely performed as that of Gershwin is clearly beyond the scope of the present volume and could readily fill a book of its own. Nevertheless, a quest to understand what "style" really means in Gershwin's case must take into some account the invaluable surviving recordings of the composer performing his own music, and the contemporaneous recordings of his music by others who are known to have worked directly with him. These documents can reveal, better than any other kind of source, how Gershwin wanted his music to sound—what he had in mind when he notated his creations, and what essential qualities of his work inevitably eluded precise notation.

The period recordings reflect, to a remarkable extent, the aesthetic desideratum articulated by the composer himself in the introduction to *George Gershwin's Song-book*: "our popular music asks for *staccato* effects, for almost a stencilled style. The rhythms of American popular music are more or less brittle; they should be made to snap, and at times to cackle. The more sharply the music is played, the more effective it sounds."[32] That Gershwin concerned himself to a considerable extent with the rhythmic character of performance does not surprise. That his description applies to the recordings of the concert music just as well as it applies to the recordings of the songs might initially surprise, but it shouldn't. Here is yet another indication of the extent to which Gershwin's diverse oeuvre demonstrates an integrated— rather than bifurcated or fragmented—aesthetic.[33] And while the quoted passage about style and rhythms was addressed by Gershwin directly to pianists wishing to perform the *Song-book* arrangements in an appropriate manner, it proves equally descriptive of the vocal styles of singers who worked successfully with the composer on his music.

Gershwin was above all else a man of the keyboard, and virtually all of his music took root at the piano. While his recordings of his piano music reveal how he preferred to hear these works performed, his recordings of piano arrangements of his songs reveal much about how he conceived the flavor of his vocal music. The recordings by Fred and Adele Astaire with Gershwin accompanying them at the piano offer a complete miniature textbook on "the Gershwin style" in performance; these records present songs from *Lady, Be Good!* and were made in 1926, the year of that show's successful opening in

London.[34] The renditions are models of rhythmic crispness. What is particularly noticeable is how scrupulously the Astaires honor the rests in Gershwin's scores, allowing the music (and the singers) to breathe liberally. Long notes in the vocal melodies are never prolonged beyond their notated values; if anything, they are frequently shortened, and this creates an even greater feeling of airiness. What is conspicuously avoided is the legato approach that Gershwin cautions against in the *Song-book*.[35] Fred Astaire retained this understanding of the Gershwin performance style throughout his long association with the composer, a fact documented in the films *Shall We Dance* and *A Damsel in Distress*. (These scores were the last projects completed by Gershwin prior to his death.) A very different but equally "authentic" testament to this style of performance is the recording of Gershwin songs made by his sister, Frances, in 1973 (when she was sixty-six years old); it is a remarkably youthful-sounding evocation of the sounds in which she obviously was immersed during her own youth and early adulthood.[36]

The presence of duo pianists Phil Ohman and Victor Arden in the pit during Broadway runs of the major Gershwin shows in the 1920s assured that an appropriate keyboard style would help define the characteristic sound of these musicals.[37] Ohman and Arden appeared first in the pivotal *Lady, Be Good!* (1924), and thereafter in *Tip-Toes* (1925), *Oh, Kay!* (1926), and *Funny Face* (1927), as well as in the markedly less successful *Treasure Girl* (1928). In his review of *Tip-Toes* for the *New York World*, Alexander Woollcott praised the "staccato of a trained tandem piano" provided by the duo pianists.[38]

Gershwin's embrace of the piano as primarily a rhythm instrument linked his playing and his composing to significant contemporary trends in both the popular and the classical spheres. The debt to the ragtime pianists is obvious, as is Gershwin's relationship to early jazz stylists such as Willie "The Lion" Smith and James P. Johnson. Less obvious, perhaps, but no less significant is the conceptual kinship to be found between Gershwin's approach to the keyboard and the "percussive" treatment of the piano that characterizes the work of modernist composers such as Bartók and Stravinsky.[39] All these relationships help underline and reinforce an essential characteristic of Gershwin's music—shared with ragtime and early jazz, with modernism, and above all with the lyrics his brother Ira wrote for it—which is its tendency to avoid sentimentality.

In sum, suspicion should greet all generalizations regarding Gershwin's style, and this must include generalizations about performance. Surely not every Gershwin song should snap and cackle; that approach would be inappropriate for the "Brahmsian" "Love Walked In" and for the more obviously operatic portions of *Porgy and Bess*, to cite only two obvious instances. Furthermore, Gershwin's music is well-written and versatile enough to survive—even to welcome—approaches to performance that lie at some distance from Gershwin's own recordings and stated ideals.[40] Such versatility is a hallmark of all music that endures meaningfully beyond the confines of its original era.

 CHAPTER 3

In Search of the Gershwin Musical, Featuring *Lady, Be Good!*

With Special Appearances by Oh, Kay!
and Other Surprise Guests

T HE 1920S MUSICAL COMEDY WAS AN ELUSIVE PHENOMENON. AT-
tempts to define it prove even more perplexing than attempts to
define the style of musical comedy composers. Some of the issues
involved are analogous. The 1920s musical was a polyglot creation, incorporating influences from vaudeville and the revue, from operetta, from
ethnic theater, and from contemporary popular music, with little or no concern evinced for stylistic unity or consistency (as traditionally conceived)
from either a musical or a dramatic standpoint.[1] The very category "musical
comedy" seemed fluid during a period on Broadway when revues, operettas,
and shows labeled explicitly as "musical comedies" were running concur-
rently, competing among themselves for public recognition and commercial dominance, and when the genres themselves appeared to be in compe-
tition for the affection and allegiance of prominent composers. No less an
authority than Gershwin himself characterized Kern's *Show Boat*—certainly
a musical, but less certainly a musical *comedy*—as "the finest light opera
achievement in the history of American music." This was in 1932, the year
following the premiere of Gershwin's own smash hit show (musical comedy?
operetta? "light opera"?) *Of Thee I Sing*.[2]

It seems best to say that the 1920s musical was intentionally elusive, in the
sense that it was a porous, unfixed kind of show. It had to be flexible enough
to absorb changes as it went along—especially those mandated by alterations
in casts and performing venues, as well as changes introduced from within by
those star performers with a penchant for improvisation. This was theater designed to be transient entertainment, just like the songs that were written for

it. The concept of creating a show that would achieve a definitive, final form in which it would endure as a "work" was utterly foreign to the ethos of the 1920s musical.

It is the conventional notion of a "work" that proves to be problematic here, even more so than the conventional notion of "style" proved confounding in the preceding chapter. To begin with, musicals are inevitably collaborative creations. This is not inherently a problem; the Rodgers and Hammerstein shows that have come to emblematize the mature, "classic" Broadway musical are readily understood as works in the traditional sense. But Rodgers and Hammerstein did not simply provide the books, lyrics, and music for their shows. They functioned essentially as "auteurs" by virtue of their continuing and intense involvement in casting, production, and rehearsals, an involvement that assured them tight creative control over the interpretation and performance of their material. Gershwin achieved something like this level of control only with *Porgy and Bess*, and that was because of the special status that adhered to the work (there's that word again, and here it's unproblematic) because it was deemed an *opera*. When he began his Broadway career, Gershwin found the composer's status, while not negligible, to be decidedly secondary in the musical's hierarchy of importance. His musicals of the 1920s revolved principally around performers, and the particular collaborative nature of these "works" entailed the interrelationships among star performers, the composer, the lyricists, the authors of the books, and the many others involved in production. At the heart of these musicals thus lay a certain fluidity that is bound to make those tied to more stable notions of the creative "work" uneasy.

An effective testimony to the hierarchy that seemed to govern both the creation and the reception of 1920s musicals is provided by the (unsigned) review of *Lady, Be Good!* that appeared in the *New York Times* on December 2, 1924, the morning after the show's Broadway opening.[3] The headline reads "Adele Astaire Fascinates," and the entire first half of the review is devoted to praise of the dancing star. Her brother Fred gets acknowledged in the fourth paragraph, whereupon the critic segues into a discussion of other major performers in the show. Gershwin's score is not mentioned until the sixth paragraph (out of eight), despite the fact that Gershwin was by this time well known and widely celebrated as the composer of *Rhapsody in Blue*. His score for *Lady, Be Good!* is characterized simply as "excellent," and the critic anticipates—correctly—that certain of the songs will go on to have a successful life outside the show. The issue of how or even whether

Gershwin's music functions in a manner appropriate to the show's characters and dramatic situations is not so much as raised. In fact it is only in the final paragraph that the book for *Lady, Be Good!* gets mentioned at all, and the initial sentence of this paragraph neatly clarifies the critic's entire approach to the musical: "The book of the piece contains just enough story to call Miss Astaire on stage at frequent intervals, which thus makes it an excellent book." Although this review may represent something of an extreme case insofar as it embodies a scarcely disguised mash note from the critic to Adele Astaire, its overwhelming emphasis on performers over any of the others involved with the show is typical for its time.[4] A more accessible example of this tendency is the review of *Lady, Be Good!* from the *New York Telegram and Evening Mail* that is reprinted in *Gershwin in His Time*; although Gershwin's name achieved a place in the headline (along with those of the Astaires and comedian Walter Catlett), his "nervous" music is the specific subject of only two sentences in the final paragraph of the review, which is otherwise concerned almost exclusively with the performers — and particularly with Adele Astaire.[5]

The secondary status of the composer within this creative environment was reflected even in published sheet music. Contemporary publications of songs from *Lady, Be Good!* had title pages in which George Gershwin's name was the last to be listed: beneath the names of the producers, (in some cases) the star performers, the authors of the book, and the lyricist.[6] With the passage of time and the steady growth in Gershwin's reputation as a Broadway composer, his name came to be featured more prominently in such publications. For instance, a title page for "Yankee Doodle Rhythm" from the ill-fated 1927 version of *Strike Up the Band* refers to the musical as "the Gershwin-Kaufman musical play" directly under the name of producer Edgar Selwyn — a tribute in effect to the significance and salability by this time of the Gershwin moniker (encompassing Ira as well as George) in addition to that of book author George S. Kaufman.[7] And Gershwin certainly employed his increasing prominence to influence the course of development of the musical in the later 1920s and 1930s. Nevertheless, the model so well represented by *Lady, Be Good!* — reflected abundantly in the immediately following Gershwin shows through *Oh, Kay!* in 1926 — retained an obvious influence upon virtually all the Gershwin musicals, at least through *Girl Crazy* in 1930. This chapter aims to foster a better understanding of the nature and virtues, as well as the limitations, of this particular type of show.

An appropriately sympathetic study of these musicals demands a fresh approach to the conception of a "work." We are not dealing here with the "inte-

Figure 3.1. Fred and Adele Astaire in 1924

grated" musical, but with a kind of theater that is thoroughly performer- and performance-centered. Such works were in fact the norm throughout much of the history of spoken drama and musical theater, including opera. The centrality of performers came to be challenged chiefly by the quasi deification of authors and composers that was a hallmark of the Romantic era and that continued into the period of modernism and beyond, but the musical theater of Gershwin's time remained resistant to this development. The reason for the resistance is obvious: the names of musical performers, to an overwhelming extent, were what brought in the paying public.

Although the mythology surrounding the notion of the great, freestanding creative work dies hard, there is no need for condescension toward performance-centered music theater, or toward its goal of pleasing a large audience. Much recent scholarship and criticism in the arts has moved in the direction of reaffirming the central importance of performers, readers, viewers, and spectators.[8] In his comprehensive history of American music, Richard Crawford deliberately takes "performance rather than composition as a starting point," and proposes "a categorical distinction between 'composers' music,' for works whose notation embodies the authority of the composer, and 'performers' music,' for works whose notation is intended as an outline to be shaped by performers as they see fit."[9] Clearly the 1920s musical, in its script and staging as well as its songs, corresponds more closely to Crawford's category of "performers' music."

There is also no necessity to regard the 1920s musical as a dead genre, permanently surpassed and buried by the integrated musical of the Rodgers and Hammerstein era. Leonard Bernstein, responsible for two of the most celebrated scores of the 1950s, West Side Story—an integrated musical if there ever was one—and the virtually operatic Candide, preceded them both in 1953 with a show that recalls in many significant ways the ethos of the 1920s musical: Wonderful Town. Wonderful Town was designed as a performer-centered show for Rosalind Russell, and the musical came to be identified with her so thoroughly that its Broadway run quickly terminated upon her departure from the cast.[10] The show had a light and loosely structured book (based on the 1940 play My Sister Eileen, which in turn was derived from a series of stories by Ruth McKenney) that placed no impediments upon the introduction of songs that bore little essential relationship to the ongoing plot or to character development. In fact, the show's biggest production number, "Conga!," broadly inflates the silliest scene from the original play, but "Conga!" is in the show and it works, simply because it's a great number. Similarly, the sisters' duet "The Wrong Note Rag" fills a slot that could be filled as readily by any upbeat, crowd-pleasing song in an analogous style. These instances reflect what we may call 1920s-type thinking, and what is worth pondering is not simply that such thinking still yielded effective theater in the 1950s, but that such theater continues to be effective today. For at the dawn of the twenty-first century, Wonderful Town was (and continues to be) very successfully revived, and the show is arguably now on the verge of entering the Broadway "canon" that for a long while has included West Side Story and (at least as a succès d'estime) Candide.

In 1971 Stephen Sondheim's Follies took as its actual subject matter the styles of music and the kinds of performers that had defined the musical of the 1920s and 1930s and, in a masterful inversion of the strategy typical of earlier times, employed original songs to tell us everything we need to know about the stories of these fictional performers. Perhaps the greatest, and certainly the archetypical, example is "I'm Still Here," which summarizes a lifetime on (and off) the stage in the space of a five-minute solo specialty number. Like every mature Sondheim show, *Follies* is unique, but it is also unlike any other Sondheim show insofar as it owes its very purpose and existence to the preintegrated musical.

In the last decades of the twentieth century, a "new" phenomenon appeared on Broadway: the hit show designed around a particular preexisting song repertoire. Such revues had appeared previously, of course, but the huge success of the Fats Waller tribute *Ain't Misbehavin'* (1978) demonstrated that this type of show need not be an intimate production intended only for occasional short runs. With *Smokey Joe's Cafe: The Songs of Leiber and Stoller* (1995), the door opened for a rapid succession of analogous shows aimed principally at the aging baby-boom generation, musicals based on the already famous work of either songwriters or performers (the group ABBA, Elvis Presley, the Four Seasons) and designed with substantial production values in the hope of achieving long runs and public acclaim. It can be argued that these shows essentially revived the ethos of 1920s musicals, but with a new kind of twist: here, the "performers" that drew in the audience were the celebrated songs themselves.[11] The underlying and often correct assumption was that people would flock to the theater to hear these beloved oldies in a fresh context, presented by new performers and linked together by simple and functional, even skeletal, plots. The target audience for such "jukebox musicals" had come to know the songs through the media of radio and recordings, and thus presumably would find the theatrical presentation of the repertoire to be novel and reinvigorating.

Could such an audience, along with those who welcome revivals of musicals such as *Wonderful Town* and *Follies*, be ready to look afresh at the Gershwin musicals of the 1920s? In any case the intellectual climate certainly seems ripe for a reevaluation of these shows.

Lady, Be Good! as Arrival and Commencement

There are many reasons why *Lady, Be Good!* is commonly viewed as a crucial arrival point in Gershwin's Broadway career. Most significant, it was the first Broadway musical to feature a complete score uniting George's music with Ira's lyrics, and the show's great success certified the brothers' fertile partnership, which ended only with George's death.[12] But the Gershwin team was not the only partnership to receive a significant career boost through *Lady, Be Good!* The show marked the return of the Astaires to the United States following an extended period of performing in England and consequently helped to cement their status as major stars in their own country. It also introduced to Broadway the versatile production team of Alex A. Aarons and Vinton Freedley. The book was the work of Guy Bolton and Fred Thompson (Jerome Kern's frequent librettists in the 1910s), who—individually and together—made numerous further contributions to the Broadway musical theater, including the books for several later Gershwin shows. And then there was the duo piano team of Phil Ohman and Victor Arden; the two created a sensation both in the pit and on the stage in *Lady, Be Good!* and helped assure a style of musical performance that was up-to-date and idiomatically "Gershwinesque."[13]

It seems a safe surmise that these creative teams all working together on *Lady, Be Good!* must have produced an energetic synergy that accounts not only for the show's success but also for the fact that these teams sought out one another on subsequent occasions, in attempts to re-create or even enhance the magic. The eminently quotable Ethan Mordden offers a fine formulation of this synergy: after claiming baldly that "*Lady, Be Good!* isn't about anything," he corrects himself by stating "*Lady, Be Good!* is about the treat of seeing the Astaires in an Aarons–Freedley musical with a Gershwin score."[14] In addition to Bolton and Thompson, the Gershwin brothers worked again with the Astaires (and later with Fred Astaire individually), with Ohman and Arden, and most frequently with Aarons and Freedley, who produced a total of seven Broadway shows for the Gershwins. But if *Lady, Be Good!* marked in many respects a fresh beginning for those involved with it, establishing a new kind of benchmark for the 1920s musical, it also represented the achievement of a goal—writing the score for a smash-hit Broadway musical comedy—toward which both George and Ira Gershwin had labored for years.

When *Lady, Be Good!* had its New York opening late in 1924, neither Ira nor George was a newcomer to Broadway. George in particular had under his belt an early and a recent success with musical comedy (*La-La-Lucille!*, 1919; *Sweet Little Devil*, 1924) along with five consecutive years of work beginning in 1920 as the sole composer for *George White's Scandals*. The *Scandals* experience served Gershwin exceptionally well as preparation for writing his mature musical comedy scores. (After the success of *Lady, Be Good!* he never worked for White again.) The *Scandals* shows were revues, and the objection might be raised that revues rarely required that songs illuminate character or plot. But neither did 1920s musical comedies tend to require songs that provided such illumination; what they needed was in fact akin to what was needed in revues: songs designed to help performers seize a moment onstage and make an indelible impression with it. In effect, successful songs in both revues and musicals of this period provided their performers with distinctive roles to fill and suggested appropriate accompanying actions for the duration of the number. The roles could be "exotic" ("Rose of Madrid" in *George White's Scandals of 1924*, "Juanita" and "Swiss Miss" in *Lady, Be Good!*) or romantic ("Somebody Loves Me" in *George White's Scandals of 1924*, the lovers' duet "So Am I" in *Lady, Be Good!*), and might imply dancing ("I'll Build a Stairway to Paradise" in *George White's Scandals of 1922*, "The Half of It, Dearie, Blues"—complete with dancing breaks for Fred Astaire—in *Lady, Be Good!*[15]), to mention just some of the possibilities.[16] Gershwin thus came to *Lady, Be Good!* prepared to write music for any stage situation. Although the *Scandals* apparently never required him to write for performing animals, he never viewed himself as being above such necessities even late in his career, as the delightful instrumental music "Walking the Dog" (also called "Promenade") from the 1937 film *Shall We Dance* demonstrates.

It is tempting to portray the trajectory of Gershwin's career in the crucial year 1924 as essentially a linear progression: from his last "immature" musical *Sweet Little Devil* and his final *Scandals* score—with one important detour in between, into the concert hall to hone his distinctively American voice in *Rhapsody in Blue*—to the great defining triumph of *Lady, Be Good!* at year's end, a triumph that established at once the model for the "mature" Gershwin musical and for the characteristic 1920s Broadway musical comedy. Telling the story in this fashion, however, omits a second detour that destroys the impression of linear progression. Less than two months before *Lady, Be Good!* began its out-of-town tryout in Philadelphia, Gershwin's musical comedy *Primrose* made its successful debut in London. This was a show tailored for British audiences, so much so that, despite its long run in London, the show was never exported to American shores.

The score of *Primrose* reveals a composer thoroughly familiar and remarkably at home with British show idioms.[17] Even those who feel they know their Gershwin might have trouble recognizing the composer of such numbers as "Berkeley Square and Kew," "Isn't It Terrible What They Did to Mary,

Queen of Scots?" and "That New-Fangled Mother of Mine"—all of which lie at a substantial distance, stylistically as well as temporally, from a song such as Gershwin's later American-in-London love song, "A Foggy Day." Only occasionally, as in "Naughty Baby" (a song that only later became well known), did Gershwin permit his "jazzy" American idiom to emerge in *Primrose*. But if *Primrose* makes the story of Gershwin in 1924 less linear, it also makes the story richer and better, insofar as it unequivocally affirms the level of versatility Gershwin had attained as a stage composer at this time. Furthermore, there are two important and direct links between *Primrose* and *Lady, Be Good!*: Ira Gershwin assisted with the *Primrose* lyrics (which were mainly the work of Londoner Desmond Carter), and Guy Bolton coauthored the book (along with George Grossmith).[18]

While it seems obvious, especially with the benefit of hindsight, that something important had arrived with *Lady, Be Good!* it is still not a simple matter to define precisely what that something was. Valuable materials are available to the present-day researcher and listener. The general collection of the Music Division of the Library of Congress has a script for *Lady, Be Good!* (including the lyrics) that is cataloged as a "libretto, corrected to December 6, 1924." There are recordings of individual songs made between 1924 and 1926 by members of the original New York and London casts, including the Astaires, Cliff Edwards (who introduced "Fascinating Rhythm"), and Ohman and Arden.[19] And there is the 1992 recording of Tommy Krasker's restoration of the entire score, with orchestrations and performances in "period" style.[20] These all lead toward some understanding of what was presented to Broadway audiences on the opening night of December 1, 1924, and on 329 occasions thereafter, but the essence of the show remains elusive.

A sampling of reactions from knowledgeable individuals—those intimately involved with the original production, and latter-day experts on the show—provides little in the way of clarification. Ira Gershwin, in a letter he wrote to close friends five days before the Broadway opening, lamented that "the show needs lots of fixing," adding "I don't think it can be remedied either, before we open in New York City." Obviously not anticipating a big hit, Ira thought the show might "take for a nice few months anyway."[21] Fred Astaire, however, in his 1959 autobiography, claimed "From the very beginning, it seemed, *Lady, Be Good!* was one of those naturals that jelled."[22] Astaire was writing with the benefit of hindsight, but even so it was his strong opinion that the book for this musical had nothing to do with the jelling. He does not mince words: "What the plot of *Lady, Be Good!* was I really can't remember, but I do know that it was pretty stupid," and he goes on to quote sister Adele's qualms just prior to the New York opening: "Do you think they'll stand for this tacky book?"[23] The Astaires clearly felt that the show succeeded in spite of its book.

Yet it is difficult to square these comments about the book with those of Deena Rosenberg, author of the well-regarded study *Fascinating Rhythm: The Collaboration of George and Ira Gershwin,* who claims that the book for *Lady, Be Good!* "got more attention than most," including early and sustained attention from Fred Astaire. To support her argument, she quotes a letter written early in July 1924 from producer Alex Aarons to Ira Gershwin that stated: "Fred Astaire and I have spent a lot of time recently discussing the type of plot we want, also the kind of story, settings, characters, numbers, lyrics, etc."[24] In terms of conception at least, this makes *Lady, Be Good!* appear virtually akin to a latter-day integrated musical. Of course it was nothing of the sort, and it is worth noting that, despite Aarons's implied hierarchy of "story, settings, characters," some of the "numbers and lyrics" preceded the actual writing of the book.[25]

The plot thickens, so to speak, when considering the reminiscences of Kay Swift, who stressed the centrality that the book of a musical always had for George and Ira Gershwin. Swift wrote that the brothers' "major preoccupation in writing for the theater . . . was, simply, to provide a suitable musical and lyrical background for the book," and she went on to quote George: "Music and lyrics, no matter how good, can never pull a show through by themselves. . . . Oh, if a song steps out of a show and becomes a hit, of course we're happy. But the main thing we try for is appropriateness—music and lyrics must serve the book, pointing it up and moving it along."[26] Swift's comments (and, one assumes, those of Gershwin) pertained to the brothers' work in general and not to *Lady, Be Good!* in particular. Nevertheless, and even if these quotations are presumed to represent deliberate overstatements, there is an intense dichotomy emerging here between the viewpoint that the book for *Lady, Be Good!* was negligible—if not in fact an impediment—and the viewpoint that the book was somehow central to the enterprise and essential to its success. Whatever Fred Astaire may have thought about the book for *Lady, Be Good!* or about books for musicals in general, he did say this in a 1978 interview: "The placement of songs and their relationship with plot and characters mattered to George a great deal. He wanted the song to work in context, to have a good reason why a character would break into song at a particular point."[27]

Tommy Krasker views the interrelationship of book and score analogously, but reasons from the latter to the former. Writing specifically of *Lady, Be Good!* he states "The [Gershwin] brothers' inventiveness found dramatic form through librettists Guy Bolton and Fred Thompson, who crafted a plot with ample room for star turns."[28] This circles right back to the essentiality of the performers, and brings to mind Mordden's later formulation: "A script like *Lady, Be Good!*'s didn't give its characters personality: its performers did."[29] The attempt to capture the essence of this show brings to mind the famous story of the blind men and the elephant. Krasker's essay on *Lady, Be Good!* even returns us to the ambiguities regarding the genre of 1920s musical comedy itself, with which this chapter began. Labeling the show first as a "musical," he shortly thereafter writes, "A celebration of talent, it was as much revue as musical comedy," and characterizes it as a "bright hodgepodge of entertainment."[30] Krasker then discusses the role that performers' alterations and improvisations played in the continuing run of the show: "Even the surviving material failed to reveal a 'definitive' version of *Lady, Be Good!* Rather, manuscripts indicated how much the original production varied from night to night—and evolved over its long run—as the performers (in true vaudeville fashion) adjusted, shaped, and stretched their material. . . . *Lady, Be Good!* was a perpetual work-in-progress; its only constant was its success."[31] The fact that a music theater specialist, one who probably knows as much about *Lady, Be Good!* as there is to be known, moves within the course of a brief essay from the term "musical" through the term "revue" to the term "vaudeville" in seeking to describe it, strongly reinforces the slippery character both of the show itself and of 1920s musical theater in general.

The one 1920s genre that played no role in defining the character of *Lady, Be Good!* was operetta. The book and the score do not evoke Europe, the past, or traditional aristocracy; indeed, such evocations would have been egregiously out of place in a musical that parades its Americanism and contemporaneity as aggressively as *Lady, Be Good!* The single exception is the specialty number "Swiss Miss"; both the elaborate structure and the melodic character of this song recall operetta, and its "exotic" subject matter would have been right at home in that genre. It is worth recalling, though, that "Swiss Miss" originated independently of *Lady, Be Good!* and was incorporated into the score for the sole purpose of providing the Astaires with an "11 o'clock number."[32] While denying operetta any role in formulating an approach to his most characteristic 1920s musicals, Gershwin did admit significant influences from operetta in his political musicals; his longest-running

Figure 3.2. George and Ira Gershwin publicity portrait, 1928

Broadway triumph, *Of Thee I Sing* (1931), was and is widely regarded as a distinctively American operetta.

There remain a few things of which we can be certain in regard to *Lady, Be Good!* That the Gershwins' score was—and is—outstanding, that the Astaires together and individually were brilliant performers, and that the combination of the Gershwins and the Astaires produced novel and superior theatrical results, all seem uncontroversial claims. This was not all there was to *Lady, Be Good!* but it may have been enough. The crucial significance of the show to the partnership of George and Ira Gershwin is affirmed by many commentators; perhaps S. N. Behrman, who knew both brothers well, summed it up most memorably and succinctly: "In it [*Lady, Be Good!*] the brothers found each other; their wanderings ceased."[33] As for the Gershwins and the Astaires, the idea that George might one day compose the score for a musical featuring the dancing siblings apparently had had its origins many years before *Lady, Be Good!* It was a dream dating from the time when George was a "piano pounder" demonstrating songs at Jerome Remick's sheet music firm (1914–17), where he first made the acquaintance of Fred Astaire.[34] *Lady, Be Good!* thus represented the achievement of a long-sought goal for George and Fred as well as for George and Ira, and realizing this helps to explain further the special magic that must have informed the production. The striking rapport of the Gershwin-Astaire partnership was captured well by Alexander Woollcott in his review of the other Broadway musical that united the two sets of siblings, *Funny Face* (1927). Woollcott wrote "I do not know whether Gershwin was born into this world to write rhythms for Fred Astaire's feet or whether Astaire was born into this world to show how the Gershwin music should really be danced. But surely they were written in the same key, these two."[35]

Fred Astaire himself fell back on the word "magic" to account for what made the show work: "It didn't matter, that weak plot. Somehow there was an indefinable magic about the show." He added that "the whole thing had a new look to it, a flow, and also a new sound with Phil Ohman and Vic Arden playing their two specialty pianos in the pit orchestra with Gershwin's best score to date." Rather than being a "hackneyed ordinary musical comedy," this show "was slick and tongue-in-cheek."[36] Turning to more recent commentaries, Rosenberg simply states that *Lady, Be Good!* "introduced a new kind of dramatic and American song and dance to musical comedy."[37] And Mordden reduces the essence of all this to a single word: "Seeking the musical that says *now*, we should talk about *Lady, Be Good!*"[38] What the show obviously projected was a new *tone* for the American musical. *Lady, Be Good!* had energy to burn; it had pizzazz; to use an anachronistic, more up-to-date term, it had attitude. This attitude—an insouciant, unsentimental, "jazzy," utterly "modern" tone—was projected not just by the score and the performers, but by all of the show's ingredients, including the book (weaknesses notwithstanding). It must have provided *Lady, Be Good!* with an individual and highly original kind of stylistic unity.

The unity of tone in *Lady, Be Good!* is demonstrated not only by what was included in the show, but by what was taken out. "The Man I Love" was originally incorporated into *Lady, Be Good!* as a solo for Adele Astaire.[39] It was arguably the finest song in the entire score, yet was dropped quickly during the out-of-town tryouts, and the decision to drop it could not have been more astute.[40] "The Man I Love" has an intimate, introspective, yearning quality that is completely at odds with the externalized, insistently upbeat tone that came to define *Lady, Be Good!* The sole number in the Broadway score even to approach the darker emotional hues is "The Half of It, Dearie, Blues," whose title alone indicates the distance this song of self-mockery lies from deep seriousness. Clearly the makers of this show understood, at least intuitively, what *Lady, Be Good!* was "about."

In a city that was in every respect the cultural center of the United States, and at a time when styles in theater, music, fashion, and mores were metamorphosing at a breathless pace, the Broadway audiences for *Lady, Be Good!* were treated to a show that encouraged them to feel up-to-date, trendy, and "with it" — in a sophisticated yet unpretentious way. This was no small achievement. But conceptualizing the achievement in this way also helps illuminate why *Lady, Be Good!* would be almost impossible to revive both faithfully and successfully. The problem lies not with the show's weaknesses, but with the particular nature of its strengths. Even if a dancing duo with gifts comparable to those of the Astaires could be found today; and even if that duo could also play convincingly at being brother and sister (assuming the two weren't already so related), as the show's book demands; and even if a comedian as skilled at 1920s-style verbal and physical humor as Walter Catlett could be found, along with a "specialty" musician as capable as Cliff Edwards, and duo pianists versed in the techniques of Ohman and Arden, and many others to fill the remaining roles; and even if everyone involved labored intensively to capture the appropriate performance style in dialogue, action, dance, and song (including improvisation) — what would be the result? Not a "musical that says *now*," surely, but at best an obvious period piece. And an inevitable conundrum arises from the fact that if there is anything *Lady, Be Good!* most emphatically was *not* for its original Broadway public, it was not a period piece. There is no way for a production or an audience of today to recapture the frisson of "modernity" that was exuded by *Lady, Be Good!* in the 1920s. Even were many aspects of the show to be updated — always a dangerous proposition — it remains an unfortunate truth that the Gershwin score itself, timeless though it may be, can never say "*now*" to a twenty-first century audience. Could that audience take to its heart a musical that says "*then*"?

The Many Charms of a Good *Lady*

Revivable or not, *Lady, Be Good!* represents the cornerstone for an understanding of Gershwin's Broadway career. Consequently, an investigation
of its elements is now in order, beginning with the much-maligned book.[41]
Bolton and Thompson did not base their work directly on any known preexisting source, but *Lady, Be Good!* was fashioned in a manner akin to most
comedies, insofar as its plot revolves around love—the course of which, naturally, does not run smooth. There are the classic ingredients of a love triangle,
love at first sight, poverty as obstacle, and wealth as enticement. The comic
figure central to the show is an archetypical one: the shady (but not truly malevolent) lawyer. There is a character in disguise, whose mistaken identity is
the source of much humorous confusion. The concept of the exotic "Other"
receives more than its due: one Mexican man, one American woman posing
as a Mexican, and the same woman dressed (later on) as a Swiss yodeler.
The script abounds in wordplay, including some good (and many bad) puns,
along with much pseudo-Spanish gobbledygook to enliven the "Mexican"
thread. The book also offers much opportunity for physical comedy. Similar
or analogous elements recur in the books for many of Gershwin's later shows.

To these typical elements were added features tailored especially for the
cast and the audience of *Lady, Be Good!* in order to render the show distinctive and up-to-date. The "couple" around whose fortunes the plot revolves
are not lovers but siblings, who just happen to love dancing together. The
construction of the book around the real-life identity of the Astaires may be
the most obvious indication of how profoundly *Lady, Be Good!* was shaped
by its star performers. In addition, both the cast and the audience probably
were delighted by specific contemporary references in the dialogue. The first
scene is barely under way when the "silver flask on your hip" makes a not-
so-veiled allusion to Prohibition, and in act 1, scene 3, a mention of "hard-
hearted Hannah" refers to the title of a 1924 hit song.[42] The lyrics in *Lady, Be
Good!* have their trendy aspects as well. In act 1, scene 3, the second verse of
"We're Here Because" presents the phrase "psycho-analyze the question a la
Freud," and later in the same scene, the famous "Fascinating Rhythm" employs the then-current slang term "flivver" for an ailing automobile.[43] In the
second act, the phrase "You don't know the half of it, dearie," popularized at
the time by the *Ziegfeld Follies*, provides an important song from *Lady, Be
Good!* with both its title and its recurrent verbal hook.[44]

The plot of *Lady, Be Good!* lends itself readily to summary, if not to rational comprehension. The curtain rises on the "old Trevor Homestead" in Rhode Island, where siblings Dick and Susie Trevor have fallen on hard times; as the show opens, they are being evicted from their home for nonpayment of rent. While Dick goes off to call lawyer J. Watterson "Watty" Watkins for possible assistance, Jack Robinson—another impoverished character, who is returning home after wandering all the way to Mexico—encounters Susie on the street. Since Jack and Susie share starry-eyed youth and recent misfortune in common, naturally they fall in love instantly, but their mutual lack of means poses an initial impediment to the fruition of any relationship. When Jack leaves, Dick returns with a plan: he's going to marry wealthy Josephine Vanderwater, who lives nearby, and thereby solve his and Susie's money problems once and for all. (We learn later in the act that Vanderwater, whose uncle owns the Trevors' house, actually arranged for their eviction in hopes of facilitating the identical outcome.) Susie protests that Dick is really in love with Shirley Vernon. This is true, but since poor Shirley lacks financial resources of her own, Dick sees this as a relationship without a future—and the audience will note the resemblance to the situation of Jack and Susie.

All of this is efficiently conveyed by the brief first scene, even before any song is performed. Love at first sight (Jack and Susie), the love triangle (Dick–Shirley–Josephine), the lawyer (Watkins), and a hint about Mexico are all in place within a few minutes' stage time. The scene is also framed extremely well, opening with hilarious slapstick potential as items are hurled out of the Trevors' house and Susie is carried out protesting on her bed, and concluding with the first sung number in the show, the siblings' attractive and upbeat duet "Hang On to Me." Those who esteem sophisticated dramaturgy will find the book of *Lady, Be Good!* a steady downhill plunge from here, unfortunately. Still, this first scene demonstrates the craft of which writers Bolton and Thompson were capable.

It turns out that while Jack was in Mexico, his estranged uncle died, leaving the young fellow a large inheritance—of which Jack is unaware. The resolution of the plot hinges upon Jack's discovery of his good fortune. The book's authors could have achieved this resolution quite quickly, of course, after which Jack and Susie would marry and the newly rich Susie would help her brother back on his feet, following which Dick and Shirley would wed, and Jo Vanderwater could seek some other eligible bachelor who'd enjoy marrying into money. But this wouldn't be a comedy or a musical if the resolution were to occur so simply and efficiently. The complications that Bolton and Thompson devised are rather mind-boggling, requiring the acceptance of any number of improbabilities. Apparently lawyer Watkins has heard about Jack's inheritance and, presuming the young man to be permanently missing, has become involved in a scam to represent Jack as deceased and a Mexican woman as Jack's widow (entitling her to collect the inheritance), with a sizable sum going to Watkins for his lawyerly efforts. It gets better: the "señora" is unable to come to the States and collect, for she has been imprisoned in Mexico. Consequently Watkins tries to pressure Susie to disguise herself as the widow, offering as incentive a nice cut from his own anticipated take. At first Susie rejects this idea, but when she learns of brother Dick's proposal of marriage to Jo Vanderwater, her sense of probity is sufficiently offended to make her reconsider and accept Watkins's illegal scheme. After much, much ado, Jack is at last discovered to be very much alive, present on the scene, and unmarried; Susie is discovered to be very much American, no widow, and unmarried; and Jo is so offended by the revealed pretense of Susie that she breaks off her engagement with Dick. Then, as quickly as you can say "fascinating wedding," the finale is upon us, as no fewer than four couples prepare to take vows—all to the tune of "Fascinating Rhythm," naturally. In addition to Dick and Shirley, and Susie and Jack, the comic pair Daisy Parke and Bertie Bassett (who have been billing and cooing sporadically throughout the show) announce their intention to tie the knot, and Watkins is at hand to offer his hand to Jo (for whom he evinced an obvious attraction previously, in the third scene of the first act).

Obviously the audience was not supposed to ask whether any of this made sense, including the basic issue of why Jack would have journeyed as far as Mexico after falling out with his uncle. The assumption, which turned out to be correct, was that the public would be so thoroughly beguiled by Walter Catlett's comic performance as Watkins, by Adele Astaire's charm and Mexican costume, by the proliferating bilingual malapropisms, and by all the other stage shenanigans prescribed by the book or improvised around it, that there would be neither time nor energy for concerns of logic.[45] The only criterion that mattered was entertainment value. And admittedly the book, ridiculous as it is, offers a good deal of that. There is one particularly delicious scene occasioned by the unraveling of Watkins's scheme: Jack, after initially helping Susie to save face in public by proclaiming her to be his Mexican wife, then continues to insist in private with her that they are married.[46] By this point the audience would probably empathize with Jack's desire to derive a little fun for himself from the outrageous situation before all the strands of the plot get finally untangled.

The Gershwin songs are inserted into and intertwine with the book in various ways, sometimes casually and sometimes more intricately. Table 3.1 lists all the musical numbers included in the libretto of December 6, 1924 (dated five days following the Broadway premiere), in order of performance; this table will be employed as a reference to facilitate the discussion to follow. It will be noticed in the table that the singing cast includes a character named Jeff, who has not been mentioned in the previous discussion simply because he plays no significant role whatsoever in the plot. Jeff was Cliff Edwards, popularly known as Ukulele Ike, whose function in the plot and in the show was only to provide additional entertainment. In act 1, he played the part of a hired musician at Jo Vanderwater's party, and his "specialty" spot in act 2 was performed in front of the curtain following a blackout between the second and final scenes—a long-standing if soon to be antiquated theatrical tradition.[47] Table 3.1 also characterizes each musical selection in terms of its dramatic function in *Lady, Be Good!* "Defining" numbers play a critical role in delineating characters and relationships; "action" numbers, involving an ensemble, serve to move the stage action forward, but typically are not critical to the ongoing plot to the extent of "defining" numbers; and "specialty" numbers are usually superfluous to the plot per se, but add measurably either to the musical substance or to the effective showcasing of performers (and sometimes, as is the case with "Fascinating Rhythm," to both).[48]

Table 3.1 demonstrates that the music of *Lady, Be Good!* was effectively sequenced to maximize variety among solos, duets, and ensembles, and among defining, action, and specialty numbers. Given the ethos of the 1920s musical, it should not surprise us that there are relatively few defining numbers. It is striking that the essential defining numbers—"Hang On to Me," "We're Here Because," "So Am I," and "The Half of It, Dearie, Blues"—are all duets, and that they have been strategically placed within the show so as to emerge prominently, and quite possibly to invite comparison with one another. Each of these duets characterizes both a relationship and the individuals in it at a pivotal dramatic moment. "Hang On to Me," the first song, positions the siblings Dick and Susie (as well as Fred and Adele Astaire) at the center of the show, clearly portraying the mutuality of their affection, concern, and support for one another (with art in this case imitating life). The remaining three duets depict three different love relationships, each at a different stage of development. "We're Here Because" presents the minor couple Daisy and Bertie as simply, happily, and sappily obsessed with each other; given the characters and the rather generic sentiment, this number is

Table 3.1. Musical Numbers in *Lady, Be Good!*

Title	Cast	Function
Act 1		
1. Hang On to Me	Dick and Susie (duet)	Defining
2. Wonderful Party	Ensemble	Action
segue: Hang On to Me	[Orchestra; Dick and Susie dance]	Action
3. End of a String	Ensemble	Action
4. We're Here Because	Daisy and Bertie (duet)	Defining
5. Fascinating Rhythm	Jeff, then Ensemble	Specialty
6. So Am I	Jack and Susie (duet)	Defining
7. Oh, Lady Be Good!	Watty Watkins and Girls of Ensemble	Specialty
8. Fascinating Rhythm	[Orchestra, for dancing]	Action
9. "Piano Speciality"	Ohman and Arden, duo pianists	Specialty
10. Finale:		Action
"Ting-a-ling, the wedding bells";[49]	Ensemble	
Oh, Lady Be Good! brief reprise	Watkins	
segue: Fascinating Rhythm, reprise[50]	Ensemble	
Act 2		
11. Linger in the Lobby	Ensemble	Action
12. The Half of It, Dearie, Blues	Dick and Shirley (duet)	Defining
13. Juanita	Boys of Ensemble	Specialty
14. So Am I, reprise	Susie and Jack (duet)	Defining(?)*
15. Oh, Lady Be Good! reprise	Jack	Defining(?)*
16. Little Jazz Bird[51]	Jeff (Cliff Edwards)	Specialty
17. Carnival Time	[Orchestra, for dancing]	Action
18. Swiss Miss	Susie and Dick (duet)	Specialty
19. Finale: Fascinating Rhythm, reprise (as Fascinating Wedding)[52]	Ensemble	Defining

*In terms of the immediate plot circumstances, these reprises may be viewed as "defining" numbers, but they differ from the other numbers I have called "defining" because what they define involves deception as well as reality. In "So Am I," Susie is continuing to impersonate the Mexican "widow" of the supposedly deceased Jack; as she relates the many fine characteristics her "husband" possessed, Jack is able to employ the words of the song's title repeatedly to assert his own possession of these same characteristics (e.g., Susie: "He was grand, how I sigh, what a man!"; Jack: "So am I!"). The concealed reality here is that Susie is truly enamored of Jack, albeit without knowing his true identity. In "Oh, Lady Be Good!" Jack, with both his identity and his live status clearly revealed, insists to Susie that she is truly his wife: "I've put an end to your widowhood so, wifie, be good to me!" This brings the deception full circle but again hints at concealed reality, since Jack would like nothing better than actually to marry Susie. These two reprises are minor events in the show as a whole, but they present exceptionally clever employment of previously heard material — real additions, rather than mere repetitions.

appropriately the least individualized of all the duets in terms of both music and lyrics. As Jack and Susie sing "So Am I" in act 1, they are in the process of falling in love—something they mutually confess as the song ends. And "The Half of It, Dearie, Blues" presents Dick and Shirley at what would seem to be a hopeless crossroads, since Dick has become engaged to Jo Vanderwater, yet the number allows the apparently estranged couple to articulate through music their shared unhappiness with the situation and thus suggests (to the audience, at least) a spark of hope for their relationship.

Before proceeding further, a clarification of what makes a song "defining" in this show is appropriate. It is obviously not a matter of a song that could arise only from this particular book and couldn't conceivably be useful for a different show without significant alterations in lyrics or music or both. The score of *Lady, Be Good!* offers no numbers remotely akin to "Pore Jud Is Daid" from *Oklahoma!* "Soliloquy" from *Carousel*, the "Jet Song" from *West Side Story*, "Roxie" from *Chicago*, or "A Little Priest" from *Sweeney Todd*. But without the four defining duets in *Lady, Be Good!* there would be holes in the script, and an understanding of plot, character, and motivation would consequently be impaired. Given the extensive slighting the book for *Lady, Be Good!* has suffered in these pages, perhaps the last sentence should be amended to state that without these duets there would be *more* holes in the script, and even an *elementary* understanding of plot, character, and motivation would be impaired. Yet it is not disingenuous to engage concepts such as plot, character, and motivation seriously in reference to *Lady, Be Good!* and the employment of such terms does not deflect the case that has been made for the centrality of song, dance, and performance in this show. Rather, numbers such as "Hang On to Me," "So Am I," and "The Half of It, Dearie, Blues" demonstrate the extent to which the score proves essential to any sense of internal coherence at certain critical points in the script. If the specialty numbers tend toward the opposite pole, they serve to remind us that the 1920s Gershwin musical was a mongrel creature, a heterogeneous and exuberantly messy phenomenon that no sooner seems to point tentatively forward to integrated book musicals than, in the wink of an eye, it skips merrily back toward vaudeville.

If "Hang On to Me" were to be omitted, the upbeat mood that colors the entire show would fail to achieve articulation in the opening scene. As it is, the initial duet caps the first scene effectively by attesting to Dick and Susie's resilience in the face of their misfortune—a resilience that stems from the positive strength of their familial bond. After hearing this number, one is led to suspect that, despite the ins and outs of the plot, the siblings are unlikely to stick with any course of action that might have an enduringly negative impact on their relationship, and in the end this suspicion is validated. The importance of "Hang On to Me" is underlined by its instrumental recurrence shortly after it is sung, as Dick and Susie talk and dance their way into Jo Vanderwater's party. "We're Here Because" is admittedly much less important than the other definitive duets, but without it we wouldn't know the extent to which Daisy and Bertie are truly, hopelessly enamored of each other. "So Am I" and "The Half of It, Dearie, Blues" convince us, in their very different ways, that the couples involved must end up together—not simply because the plot demands it, but because they are revealed truly to care.

Musically, the three act 1 duets express straightforward affection by dwelling on simple repeated motifs. In "Hang On to Me," the two-note diatonic motif moves sequentially up the notes of a major triad; this simplicity of pitch structure reflects perhaps the basic nature of the sibling relationship.[53] The two-note chromatic motif that informs "We're Here Because" effectively conveys the urgency of Daisy's and Bertie's passion, especially when it is sung at the headlong tempo that characterizes this number. In the case of "So Am I," the central motif has grown to three notes, the last one consistently prolonged for several beats, as if attesting to the new lovers' reluctance to part. "The Half of It, Dearie, Blues" (in act 2) is constructed along different lines, as befits a duet expressing frustrated feelings in a negative situation. Here the dominating idea is not a brief motif, but rather an arch-shaped idea extending over thirteen notes and (counting the final long note) four measures.

The general family resemblance among the three act 1 duets is emphasized in the overture to *Lady, Be Good!* Gershwin cleverly structured the overture so that the three tunes would seem almost to grow one from another. After opening with a big statement of the musical's title song, the overture presents "We're Here Because," followed by "Hang On to Me," and then "So Am I"; in this sequence the listener may hear a two-note chromatic motif metamorphose into a two-note diatonic motif, which is in turn extended to a three-note diatonic motif. (The overture then moves to "Fascinating Rhythm," after which it rounds itself off with a restatement of "Oh, Lady, Be Good!") Clearly Gershwin was interested in giving meaningful shape to the usually amorphous overture for musicals, even this early in his career. Was he perhaps drawing on his recent experience with independent instrumental form provided by the composition of *Rhapsody in Blue*? In any case, the appearance of "We're Here Because" in the overture seems an obvious instance of foregrounding structural considerations over others, since in the show itself this number is a song of secondary importance performed by secondary characters. Unlike all the other numbers heard in the overture, "We're Here Because" is presented only once after the curtain rises.

The "action" numbers in *Lady, Be Good!* provide purely functional music. They serve to introduce and conclude scenes, to accompany movement on the stage, and to give members of a group something to sing while they mill about or move decisively from one position to another. Although songs such as "A Wonderful Party" and "Linger in the Lobby" do accomplish a measure of scene setting, they are in no way essential to the drama. What is noteworthy about Gershwin's action numbers is how well made they are. A musical slot that could have called forth mere busywork from a lesser composer became, in Gershwin's hands, the occasion for highly skilled craftsmanship. "End of a String" and particularly "Linger in the Lobby" inspire admiration for their formal and rhythmic inventiveness. Although the action numbers from *Lady, Be Good!* were not the big hits of the show—and were not designed to be—the opportunities they afforded Gershwin to write for vocal ensemble helped develop this aspect of his compositional technique. These opportunities thus prepared him for the challenges in ensemble writing that he would later set himself in *Strike Up the Band, Of Thee I Sing, Let 'Em Eat Cake,* and especially *Porgy and Bess.*

When we turn at last to the specialty numbers, the peculiar and eclectic nature of the 1920s Gershwin musical confronts us baldly. "Fascinating Rhythm" is the song most frequently used in *Lady, Be Good!* One of two immediately popular songs from this musical (the other being the title song), it remains surely the most performed and admired number to come from the score. Yet it is introduced as a specialty number, utterly incidental in terms of the developing plot. More remarkably, the title song itself has nothing essential to do with the show. Its opening lyrics are linked to the book in a makeshift and ultimately tenuous way through the substitution of "Susie" for "lady": "Oh, sweet and lovely Susie, be good!"[54] At this point Watkins is pleading with Susie to participate in his scheme to obtain the Robinson inheritance—and the crucial word "good" does take on an effective ironic tinge in this context. But the lyrics that follow make progressively less sense in relation both to the plot and to the nature of Watkins's character; the wily lawyer is hardly "all alone in this big city" and is quite far from being what anyone would describe as "a lonesome babe in the wood." As the song progresses, all pretense of plot relevance is quickly abandoned, and "Oh, Lady Be Good!" reveals its true nature as a big production number: Susie exits, a chorus of girls enters, and Watkins proceeds to have a grand old time playing up to the young ladies individually and together. This was comedian Walter Catlett's biggest moment in the show, and he evidently made the most of it. According to Gershwin himself, "Walter was a funny man, and, like a lot of comedians, even his voice was funny—in fact, it was terrible. And what he did to '[Oh,] Lady, Be Good!' was nobody's business."[55]

If "Oh, Lady Be Good!" gloriously flaunts its irrelevance in the show, something rather different happens to "Fascinating Rhythm" as it makes its several reappearances. Introduced as party entertainment for the characters onstage (as opposed to Cliff Edwards's act 2 specialty, which is presented strictly as entertainment for the audience in the theater), "Fascinating Rhythm" insinuates itself into the action as it is employed for dance music at the party, and it eventually forms the climax of the act 1 finale. "Fascinating Rhythm" also concludes act 2, with its new lyrics ("fascinating wedding") now conveying information essential to the resolution of the plot: the confirmed reconciliation and impending nuptials of four couples. By this time the originally ornamental specialty number has become the defining culmination of the show. In the abstract this would seem to be quite a conceptual and dramatic coup. It is difficult to know, however, the extent to which this evolution of "Fascinating Rhythm" was consciously planned by the show's creators. Perhaps it was just a particularly intriguing by-product of the serendipity that surrounded the making of *Lady, Be Good!*—especially since the act 2 finale arrives and departs so quickly. In any case, it comes as no surprise that "Fascinating Rhythm" was featured so extensively in the show. The creators recognized a great musical theater number when they had one. Furthermore, the extent to which the essence of *Lady, Be Good!* may be seen ultimately as resting upon the freshness and novelty of its music and dancing is precisely the extent to which the show is ultimately *about* "Fascinating Rhythm." Viewed in this light, the "specialty" number not only evolves into something essential; rather, "Fascinating Rhythm" embodies the core of the show from the moment of its first appearance.

A consideration of the ways in which "Fascinating Rhythm" functions in *Lady, Be Good!* raises one other provocative issue. To frame it as a question: to what extent are the characters in this show—as distinct from the performers and the audience—presumed to be aware of the music? There is a certain amount of obviously diegetic music in *Lady, Be Good!* It is apparent that the onstage characters all hear Jeff perform "Fascinating Rhythm" as a *song*, complete with onstage ukulele, and that they are later aware of it being played as music for their dancing at Jo Vanderwater's party. Furthermore, they are aware of this dance music as being specifically "Fascinating Rhythm"; when it starts up again during the finale to act 1, Dick pointedly asks Susie, "Why is it every time we are having a good fight somebody has to play that tune?"[56] This is not the only point in the show at which the performers seem to be sharing a joke with the audience at the expense of music theater itself, mocking its basic artificiality. Earlier in the act 1 finale, just as the ensemble has completed singing its congratulations to Jo and Dick on the occasion of their engagement, Watkins enters and, realizing that the chorus has been singing, laments "Oh, dear, I've forgotten my music."[57] Such play with the conventions of musical comedy definitely contributes to the distinctive character of *Lady, Be Good!* and must have been, for audiences of the 1920s, yet another facet of its nowness.[58]

The remaining specialty numbers require little comment. "Juanita" is marginally connected to the plot, insofar as it celebrates Susie's "Mexican" persona. Gershwin's music for "Juanita" offers little in the way of "exotic" atmosphere, however, and simply presents the opportunity for a colorful stage number. "Swiss Miss" is as gleefully irrelevant to the story as Cliff Edwards's act 2 numbers—unless we are supposed to take seriously the idea that Susie has abruptly landed a job as a Swiss yodeler!—and had no more (or less) important a function than providing the Astaires with a spectacular star turn just before the show's conclusion.

This discussion has so far avoided selecting individual songs for musical and lyrical analysis outside the context of the show. Since so many of Gershwin's songs remain well known, while the shows from which they came have become virtually unknown, recontextualization is particularly illuminating. Let us now, however, consider two numbers from *Lady, Be Good!* to examine more fully the artistry of George Gershwin's music and of his brother's lyrics.

As the opening number, "Hang On to Me" has to be a fine and memorable song in and of itself, while successfully establishing an appropriate tone and stylistic point of reference for the musical's entire score. The song performs its multiple tasks admirably, with both efficiency and grace. Considering the refrain first, it opens with a two-note melodic motif that is immediately restated twice in a syncopated rhythmic pattern (see ex. 3.1). This in turn creates a two-measure melodic and rhythmic unit that is directly echoed in

Example 3.1. "Hang On to Me," refrain, mm. 1–8

mm. 3–4 and 5–6 as the tune makes its way up the pitches of a tonic triad. All this seems as basic and natural as the sibling relationship being celebrated in the lyrics—as does the descent to the tonic note in m. 7. What is completely unexpected, however, is the parenthetical appendage of m. 8 ("Forever and a day") and its introduction of new pitches, including the striking blue third B-flat. This "jazzy" touch is like a fashionable wink from Gershwin, assuring his performers and listeners that, despite all the straightforward triads, this is indeed the jazz age.[59] Eight bars into the refrain of its opening number, *Lady, Be Good!* had thus initiated its audience into the delights of syncopation and blue notes, trendy musical characteristics that reappear abundantly in the score.

Syncopation even occurs directly at the outset of the introductory verse in "Hang On to Me" (see ex. 3.2). The verse also anticipates the arpeggiated melodic line of the refrain, although the essential direction of the line in the verse is downward rather than upward. This is appropriate, as the lyrics of

Example 3.2. "Hang On to Me," verse, mm. 1–4

the verse refer to the troubled situation in which Dick and Susie find themselves, while the lyrics of the refrain convey optimism and reassurance. The basic motif of the verse spans the dissonant interval of a seventh (D down to E), as opposed to the intervals of the tonic triad articulated in the refrain. Nevertheless, the melodic leaps of a third that are consistently present in this song—these leaps also permeate the bridge section of the refrain—serve as an obvious source of unity.

In terms of form, "Hang On to Me" is as uncomplicated as the sentiments it communicates. The verse has a sixteen-measure structure comprised of four four-bar sections in the pattern AA'AB, while the thirty-two measures of the refrain present the typical AABA arrangement of four eight-bar sections.[60] These formal patterns reappear in the other songs of the score, either literally or in varied manifestations.

The lyrics Ira Gershwin provided for "Hang On to Me" demonstrate a simplicity concealing artistry that complements his brother's music perfectly. Graceful yet unexpected rhymes ("For like Hansel and Gretel / We will prove our mettle") and a skillful employment of internal rhyme ("Don't *sigh*, we'll get along; / Just *try* humming a song") are typical of Ira's essential contributions to the spirit and sparkle of *Lady, Be Good!*

Turning to "Fascinating Rhythm," we encounter a song of much greater complexity than "Hang On to Me"—as befits the most highlighted specialty tune in the show. "Fascinating Rhythm" is a celebrated and frequently discussed Gershwin song; because of this and because of its intricacy, a comprehensive discussion of the number will not be attempted here.[61] Rather, attention will be directed to significant similarities and differences between "Fascinating Rhythm" and "Hang On to Me" and to a few infrequently re-marked details.

Nobody who has heard "Fascinating Rhythm" even once will need to be told about syncopation and blue notes in this song; it provides a classic in-stance of the "Gershwin style" as most traditionally (and narrowly) defined. One important similarity between this number and "Hang On to Me" is the way in which the verse introduces musical ideas that will be carried into the refrain, albeit in a contrasting manner. This is a compositional practice evi-dent in many Gershwin songs. (See, for another example, the discussion of "The Man I Love" in chapter 2.) In the case of "Fascinating Rhythm," it is the virtually obsessive reiteration of a basic melodic and rhythmic motif that links the verse with the refrain, although each part of the song is given an individual motif. In the verse it is the three-note descending figure first heard on the words "rhythm, a rhythm, a," while in the refrain it is the six-note idea (plus an eighth-note rest) to which the words of the song's title are set (see ex. 3.3).

Another similarity between "Hang On to Me" and "Fascinating Rhythm" involves the role harmony plays in defining the basic character of each song, although the two songs are so contrasting in character that this conceptual analogy between them becomes also a source of visceral difference. Looking at the refrains, it is striking the extent to which "Hang On to Me" is an-chored to the stable, steady consonance of its tonic triad, while "Fascinating Rhythm" is appropriately awash in jittery, unresolved harmony. The differ-ence extends so far as to render the two numbers virtual opposites harmoni-cally: while the refrain of "Hang On to Me" begins firmly on its tonic chord, with the tonic note strongly reinforced by the vocal line, one must wait until the very end of the refrain in "Fascinating Rhythm" to hear the voice and the accompaniment arrive, together and unequivocally, on a stable tonic.

The attention that commentators on "Fascinating Rhythm" usually de-vote, justifiably, to the song's exceptional rhythmic ingenuity has tended — understandably but unfortunately — to suppress awareness of its equally remarkable harmonic dimension. The off-tonic opening of the refrain is in-herently unstable, but this instability is underlined in two distinct ways. First of all, the chords of the accompaniment are arranged in a way such as to maximize dissonance (see ex. 3.3); musicians would particularly note the absence of chordal roots in the bass line of this passage. Furthermore, the preceding verse has generated harmonic instability in its own way (by so in-

Example 3.3 "Fascinating Rhythm," mm. 1–4 of the verse and mm. 1–4 of the refrain

sisting on blue thirds that the song opens de facto in a minor key), and has consequently established a particular expectation of resolution that fails to materialize with the refrain.

Ira's lyrics for George's fascinating rhythms are replete with felicitous touches. In the first four measures of the refrain, for instance, observe how the verbal accent pattern shifts with each successive six-syllable unit, in order to accommodate precisely the changing metrical position of the six-note motif (see ex. 3.3): "*Fas*-ci-nat-ing Rhythm, / You've *got* me on the go! / Fas-ci-*nat*-ing Rhythm, / I'm all a-*qui*-ver." Ira's choice of the adjective "fascinating" is particularly admirable; in addition to its descriptive aptness, the word's primary and secondary accents suit it perfectly for the double duty it fulfills in these four measures. In the verse, Ira's gift for playful and intricate rhyme is again on display, as he describes the rhythm:

Comes in the morning
Without any warning,
And hangs around me all day.
I'll have to sneak up to it
Someday, and speak up to it.
I hope it listens when I say . . .[62]

The verse of "Fascinating Rhythm" is sixteen measures long, with four four-bar sections in an AA'A"B pattern; the formal similarity to the verse of "Hang On to Me" is evident. The refrain of "Fascinating Rhythm" is comprised of the usual four eight-measure sections, although the pattern here is ABAC. In the last four bars of the C section, however, Gershwin reiterates the opening motif of A, and in so doing makes effective reference to the kind of formal rounding that characterizes an AABA refrain. This strategy is not atypical of Gershwin songs with refrains in an ABAC pattern.

"Hang On to Me" and "Fascinating Rhythm" together demonstrate the wide stylistic range Gershwin was already exploring in his Broadway music by 1924. The quiet mastery of the former contrasts most effectively with the latter's aggressive brilliance. A wide and wonderful musical palette vivified the score of *Lady, Be Good!* at every turn and made an inestimable contribution to the treat this show offered its audiences.

The Model of *Lady, Be Good!* as Reflected in Later Musicals

Lady, Be Good! was performed on Broadway 330 times, and it represented Gershwin's greatest success of the 1920s in terms of performance longevity.[63] By this standard, in second place is *Oh, Kay!*, whose Broadway opening in November 1926 took place nearly two years after that of *Lady, Be Good! Oh, Kay!* ran for 256 performances. (In between *Lady, Be Good!* and *Oh, Kay!* Gershwin worked in 1925 on three shows, two of which—*Tell Me More!* and *Tip-Toes*—employed members of the creative team that produced *Lady, Be Good!* The other show was the operetta *Song of the Flame*, featuring music by both Gershwin and Herbert Stothart.) *Oh, Kay!* won a place in Broadway history thanks to the spectacular success of Gertrude Lawrence in the title role of this first show written explicitly for her. The show also won the enduring esteem of both Gershwin aficionados and lovers of music theater by virtue of its bejeweled score. With gems such as "Maybe," "Clap Yo' Hands," "Do, Do, Do," "Someone to Watch Over Me," and "Fidgety Feet" adorning it, the score of *Oh, Kay!* as a whole arguably surpasses even that of *Lady, Be Good!* A brief examination of *Oh, Kay!* will prove useful by revealing concepts and operating principles that were retained from the earlier musical, along with those that evolved, metamorphosed, had to be discarded, or were invented anew to fit the new circumstances.

To begin with the personnel involved, many veterans from *Lady, Be Good!* played crucial creative roles in *Oh, Kay!* —George and Ira Gershwin, producers Aarons and Freedley, and Guy Bolton, who coauthored the book this time with his frequent collaborator P. G. Wodehouse. The cast was different, but continuity with the now established standards of appropriate Gershwin style in performance was guaranteed by the presence of duo pianists Ohman and Arden in the pit.

The performers may have been new to a Gershwin show, but the idea of structuring a Gershwin show around performers certainly was not. In this case it was a single performer, the multitalented Gertrude Lawrence, who defined the show. This naturally led to a show substantially different from *Lady, Be Good!* insofar as Lawrence was not a member of a performing duo, nor was she known as a dancer. Consequently there was no parallel in *Oh, Kay!* to the proliferation of duets in *Lady, Be Good!* (although Lawrence got to sing two fine duets, "Maybe" and "Do, Do, Do," with her leading man, and two of the secondary characters were accorded the comic duet "Fidgety Feet"), and the show did not present an abundance of specialty numbers with dancing (although, to be sure, there were specialty numbers in the score). On the other hand, Lawrence was able to do something that even Adele Astaire evidently could not: successfully sustain a serious solo love song in the midst of an upbeat, lightweight plot. Therefore the wonderful and wistful "Someone to Watch Over Me" remained in Lawrence's show, whereas "The Man I Love" had to be excised from *Lady, Be Good!* prior to that show's Broadway opening.[64]

For all the differences, *Oh, Kay!* was still a show that said *now* to its audiences as emphatically as had *Lady, Be Good!* What could be more *now* in 1926 than a show whose very subject matter revolved around Prohibition? (Of course this would unavoidably render any revival of the show a period piece.) And naturally there were those Gershwin songs, with their characteristically up-to-date rhythms, melodic inflections, and harmonic color.

The book for *Oh, Kay!* is somewhat more coherent and more literate, if no more serious, than that of *Lady, Be Good!* At least there is no plot thread involving an unclaimed inheritance and a bogus Mexican widow, although the marital status of the leading male character Jimmy Winter vacillates rather nonsensically at points. To be sure, love takes center stage once again in *Oh, Kay!* and the love triangle involving Kay, Jimmy, and Jimmy's bride (or bride-to-be) Constance is the hinge upon which the plot turns. Since Kay is the sister of a bootlegger, her strategies for avoiding a troublesome revenue officer present numerous opportunities for disguise and mistaken identity; first she poses as Jimmy's wife, and later as his maid. The legal profession is represented in *Oh, Kay!* by a comic judge who is Constance's father, rather than by the shady lawyer of *Lady, Be Good!* One final jab is accorded the spirit of the law in *Oh, Kay!* when the persistent revenue officer turns out himself to be a bootlegger in disguise. The exotic "Other" receives just token recognition in *Oh, Kay!* via the "mammy song" performed by one of the bootleggers as a specialty number to entertain the others onstage, "Clap Yo' Hands." There is the usual array of puns besprinkled throughout the script, and many an occasion for physical comedy.

Several of the songs Gershwin wrote for *Oh, Kay!* demonstrate family resemblances to those in *Lady, Be Good!* and the score of the later musical as a whole reflects a similar attention to variety—in terms both of personnel required for the performance of successive numbers, and of the dramatic functions served by those numbers. For example, in Tommy Krasker's restoration of the score, act 2 commences with the ensemble "Bride and Groom," followed in turn by a trio ("Ain't It Romantic?" for Kay, Jimmy, and the comic lead "Shorty" McGee); a duet for two characters who were not heard in the trio ("Fidgety Feet"); and a solo for Jimmy, in which the chorus eventually joins ("Heaven on Earth").[65] "Bride and Groom" is an action number depicting preparations for the anticipated nuptials of Jimmy and Constance. "Ain't It Romantic?" is a comic defining number that allows Kay and Jimmy to express their feelings for one another in an apparently tongue-in-cheek fashion. "Fidgety Feet" is an obvious specialty selection, while the function of "Heaven on Earth" is more ambiguous; Jimmy's solo seems something of an aside as he prepares for what is shaping up to be an unavoidable union with Constance, but "Heaven on Earth" also hints at the possibility of a more satisfying outcome. In the event, Constance calls off the wedding and leaves Jimmy free to marry his true love, Kay.

"Bride and Groom" is analogous to "Linger in the Lobby," the opening act 2 ensemble of *Lady, Be Good!* Both are complex, multisectioned action numbers that push the show forward musically, as well as dramatically, by never returning to their opening strains. "Ain't It Romantic?" demonstrates an obvious kinship in tone to the similarly positioned "The Half of It, Dearie, Blues" in *Lady, Be Good!* And "Fidgety Feet" is, in effect, the "Fascinating Rhythm" of *Oh, Kay!*—at least from the musical point of view, with its pairing of metrical displacement and harmonic instability. It should also be noted that the refrains of "Fascinating Rhythm" and "Fidgety Feet" share an off-tonic opening (on the dominant seventh chord) and a thirty-two-bar ABAC form, in which the final C section refers pointedly back to the defining motif of A. Nevertheless, Gershwin's unflagging inventiveness is ever manifest in the score of *Oh, Kay!* Neither "Fidgety Feet" nor any other number in this musical sounds merely derivative of an earlier Gershwin song.[66]

Clearly there were many lessons to be gleaned from the success of *Lady, Be Good!* and Gershwin's understanding of them is reflected abundantly in the score of *Oh, Kay!* The persistent influence of the *Lady, Be Good!* model is further revealed by moving forward to 1930 and demonstrating the extent to which that model still exercised its hold on Gershwin's biggest hit of that year, *Girl Crazy.*

Girl Crazy represents the last grand hurrah for the 1920s Gershwin musical. Coming as it did after Kern and Hammerstein's revolutionary *Show Boat* (1927), the stock market crash of 1929, and Gershwin's previous 1930 success with the forward-looking political satire *Strike Up the Band,* *Girl Crazy* may have constituted both for its creators and for its audience a broad and affectionate gesture toward a Broadway style that was rapidly becoming antiquated.[67] Certainly it was the last successful Gershwin show in the mold of *Lady, Be Good!* and, with the single exception of the strikingly unsuccessful *Pardon My English,* the last show Gershwin wrote along those lines. For Gershwin the 1930s would be defined by political operetta, grand opera, and film scores. Still, *Girl Crazy* marks the splendid end of a line that includes *Funny Face* along with *Lady, Be Good!* and *Oh, Kay!,* and among this group only *Lady, Be Good!* had a longer Broadway run than *Girl Crazy.* (In addition to the 1927 *Funny Face* written for the Astaires, between *Oh, Kay!* and *Girl Crazy* Gershwin collaborated with Sigmund Romberg on *Rosalie,* starring Marilyn Miller, and wrote two other musicals: *Treasure Girl* (1928)—a second, unsuccessful show for Gertrude Lawrence—and *Show Girl* (1929), another failure at the box office, featuring Ruby Keeler. *Treasure Girl,* an Aarons–Freedley production that also brought along librettist Fred Thompson, comedian Walter Catlett, and duo pianists Ohman and Arden from the old *Lady, Be Good!* team, seems especially to merit reevaluation.)

Among the many Gershwin musicals centered around performers, *Girl*

Crazy possesses a peculiar distinction. It was originally intended as a vehicle for one major star who never actually appeared in it (Bert Lahr), but it proved instead to be the show that established the career of another major star (Ethel Merman).[68] Given the ethos of this type of show, it proved a less than difficult matter to reduce substantially the importance of one character while opening up increased performance opportunities for another.[69] *Girl Crazy* also gave a decisive lift to the burgeoning career of a still-teenaged Ginger Rogers. It appears more than likely that the abundant talent and youthful energy provided by Rogers and Merman helped inspire Gershwin to produce a score particularly rich in rhythmic and melodic invention.

The plot of *Girl Crazy* is as flimsy and silly as they come, and unsurprisingly it revolves around love: initial infatuation (the Danny Churchill part in the duet "Could You Use Me?"), initial rejection (the Molly Gray part in the same duet), shared passion ("Embraceable You," a later duet for Danny and Molly), obstacles and remorse ("But Not for Me"), remorse and philosophical acceptance ("Boy! What Love Has Done to Me!"), and naturally a happy ending. Along the way there are temporary love triangles and misunderstandings. There is exotica galore, beginning with the setting itself in the "Wild West"—Custerville, Arizona, home to a small all-male population until the arrival of New Yorker Danny Churchill starts the action.[70] (One can only wonder which would have seemed more exotic to Gershwin's Broadway audience: an Arizona setting, or a town without women?) The beginning of act 2 even moves the setting to Mexico. The law comes in once again for its share of ridicule, this time in the form of a comic sheriff who, in order to avoid succumbing to the local tradition of assassinating sheriffs, disguises himself—first as a Native American and then as a woman. The script is replete with the expected puns and occasions for horseplay.[71]

Despite its novel setting, the basic nature of *Girl Crazy* was old-fashioned for an audience of 1930. What distinguished the show, and what must have said "now" (if indeed anything did), was Gershwin's score—remarkable by any standards, even his own—and its performance by a pit band that included a group of up-and-coming jazz stars: Benny Goodman, Glenn Miller, Red Nichols, and Gene Krupa.[72]

Several numbers from *Girl Crazy* suggest significant analogies to earlier types. "Embraceable You" depicts Danny and Molly expressing their now mutual attraction in much the same fashion that "So Am I" from *Lady, Be Good!* certifies the mutual infatuation of Jack and Susie. "But Not for Me" resembles "Someone to Watch Over Me" from *Oh, Kay!* insofar as it is wistful song for a female character separated by circumstances (temporarily, in both cases) from the man she loves.[73] And "I Got Rhythm" is, of course, the self-proclaimed rhythm specialty tune for the new show.

On the other hand, several numbers in *Girl Crazy* do not evoke obvious precedents in Gershwin musicals. "Could You Use Me?" represents a different kind of duet, in which the protagonists employ the same music to express diametrically opposite feelings. "Sam and Delilah" is a specialty solo of dark, bluesy character with lyrics conveying an overtly sexual and ultimately violent story. The recurring male quartet "Bidin' My Time" functions almost like a performer who reappears regularly in the show, and whose role is to lazily entertain the audience during changes of scene.[74] The score of *Girl Crazy* is so rich that even a purely functional action number such as the ensemble "Bronco Busters" is lifted out of the ordinary at every turn with unexpected harmonic coloration and striking syncopation. And "Treat Me Rough," essentially a throwaway comic number that in another composer's hands might have called forth a minimal effort, becomes through Gershwin's artistry a celebration of aggressive rhythmic virtuosity.

It was probably the enormous popularity of *Girl Crazy* that accounts, at least in part, for the fact that the show was fashioned into a movie twice within the period of a mere thirteen years following its Broadway debut. The second of these films, the 1943 *Girl Crazy* with Mickey Rooney and Judy Garland, became and remains popular. But the reach of *Girl Crazy* extended well beyond this. Some basic elements of the story and six songs from the score eventually provided the basis for a "new Gershwin musical comedy," *Crazy for You*, which became a smash hit on Broadway in 1992 and is proving to have an extensive stage life of its own. Although *Crazy for You* is quite far removed from the original *Girl Crazy*, it is perhaps not beyond credibility to conjecture that the 1992 show is what *Girl Crazy* might have evolved into—had it somehow been able to run for six decades on Broadway, always maintaining the practice of continual improvisation, rewriting, refreshment, and reinvention that represented the true heritage of the 1920s Gershwin musical.

CHAPTER 4

Entr'acte

The Showman in the Concert Hall

ERSHWIN'S EXTENSIVE AND SUCCESSFUL CAREER IN MUSIC THE-
ater has too often been employed by critics as a foundation upon
which to attack his legitimacy and achievement as a composer for
the concert hall. Fortunately, it is no longer necessary to validate Gershwin's "classical" works by taking extensive pains to differentiate them from
the rest of his output; a growing body of scholarly writing on this music is
cementing the argument for its essential status.[1] Although the focus of the
present volume precludes detailed examination of these works, it is relevant
and important here to underline the fundamental connections that exist between the Gershwin of Broadway and the Gershwin of Carnegie Hall. It is
also essential to look beyond obvious surface similarities in musical language
and to probe the manner in which Gershwin's ability to shape original and
convincing concert music was actively abetted by his music theater experience and expertise.

We would do well in this enterprise to follow the lead of scholar Carol
Oja, who points out as an example the curtain-raising character of the orchestral opening for Gershwin's Concerto in F, while cautioning us not to be
embarrassed by this Broadway analogy.[2] The "star" performer grandly introduced by the music that opens Gershwin's concerto is, of course, the pianist,
who then proceeds—continuing with the Broadway metaphor—to present a
substantial and intricate solo "number." Gershwin here fuses elements of the
American vernacular with a traditional Classical strategy of commencing a
concerto with an orchestral passage, during which the solo instrument remains silent, and only afterward allowing the soloist to enter prominently.

Figure 4.1. A formal George Gershwin at Lewisohn
Stadium, New York, August 1929

A synthesis of popular stylistic elements with the formal principles of
concert music was not atypical of Gershwin. In *An American in Paris*, the
"blues" and "Charleston" sections may be interpreted as filling the roles of
"slow movement" and "dance movement" (or scherzo), respectively, within
the multipartite whole. This reading of the work's form—which could easily
coexist with others, given the richness and complexity of *An American in
Paris*—would view the piece along Romantic lines as essentially a four-
movement structure compressed into a single uninterrupted span, with a
large-scale opening fast "movement" and a cumulative "finale" surrounding
the central slow and dance "movements." The ordering and proportions of

these four "movements" correspond readily to those found in a traditional symphony.

While the formal strategies employed by Gershwin in his concert works conform frequently to those characteristic of the canonic repertoire, other aspects of organization in Gershwin's "classical" output initially appear more anomalous. Such instances may often be understood, however, as clever adaptations from music theater usage. One example is the prominent new theme featuring the trumpets that appears about three minutes into *Rhapsody in Blue* (at reh. no. 9 in the published score). Preceded by two huge precadential chords supporting a long-held growl in the flutter-tongued trumpets, this unexpected but irresistible tune arrives with the power of a coup de théâtre. Blazing forth in the fresh key of C major, its straightforward melodic and harmonic content, predictable phrasing, and accompanying pounding rhythms serve perfectly to release all the accumulated tension of the preceding music—which has been moving steadily toward tonal stability and rhythmic regularity. In other words, this new theme is a beautifully prepared "number." What is odd from a structural standpoint is not the appearance of a fresh theme at this juncture, but rather the fact that this big tune is stated once only and then disappears. Every other important theme in *Rhapsody in Blue* either is elaborated extensively upon its appearance or recurs later in the work. Yet the impact of this short sixteen-measure passage is surely that of a major event; it will not do to label it a transition or an interlude to explain it away. We might think of it instead as akin to a "specialty number"—a particularly inspired one—that emerges as an "aside" from the work's ongoing "action" in order to fulfill a specific theatrical function. (It may be significant that Gershwin originally conceived the construction of the *Rhapsody* in terms of a "plot.")[3] Although the isolated "specialty number" functions effectively in *Rhapsody in Blue*, Gershwin did not employ this particular kind of theatrical strategy in his subsequent instrumental compositions, favoring rather the extensive development of all major themes that is more typical of the concert repertoire.[4]

Another noteworthy feature of the thematic organization in *Rhapsody in Blue* is the relatively late introduction of the famous E-major lyrical melody (at reh. no. 28—out of forty numbered segments). When the work is performed without or with minimal cuts, this introduces the most substantial contrasting section at a point approximately two-thirds of the way through. It would be more common in concert music to have such a contrast come either at or before the halfway point; two-thirds of the way is customarily the place for a climactic passage of development or for a significant restatement of earlier material. Rhapsodies, however, are by definition wayward creatures, and the atypical proportions of *Rhapsody in Blue* warrant further attention only because of parallel organizational features demonstrated by two movements of the Concerto in F and by *An American in Paris*.

In both the first and the second movements of Gershwin's concerto, lovely lyrical passages arise unexpectedly well past the halfway point. (In the first movement, this *Moderato cantabile* is at reh. no. 20 — out of thirty-six; in the second movement, the music is marked *Espressivo con moto*, at reh. no. 10 — out of seventeen.) While the lyrical theme in the *Rhapsody* comes across to the listener as something quite new, both passages under discussion in the concerto build obviously on music heard earlier in their respective movements. Nevertheless, all three of these melodious effusions produce the surprising effect of turning a new page, if not starting a new chapter. Gershwin's choice of a new and distant tonal center in all three cases plays a highly significant role in producing this effect, and what is particularly striking is that in all three cases the key is the same one: E major. (E major lies a tritone away from the *Rhapsody*'s home key of B-flat major; in the concerto, it is a half step away from the first movement's tonic F, and an augmented second — or an enharmonic minor third — from the second movement's D-flat center. In none of these instances would the notes of an E-major triad be found within the diatonic scale of the home key.) A further resemblance between the E-major theme in the *Rhapsody* and that in the concerto's second movement is that each is introduced by a "curtain-raising" arpeggiated dominant-seventh chord played by the piano.

The curtain-raising metaphor suggests a source for Gershwin's obvious tendency to introduce something new around the two-thirds point in his concert movements. The typical musical comedy of the 1920s (and later) had two acts, with the second significantly shorter than the first, so that the curtain would rise on the final act about two-thirds of the way into the total performance time. Is it far-fetched to posit some relationship between the large-scale temporal proportions that characterized these music theater works and the temporal proportions favored by Gershwin in structuring his "classical" works?

An American in Paris offers yet another instance of a major new event near the two-thirds point, namely the introduction of the "Charleston" theme (at reh. no. 57 — out of seventy-seven). Although this is music quite different from that in the preceding examples, it shares basic characteristics with them in terms of its relationship to the overall context of the work: new tempo, new key, new thematic focus, a shift in featured instruments. Thus all of Gershwin's large-scale concert works of the 1920s demonstrate an approach to temporal organization that might be traced in some way to the influence of music theater. Beginning with the *Second Rhapsody* for piano and orchestra, composed in 1931, Gershwin moved away from employing organizational strategies in his "classical" music that evoked the typically asymmetrical proportions of two-act musical comedies; it is perhaps not coincidental that Gershwin's 1931 musical *Of Thee I Sing* is in two acts of virtually equal length.

The fashioning of effective conclusions, which provided dramatic resolution while summarizing important earlier material, was a concern that the music theater composers of Gershwin's time shared with many nineteenth- and twentieth-century composers for the concert hall. In musical comedies, reprises of memorable tunes introduced previously in the show would often precede, or be incorporated into, the finales of both acts. The concluding material of act 1 in *Lady, Be Good!* provides examples of both these strategies. (See table 3.1 in chapter 3; in addition to the orchestral restatement of "Fascinating Rhythm," it is likely that the "Piano Speciality" number incorporated music heard earlier in the act.) There is of course no shortage of analogous instances in the Romantic and early twentieth-century opera repertoire. The telling employment of musical recurrence for grandly tragic impact was a favored technique of Verdi's, as anyone knows who has experienced the final moments of *Rigoletto* or *Otello*. In instrumental concert music, perhaps the best-known and most celebrated instances of musical recurrence are found in Beethoven's Fifth Symphony. The famous four-note opening motif casts its shadow over the entire work, making a particularly dramatic and unexpected reappearance just preceding the recapitulation in the finale.

With so many models from both the concert hall and the dramatic music repertoire upon which to draw for instruction and inspiration, Gershwin unsurprisingly incorporated musical recurrence into the conclusions of his instrumental works. The final movement of the Concerto in F offers a brilliant summary of all the prominent themes from the preceding two movements. But Gershwin's tour de force in this realm is probably the concluding section of *An American in Paris*; commencing at the *Moderato con grazia* five measures before rehearsal number 69 is an inspired potpourri of earlier themes that jostle, dovetail, overlap, and accompany one another in as fine an evocation of "metropolitan madness" as Gershwin — or anyone else — ever conceived.[5] When Gershwin came to write the final act of his own opera, he was obviously well prepared to use thematic recurrence for striking dramatic effects.

The examples in the preceding paragraphs from the repertoires of musical comedy, opera, and instrumental concert music remind us that all successful music relies to a significant degree upon methods that may be termed theatrical, or at least dramatic. Any art form dependent upon the temporal dimension may profitably employ techniques such as foreshadowing and recurrence, the gradual accumulation of tension, and the postponement and fulfillment of release. Beethoven's Fifth Symphony is an abstract, totally nonprogrammatic work, yet its impact upon audiences from the time of its premiere to the present day surely certifies its status as one of the masterpieces of musical "theater"—broadly conceived.[6] What is arresting about Gershwin's career is not the fact that he brought his showman's instincts for drama into the concert hall. It is rather the level of popular success and aesthetic sophistication he was able to achieve in both music theater and instrumental composition. To have made such substantial contributions to each of these genres within such a tragically short span is an accomplishment that should still inspire wonder, along with a sense of the further potential that was irretrievably lost when Gershwin died so young.

While these pages have had as their focus the influence exerted by Gershwin's Broadway work upon his concert music, much could be written, of course, concerning the reciprocal influence of the latter upon the former. Gershwin was fond of setting himself new challenges, and each successive challenge met helped to expand his creative range, vision, and ambition. Through the composition of instrumental music, Gershwin enlarged his working vocabulary of melody, harmony, and rhythm, as well as his grasp of form, and he applied his new knowledge and understanding to his music theater enterprises. While evidence for this assertion is abundant throughout his evolving song output, perhaps the single most outstanding illustration of it is so obvious that it is infrequently remarked—it is a fact, as it were, hidden in plain view. The fact may be revealed in the form of a pair of questions: how many Gershwin "standards" predate the composition of *Rhapsody in Blue* (early in 1924), and what explains the sudden explosion of Gershwin standards produced in the wake of his outstanding success with this first major concert work (that is, later during 1924, and following in 1925, 1926, etc. . . .)?

Paul Whiteman's commission for *Rhapsody in Blue* offered Gershwin an opportunity to work on a musical canvas of previously unimagined scope and

Figure 4.2. An informal George Gershwin with
conductor Albert Coates, Lewisohn Stadium,
New York, August 1932

flexibility. Gershwin's discovery that he could rise to this challenge probably
amounted to the greatest leap of *self*-discovery in his entire creative career
(with one possible exception: the leap of self-discovery represented by the
creation of *Porgy and Bess*). In the *Rhapsody* he was able to find, develop, and
explore his own distinctive musical personality and artistry. The sense of self
and the self-confidence that this process and its resulting success provided
are reflected in the newly assured, distinctive personality and artistic achievement of the songs Gershwin began to write soon afterward—beginning with
"The Man I Love," through the score of *Lady, Be Good!* and beyond. The ex-

perience of composing *Rhapsody in Blue* helped enable Gershwin to make a remarkably rapid transition, as a theater composer, from the status of a gifted up-and-comer who occasionally produced a truly memorable song to that of an authentic star who turned out such songs with astounding regularity. In effect the *Rhapsody* proved a gift to Broadway as much as to the concert hall, and the same may be claimed for Gershwin's other contributions to the "classical" repertoire. With Gershwin's culminating work, the distinction collapses anyway: *Porgy and Bess* was intended to be, and remains, a direct gift from the composer both to Broadway and to the opera house.

CHAPTER 5

Something Completely Different
Of Thee I Sing *and the Musical as a "Work"*

ROM THE FIRST MEASURES OF THE OVERTURE, IT WOULD HAVE been obvious to an attentive listener in Broadway's Music Box Theatre on the evening of December 26, 1931, that something unusual was afoot. There was no traditional curtain-raising musical gesture leading quickly into a memorable tune. Instead, aggressive fragmentary ideas, tossed out in rhythmically disjunct patterns of alternating triple and duple measures, yielded to an extensive unstable passage based on nervous dotted rhythms and dissonant chord structures, without establishing any clear melodic line. When a real tune seemed finally to emerge, it was subtly enclosed within the inner lines of the musical texture, coming to full prominence in the top line only in the course of its second presentation. Yet this tune ("Who Cares?"), with its many wide leaps and its almost continually dissonant relationship with the underlying harmony, was a far cry from the typical Broadway tune, appearing rather to be cut from a cloth similar to that employed for the unusual music preceding it. Then what? An unexpected cadence to minor, persistent restatements of the opening fragment ("Wintergreen for President"), and—out of nowhere—an instrumental recitative for solo violin!

By this time, that attentive listener could have been excused for wondering whether he had ventured into Carnegie Hall by mistake to hear Gershwin's latest, strikingly modernistic, "classical" offering. Was he really present at the opening night of the composer's latest Broadway show? The concluding portions of the overture brought yet further surprises: more dotted rhythms, occasional metrical hiccups (in the form of 1/4 measures), and some of the most complex harmony yet (six-note chords, no less), leading finally to a big, new, stable tune ("Of Thee I Sing") that was more akin to an anthem than to a traditional love song or to an upbeat dance or novelty number. At least the piece ended with (at last) a firm and unequivocal major-key cadence.[1]

While the typical member of a 1931 Broadway audience would probably not have been paying such close attention to the overture for *Of Thee I Sing*, the innovative qualities of that overture seem designed to impress even the most casual listener. As for those who arrived late or talked right through the overture, the message that this was no ordinary musical was delivered forcibly as soon as the curtain rose. The scene was that of a political parade, replete with banners bearing slogans such as "Vote for Prosperity and See What You Get" and "Turn the Reformers Out," while the partisans sang an opening number unlike any heard before: "Wintergreen for President."

"Wintergreen for President" is a march in 2/4 meter that lacks any significant trace of a new Gershwin "tune," a conventional harmonic organization, or a traditional song form. This number is instead a mosaic-like construction in which Gershwin's brief, gruff motifs—one setting the title phrase; another setting "He's the man the people choose," which is repeated for the text "Loves the Irish and the Jews"; and the third consisting of a choral interjection on "Ah"—alternate irregularly with equally brief quotations of celebrated rallying tunes (such as John Philip Sousa's "Stars and Stripes Forever" and Theodore Metz's "Hot Time in the Old Town Tonight"). What better way to begin a brilliant and unprecedented evening of music theater than with this brilliant and unprecedented opening scene and music?

From the outset, audiences and critics recognized *Of Thee I Sing* both as something different and as something terrific. It became the greatest Broadway success of Gershwin's career and, with a run of 441 performances, the longest-running book musical of the 1930s. The opening-night reviewers lavishly praised both the show's originality and its quality. Recognition of these merits climaxed with a further unprecedented development, namely the awarding of the Pulitzer Prize for drama to *Of Thee I Sing* on May 2, 1932—the first time a musical had received such an award. Aware of the tradition-breaking character of their choice, the Pulitzer Committee issued a statement saying, in part, that "This award may seem unusual, but the play is unusual."[2] Since there was no provision at the time for a Pulitzer Prize in music, the *Of Thee I Sing* award went to George S. Kaufman and Morrie Ryskind for the book and to Ira Gershwin for the lyrics—but ironically not to George Gershwin, an injustice that was remarked upon by Ira at the time and by many others afterward.[3] But the composer himself took undiminished pride in *Of Thee I Sing*, referring to it as "one show that I'm more proud of than any I have written."[4]

The twenty-first-century listener who first approaches *Of Thee I Sing* knowing only the Gershwin show music of the 1920s is likely to share the same level of surprise I attributed to the hypothetical opening-night listener. Indeed, the overture and "Wintergreen for President" could justifiably leave one wondering whether in fact this material is truly Gershwin's, or the work of some previously unknown but brilliant theater composer who had obviously learned a lot from Gershwin, while managing to forge a fresh and highly personal musical language of his own. As the score progresses, surface elements typical of Gershwin emerge more strongly; certainly the stereotypical syncopated rhythms and blue notes may be heard. But *Of Thee I Sing* never really *sounds* much like other Gershwin. Rather, as the listener comes to know it, it sounds most like itself: the characteristic rhythms, harmonies, phrasing, and constructive strategy of the overture and—especially—of "Wintergreen for President" inform the score as a whole, on several levels.[5] The music is of a piece. It *is* a piece. Eventually one throws up one's hands and admits it: in the most doggedly traditional, old-fashioned sense of the term, *Of Thee I Sing* is a *work*. And it is a thoroughly distinctive work as well, both in terms of Gershwin's oeuvre and in terms of the history of American musical theater.[6]

What circumstances facilitated the creation of such a work, which, it should be emphasized, represented the ultimate popular and critical success Gershwin achieved in music theater during his lifetime? And how may we best understand the depth of its specifically musical achievement, which assures the work an enduring special place in the composer's output?

What's New: Circumstances, Artistic Control, and Creative Methodology

To understand the distinctive environment that surrounded the creation, production, and reception of *Of Thee I Sing*, it will help to compare that environment with the one surrounding the appearance of *Lady, Be Good!* seven years earlier. In 1924 the brothers Gershwin were a promising but as yet unproven Broadway partnership. By 1931 they were as close as a songwriting team could be to superstars, especially since their two Broadway openings of the previous year, the revised *Strike Up the Band* and the brand-new *Girl Crazy*, had both been successful with the public and the critics—in the case of *Girl Crazy*, outstandingly so. Playwrights George S. Kaufman and Morrie

Figure 5.1. Ira and George Gershwin (top) with George S.
Kaufman (left) and Morrie Ryskind (right), New York, early 1930s

Ryskind were no Broadway novices themselves, having established enviable
reputations during the 1920s working both separately and together on both
musical and nonmusical projects. (They had collaborated informally on *The
Cocoanuts*, a Marx Brothers vehicle, in 1925 and formally on a second musical
with the Marx Brothers, *Animal Crackers*, in 1928.) Kaufman had also begun
a second successful career as a stage director in 1928 (with *The Front Page*,
by Ben Hecht and Charles MacArthur), a factor that became unexpectedly
important in the evolution of *Of Thee I Sing*. Furthermore, prior to collabo-
rating with the Gershwins on *Of Thee I Sing*, Kaufman and Ryskind had
already worked productively with the brothers on another musical that fea-

tured an unusual political slant, namely *Strike Up the Band*: Kaufman had authored the book for its original (unsuccessful) version of 1927, while Ryskind had revised it for the musical's acclaimed resurrection.

It was in fact Kaufman and Ryskind who first conceived the premise for *Of Thee I Sing* and who brought the Gershwins on board, as well as the experienced and sympathetic Broadway producer Sam H. Harris.[7] Like the creative partnership responsible for *Lady, Be Good!* this was a generously gifted group of people, anxious and pleased to work together. But there was a crucial difference between 1924 and 1931, and it is attributable not to the greater quantity and quality of collective experience that the Kaufman–Ryskind–Gershwins–Harris team brought to the table nor even to the stimulation they all must have felt, given their individual and collective reputations, not merely to meet but to surpass the public's expectations for their project. The decisive factor was rather the extraordinary amount of sheer clout that this group could bring to bear in assuring that the wishes of the authors, lyricist, and composer proved the defining factors shaping *Of Thee I Sing*.

Kaufman, Ryskind, and the Gershwins shared a distinctive vision and a remarkable creative empathy, energy, and synergy, while Harris worked shrewdly to assure that neither he nor anyone else would interfere. When Kaufman announced his decision to direct the show himself, the circle was closed and the matter was clinched: control of the show lay totally in the hands of the creative team. The departure this represented from the performer-centered 1920s musical could not be more apparent, or more significant.

Given these circumstances, it does not surprise that the casting for *Of Thee I Sing* reflected the needs and desires of the creators, instead of a chosen cast mandating or manipulating the creative decisions. In an amusing reversal of the customary situation, Kaufman's choices for the roles of president and vice president, William Gaxton and Victor Moore respectively, spontaneously became a new comedy team that went on to play successfully together in many shows—including the Gershwins' *Let 'Em Eat Cake*, Cole Porter's *Anything Goes*, and Irving Berlin's *Louisiana Purchase*. As director, Kaufman's control of his cast was firm, and he was known for his intolerance of performers' alterations and interpolations in a script either before or after a show opened—another essential divergence from the typical practice in earlier musicals, and one that assured the integrity of the play as a work. In an article that appeared during the fourth month *Of Thee I Sing* was running on Broadway, the much-praised Victor Moore was quoted as saying "I've been in

Figure 5.2. Victor Moore and William Gaxton as
Throttlebottom and Wintergreen, ca. 1932

twenty-five musical shows in the last quarter of a century and this is the first
time that I haven't been permitted to insert a line here and there." Significantly, Moore added "I'm getting reconciled now, though. The darned show
goes so well as it is that I guess it would be a case of gilding the lily if we tried
to improve it."[8]

The status of the book for *Of Thee I Sing* as a fixed text of independent
literary interest and merit was certified, in effect, by its publication in April
1932—even before the show had been awarded the Pulitzer Prize.[9] The appearance in print of what the authors significantly called their musical *play*
(italics mine) marked the first time that the libretto of an American musical

had been deemed worthy of publication, and it went through seven printings in as many months.[10] The inclusion of Ira Gershwin's lyrics in the printed play made it apparent to a reader how fully integrated those lyrics were into the whole conception; Ira's contribution was obviously considered essential to the work's literary impact and success.

From the Gershwins' side, Kaufman's and Ryskind's creative sympathy as writers and Kaufman's tight control as director made it certain that the integrity of the lyrics and music they wrote for *Of Thee I Sing* would be as scrupulously preserved in performance as the text of the book. The brothers responded to this golden opportunity with material wedded much more intricately and imaginatively to the book of the musical than was the case in any of their previous efforts. George in particular appears to have rethought the possibilities presented to him by *Of Thee I Sing* on almost every level, and he produced a score at once unique and unerringly appropriate for its purpose. Its status as a work in its own right was underlined by the publication of the complete piano-vocal score for *Of Thee I Sing*, also in 1932.[11]

The interdependence of the music, lyrics, and book in *Of Thee I Sing* makes it particularly important to understand the book, if one is to understand fully the other components. This requires not merely a knowledge of the plot, which is readily acquired, but also an understanding of the book's construction, tone, and approach to humor.

The basic story line is easily conveyed. An unnamed American political party has chosen as its presidential candidate—for no obvious reason—a man named John P. Wintergreen. According to the candidate himself, "I never expected to get the nomination. Didn't *want* the nomination. Never was so surprised as when my name came up." When he is asked by members of the National Campaign Committee just who at the nominating convention brought Wintergreen's name up by calling out the name from the back, the candidate replies without hesitation "That was me. Most spontaneous thing you ever saw. So here I am, gentlemen—nominated by the people, absolutely my own master, and ready to do any dirty work the committee suggests."[12] With this exchange, basic themes underlying the story are quickly established: American politics are haphazard, unburdened by principle, and readily swayed on the spur of the moment.

If the selection of this presidential candidate was an apparently random event, that of the vice president on the ticket was so empty of import that nobody seems able to remember the poor man's name. The identity and even the existence of Alexander Throttlebottom thus become a running joke throughout the play—and how well chosen his name was for the purpose! Obviously this undistinguished team of nominees needs an inspiring platform on which to run. And indeed such a platform is chosen by the Campaign Committee: love. As Matthew Arnold Fulton, a committee member and newspaper magnate puts it, "People *do* care more about love than anything else. . . . If we could find some way to put it over—why, we would get every vote."[13]

And so a campaign strategy is hatched. A beauty contest in Atlantic City will determine the most beautiful girl in the United States. Candidate Wintergreen will propose to her in every state, and she will accept—contingent, however, upon the success of his campaign. Then the American electorate, duly touched and unwilling to part the couple by voting against love, will sweep Wintergreen into office, and the new president will celebrate his inauguration and his nuptials on the same day.

Such a cynical view and employment of love was something new in American musical theater in 1931, and of course this campaign plan cannot be allowed to work without a hitch. The underlying dramatic principle here is not so much that the cynicism must be challenged, as that without a conflict there would be no play to speak of (or at least no second act). When Miss Diana Devereaux ("the most beautiful blossom in all the Southland") proves the winner of the contest in Atlantic City, Wintergreen states he is unwilling to marry her, because by this time he has fallen in love with Mary Turner, a campaign worker. His attraction to Miss Turner is no less pragmatically and sensually based than an attraction to the bathing-beauty winner of a politically motivated contest: Wintergreen is concerned about having a wife who can cook, and he has become entranced upon tasting Mary's "marvelous" corn muffins (culinary marvels to be sure, given Mary's assurance to Wintergreen that she is "the only person in the world who can make them without corn").[14] While the Wintergreen-Turner love affair obviously has no rational basis, at least it arises spontaneously rather than through political maneuverings, and thus falls more in line with the conventions of musical comedy.

The campaign proceeds with Wintergreen wooing Mary, and naturally he wins a decisive victory. Act 1 concludes with the Inauguration (and wedding) Day ceremonies, which proceed smoothly until Diana Devereaux appears abruptly, demanding justice and serving Wintergreen with a summons for breach of promise. Since the Supreme Court Justices are conveniently on hand—it being Inauguration Day—to adjudicate the merits of the case, framed as "corn muffins or justice," the nine sages huddle and summarily

Figure 5.3. The winning campaign: publicity still from the
original production of *Of Thee I Sing*, ca. 1932

render their verdict: "Corn muffins!" Amid general rejoicing, Diana departs
vowing revenge.

As act 2 gets under way, it becomes apparent that the Devereaux matter
is engendering a good deal of negative publicity for the Wintergreen administration. The president and Mary brush the concerns aside, but, with the arrival of the French ambassador, the affair assumes international implications
that can no longer be ignored. It seems that Diana is of French descent—
the "illegitimate daughter of an illegitimate son of an illegitimate nephew
of Napoleon," no less—and consequently the honor of France itself is involved in the commitment made by Wintergreen's campaign that he marry

the winner of the Atlantic City beauty contest. Despite this development, Wintergreen adamantly stands by Mary. When he refuses the suggestion of his advisers that he resign the presidency to resolve the crisis, the advisers proceed, in keeping with their loyalties and moral character, by threatening him with impeachment.

One positive aspect of the ensuing impeachment trial in the Senate is that it finally gives poor Throttlebottom something to do, as he must preside over it. The French ambassador and Diana and other Atlantic City contestants present their testimonies, and the senators are all set to hand down a guilty verdict when—in a dramatic moment that parallels Diana's earlier interruption of the formal Inauguration Day ceremonies—Mary appears and calls an immediate halt to the proceedings. She insists that, prior to impeaching her husband, the senators must learn of his "delicate condition." She is pregnant, and he's about to become a father! As Throttlebottom wisely points out, no precedent exists for impeaching an "expectant father," and the case against Wintergreen evaporates. (Congratulated afterward by his advisers, Wintergreen assures them that he foresaw the crisis and "planned the whole thing" months ago, asserting that "Anybody in my place would have done the same."[15])

All is not settled, however, for the affront to Diana and to France must still be redressed. The French ambassador, citing his nation's declining birth rate, demands that Wintergreen's baby be given to France as compensation. Wintergreen refuses, of course, and when Mary delivers twins (a boy and a girl), France suffers an "insult added to injury" and threatens war. Then Diana reappears, and Wintergreen offers as a solution that "she can have her own babies," not allowing any significance to her unmarried condition. The French ambassador counters that "the family has been illegitimate long enough."[16] Finally Wintergreen, finding the provisions of the U.S. Constitution useful to him for what is presumably the first time, hits upon the solution that has been hidden in plain sight: when the president is unable to fulfill his duties, the responsibility falls to the vice president. Throttlebottom thus gets to marry Diana, restoring her honor and that of France; Wintergreen gets to keep Mary and his new children; and the audience gets to go home happy.

Some of the tone and humor of the book for *Of Thee I Sing* may be gleaned from the preceding account, along with some basic conception of the libretto's construction. Perhaps the most important aspect of its construction—at least for Gershwin—remains to be acknowledged, however; that is its alternation of substantial sections consisting purely of spoken dialogue

Figure 5.4. President Wintergreen and the First Lady share adjoining desks: publicity still from the original production of *Of Thee I Sing,* ca. 1932

(which can constitute entire scenes, such as act 1, scene 2, and act 2, scene 4) with equally substantial sections that allow for extended musical treatment with few, if any, interruptions (such as the opening and concluding portions of act 1, scene 3, and the entirety of act 1, scene 6, and of act 2, scene 5). Before continuing with a detailed consideration of the composer's contributions to *Of Thee I Sing,* however, perhaps the issue of just how different its story line is from that of a more conventional musical should be addressed.

The More Things Change . . .

In the opening pages of his *Sing for Your Supper: The Broadway Musical in the 1930s,* the usually perspicacious Ethan Mordden pooh-poohs the conventional wisdom that *Of Thee I Sing* was a bracingly different kind of musical for its time. Mordden claims rather that the work was "neither daring nor breakaway," but simply a "musical comedy of traditional style" with a political mise-en-scène, "a babes-and-jokes show, albeit of unusually high satiric quality."[17] His extended consideration of the show later in the book offers a more modulated view, emphasizing some distinctive characteristics of Gershwin's score.[18] Nevertheless, a revisionist approach to *Of Thee I Sing* is worth entertaining at least momentarily; if Mordden overstates the case, scholar Howard Pollack echoes aspects of this new angle when he writes "Although commentators have traditionally viewed *Of Thee I Sing* as a political satire . . . the show proved in equal measure a romantic comedy."[19] To what extent, then, does the book for *Of Thee I Sing* represent an authentic departure?

It is documented that Kaufman and Ryskind set out self-consciously to write something fresh and uncompromising with *Of Thee I Sing*, damn the consequences.[20] But these two were experienced writers for the stage, so in no sense did they—or could they—undertake the project ab ovo, with a proverbial clean slate. Long-standing theatrical traditions and previously effective approaches to script construction naturally left imprints upon their work. Consequently, the more one searches for analogies to the books of earlier musicals in *Of Thee I Sing*, the more readily one finds them.

The plot for *Of Thee I Sing* is driven by that most enduring dramatic staple, the love triangle—even if the constellation of Wintergreen, Mary, and Diana lies at some distance from a conventional love triangle. Wintergreen and Mary undergo an experience somewhat analogous to that of love at first sight, if one admits the imaginative variant in this case of love at first *bite* (of a corn muffin, that is). There are impediments to a marriage, in two instances: Wintergreen's love for Mary prevents the anticipated fulfillment of Diana's ambition, while Diana's later demands for an annulment threaten the union of Wintergreen and Mary.

Many other traditional situations and character types are referenced in the book for *Of Thee I Sing*. The stereotypical shady lawyer or officer is represented in spades by an entire crew of unsavory politicos and their hangers-on. The exotic "Other" may be seen in the caricatured French ambassador and his attending group of French soldiers. And the standard comic device of mistaken identity gets an ingenious twist in the character and situation of Throttlebottom, the script's "invisible man," who seems at points on the verge of joining everyone else in forgetting his own name.[21] Opportunities for physical humor are afforded by the marching entrances of the Supreme Court Justices, by the marching of the French soldiers accompanying the ambassador, and above all by the campaign rally scene set in Madison Square Garden (act 1, scene 4), in which a cliché-ridden political speech is accompanied by onstage wrestling.

Looking to the details of the writing itself, the book abounds in the puns and wordplay typical of scripts from this period. (The name Throttlebottom is subjected to a good amount of verbal abuse, as would be imagined.) Contemporary references, especially of a political nature, are frequent—and of course particularly appropriate—and they helped make *Of Thee I Sing* yet another Gershwin show that said "*now*." One inspired example may be offered, from an exchange between Wintergreen and Throttlebottom at the end of act 2, scene 2, concerning presidential speeches:

> WINTERGREEN: You've got to be careful about speeches. You only make a speech when you want the stock market to go down.
> THROTTLEBOTTOM: What do you do when you want the stock market to go up?
> WINTERGREEN: (Fairly falling on his neck) Oh! Wouldn't I like to know![22]

Broadway's Depression-era audiences must have roared as the curtain came down upon these lines. Prohibition was still in effect during the run of this musical, so Kaufman and Ryskind made certain to include some uninhibited onstage drinking by their sterling representatives of American public life (in act 1, scene 2, and act 2, scene 5). Occasional internal references to music in the script tease the conventions and artificialities of music theater itself, in a manner similar to that found in the book of *Lady, Be Good!*[23]

The inevitable fallacy that hangs over this entire line of argument has to do with the fact that one tends to find what one is looking for. Many of the most striking analogies cited have important codicils attached. Are all the apparent similarities to earlier musicals significant in terms of an audience's actual experience of *Of Thee I Sing*? The safe money would seem to lie with a qualified negative: the show's book offers just enough in terms of familiar strategies to make the audience comfortable with, attentive to, and appreciative of, its considerable novelty.

If this last viewpoint is accepted, it follows that *Of Thee I Sing* is not at all a "musical comedy of traditional style" in a political setting. Instead the political setting is a device employed to facilitate the presentation of a parodic critique of musical comedy traditions—in terms of plot structure, comedic situations, and character types, and especially in the treatment of the eternal theme of love—all while the show is merrily mocking American politics itself as well. This is what Gerald Mast was getting at when he wrote that *Of Thee I Sing* (along with *Porgy and Bess*, which he provocatively paired with it) reveals "more thoroughly systematic thinking about the conventions and form of musical theater than any previous musical."[24] Mast also called attention to the "dazzling innovations in staging and stagecraft" in *Of Thee I Sing* that must have impressed contemporary theatergoers, citing the Madison Square Garden political rally-cum-wrestling scene and the election night projections on a motion picture screen (act 1, scenes 4 and 5, respectively).[25]

If the book for *Of Thee I Sing* references tradition only to the extent necessary to engage its real—and novel—agenda, the same may be said for the show's music. Naturally there is a typical variety in the musical score: solos, occasional duets, and many ensembles are heard in *Of Thee I Sing*, presenting an array of different voices and textures. Gershwin also employs some traditional Broadway song forms and styles—but these throw into relief the unconventional character of much of his score.

Returning Gershwin's music at last to the discussion points up the deeper fallacy of evaluating the nature and impact of a musical without referring directly and substantially to the contributions of its composer. In fact it is the music upon which the reputation of *Of Thee I Sing* as a groundbreaking work must rest, as implied by the description at the opening of this chapter. Commentators on *Of Thee I Sing*, beginning with the reviewers of its Broadway debut, have testified to the transformational effect of Gershwin's music upon the drama.[26]

How the Music Works

The score for *Of Thee I Sing* is intimately tied to, even inseparable from, its book. Despite the enormous popularity of the show and the quantity and quality of its music, few songs proved extractable for individual publication, and even those that did displayed both lyrical content and musical characteristics revealing their obvious identity as songs taken from *Of Thee I Sing*. Two standards that have endured from the score, "Who Cares?" and the title song, demonstrate this clearly, and so will be considered in context during the course of the following discussion.

Theater historian Stanley Green goes so far as to claim that, in the case of *Of Thee I Sing*, "the musical relationship is more firmly structured in the story than in any previous musical comedy."[27] Surely this achievement did not result from fortunate happenstance; citing an interview with Ira in the *Boston Globe*, Howard Pollack indicates that the Gershwins consciously altered their typical working methods for the creation of this score, with "the greater proportion" of the lyrics having preceded the writing of the music rather than vice versa.[28] The heightened sensitivity to specific demands of text that this new procedure must have instilled in George obviously prepared him well to undertake the composition of *Porgy and Bess*.

To fully appreciate the musical achievement represented by *Of Thee I Sing*, let us consider the special challenges posed to Gershwin by the individual nature of the project. The libretto's distinctive and thoroughgoing tone of parody called for an equally distinctive and thoroughgoing musical counterpart. Yet substantial variety in the music was also required, if the extended musical numbers invited by the book's construction were to be successfully created and sustained. Among the more common ways to achieve such variety would have been musical individuation of the characters, and the presentation and development of some elaborate musical ideas, but the parodic particularities of the book for *Of Thee I Sing* presented obstacles to both these strategies. Most of the characters in the libretto are deliberately drawn to resemble stereotypes, and part of the point is that many of them are quite similar. (The ultimate joke behind everyone's forgetting the identity of the vice president is that in this show he could indeed be anybody.) And since these characters, again deliberately, are written to express themselves via stereotypical slogans, catchphrases, and clichés (what we today would call "sound bites")—or with parodies of them—Gershwin's devising of elaborate or sustained musical lines for such expression would have been totally "out of character."

In effect, the musical requirements for this show presented Gershwin with a series of paradoxes. The overall tone had to be highly original, yet parodic. He needed to achieve consistency along with variety. He had to work with stereotypes and clichés, but in a knowing manner. Concise expression was a necessity, but it had to be employed in the creation of substantial musical scenes. A lesser composer would have thrown up his hands and either given up or contented himself with a modest effort toward one or two of these goals. Gershwin went to work, and created a work. And his work was a remarkably integrated and systematic achievement, such that an understanding of its overall methodology may proceed directly from a careful analysis of the very opening number, "Wintergreen for President."

Important characteristics of "Wintergreen for President" were men-

tioned at the beginning of this chapter, including its mosaic-like construction based on the irregular placement of brief recurring motifs and equally
brief quotations of famous tunes; the formal unpredictability that is a direct
consequence of this means of construction; and the song's completely untra-
ditional harmonic organization. Immediately obvious from the outset of the
number, but by no means less significant, are Gershwin's choice of a minor
key and his employment of a 2/4 *Tempo di Marcia* rhythmic character. The
introduction starts with symmetrical phrasing, alternating orchestral out-
bursts with an offstage chorus, but it comes to a halt abruptly after eleven
measures, effectively preparing the rhythmic asymmetries that will ensue.
Every aspect of "Wintergreen for President" is thus designed to defeat expectations of how the opening number of a musical should behave, and to establish instead expectations of an unconventional show to follow. Above and
beyond these considerations, however, is the singularly important fact that
"Wintergreen for President" establishes patterns of musical expression and
construction that prove to be characteristic throughout the subsequent score.

"Wintergreen for President" embodies a pivotal discovery on Gershwin's
part that addressed several of the paradoxical challenges posed by the musical's book. The discovery was that short, straightforward, easily remembered
musical motifs—the sort that ideally suited the show's characters, situations,
and language, and which could occasionally be deliberate clichés or even
quotations—might be fashioned and employed in a manner that enabled the
kind of open-ended, unconventional formal structuring invited by the book
as a whole. Such motifs, then, were not of necessity tied to the symmetrical
phrasing and to the closed sixteen- and thirty-two-bar structures typical of
Broadway song. Stated thus baldly, the discovery scarcely seems revelatory;
but putting it into practice on both a small and a large scale, and in a convincing and inspired manner, is something else entirely. Here Gershwin was
substantially assisted by two aspects of his previous experience. Working with
brief motifs had always been characteristic of him, and in his instrumental
compositions he had worked successfully with such motifs in an open-ended,
developmental context.[29]

Consider the three recurring motifs in "Wintergreen for President,"
shown in example 5.1. The motifs are designed to be blunt, unremarkable
musical "slogans" that nevertheless are suitable for producing a fairly extended number (ninety-six measures, not counting the repeat suggested in
the score) that would exhibit markedly unusual features. Only one of these
three melodic ideas is linked to a definite harmonic profile, and that (appro-

Example 5.1. "Wintergreen for President," mm. 12–15, 20–25, and 3–4,
with half-step melodic figures indicated

priately enough) is the setting of the title phrase, which simply arpeggiates a
minor triad over two measures of 2/4 meter. The other two motifs each involve nothing more than the presentation of a melodic half step, an interval
that harmonically is almost infinitely malleable.

In the event, Gershwin uses the "He's the man . . ." motif to effect surprising modulations in the course of the opening number, while the recurrences of the "Wintergreen for President" motif are employed, in transposi-

tion, to anchor the song temporarily in various keys. (The extent to which "Wintergreen for President" departs radically from any traditional tonal organization can be conveyed by a listing of the temporary harmonic centers articulated by the singing of the title phrase: first G minor, then A minor, then F-sharp minor, and finally G minor again.) Rhythmically, the only phrasing that remains fixed is the two-measure duration of the "Ah" motif. The "Wintergreen for President" motif usually is extended to four measures by sustaining its final note, but at the number's conclusion it is sung repeatedly in two-measure phrases—a treatment that has been anticipated by instrumental references to the motif in the accompaniment. And Example 5.1 demonstrates that the "He's the man . . ." motif consists of two statements of an ascending half step with the sequential statement foreshortened to two measures instead of four, resulting in a rhythmically asymmetrical six-measure passage.

The recurrences of the three central motifs provide "Wintergreen for President" with an obvious formal structure, but one that clearly is not reducible to any conventional pattern.[30] Scattered among these recurrences are the quotations, chosen by Gershwin not only because his Broadway audience would find them immediately recognizable and relevant to the spirit of a political rally, but also because of their relationships to his own three motifs. (The connection is most obvious in the quotations from "Stars and Stripes Forever" and "Hot Time in the Old Town Tonight," with their prominent melodic half steps, but the remaining quotations employ intervals of a minor third or a perfect fourth, which create links to the "Wintergreen for President" motif.) An additional source of continuity may be found in the persistent 2/4 march patterns that accompany the kaleidoscopic sequence of melodic events.

"Wintergreen for President" is, musically and conceptually, many things at once: a number at once startlingly original and obviously parodic, a convincingly unified composition that uses a remarkable variety of material, and a piece that references tradition within a thoroughly novel framework. The musical interspersion of new "slogans" with old "clichés" establishes the tone of the show perfectly in every respect. With "Wintergreen," Gershwin sets the stage comprehensively for the play to follow, while presenting compositional materials and techniques that serve as models and points of reference for the ensuing music.

Throughout *Of Thee I Sing*, musical numbers ranging from brief choral interjections to self-contained songs are woven from short musical motifs analogous to those Gershwin created for "Wintergreen for President." The technique employed in "Wintergreen," of composing an extended number by alternating recurrences of motifs with contrasting material, is used elsewhere on a broad scale to engender long, uninterrupted spans of music in which restatements—ranging from brief passages to entire reprises of songs—are interspersed with fresh material (also ranging from brief passages to entirely new songs). These long musical scenes provide both unity and variety, and they display characteristics of harmonic and rhythmic inventiveness analogous to those manifested in the show's opening number.

The 2/4 meter of "Wintergreen for President" is noteworthy because this meter was used rarely by Gershwin during the 1920s. Of the eighteen songs spanning his career that were selected by Gershwin himself for his 1932 *Songbook* (including "Who Cares?" from *Of Thee I Sing*), all are either in 4/4 or 2/2 ("cut") time, except for the two earliest songs ("Swanee" and "Nobody but You," both from 1919), which were written in 2/4.[31] Yet 2/4 meter appears with remarkable frequency throughout *Of Thee I Sing*, and this offers yet another indication of the extent to which "Wintergreen for President" establishes musical patterns for the entire show. Meters of 4/4 or 2/2 become virtually the exception rather than the norm in this score; other meters that seem atypical of Gershwin, such as 3/4 and 6/8, occur as well. Clearly Gershwin intended the metrical framework for *Of Thee I Sing* to be as novel as the other musical aspects.[32] There may be a parodic intent at work here as well: many of the choral passages in 2/4, and above all the French ambassador's song in 6/8 ("The Illegitimate Daughter"), are suggestive of the Gilbert and Sullivan patter songs typically written in those meters, while the 3/4 sections are obviously waltzes.[33]

One last characteristic of "Wintergreen for President" that prefigures later music in the show is the appearance of quotations. The most extensive use of quotations occurs in the final scene of act 2, creating a kind of symmetry with the opening of act 1. No. 15 in the score, "Trumpeter, Blow Your Golden Horn," has a formal arrangement similar to that of "Wintergreen for President," but on a larger scale; substantial quotations, among them "The Farmer in the Dell" and Stephen Foster's "Old Folks at Home," are sandwiched between recurrences of original music by Gershwin.

To illustrate the manner in which extended musical scenes are constructed in *Of Thee I Sing*, the large-scale concluding number of act 1, scene 3, will serve well. (This is No. 3 in the published score, which is misleadingly labeled "Finaletto, Scene IV—Act I," probably reflecting the ordering of

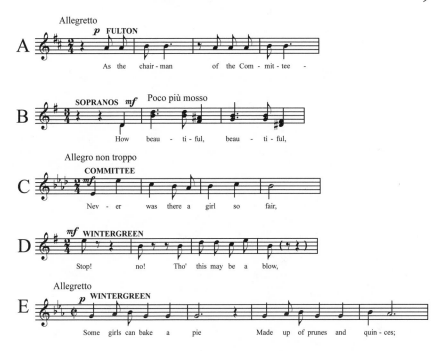

Example 5.2. Vocal motifs from *Of Thee I Sing*, vocal score, No. 3

scenes in one of the draft stages of the libretto.) The most important musical motifs employed in this number are shown in example 5.2, and a schematic musical and dramatic outline of the whole—with subdivisions defined by the occurrence and recurrence of these motifs—is provided in table 5.1. The following discussion is by no means intended to be comprehensive, and will call attention only to features of outstanding interest or importance related to the issues raised in this chapter.[34]

Among the significant surface features of this number revealed in table 5.1 are the sheer quantity of musical material; the continuity that is assured through the presence of transitions (that sometimes take the form of recitatives) and the absence of big internal cadences; Gershwin's tendency to avoid traditional formal designs, both within subdivisions and in the shaping of the number as a whole; and his employment of recurring motifs as a source of local and overall unification. The fact that the motifs, with the single exception of motif C, display prominent repeated pitches may also contribute to an overarching sense of coherence (see ex. 5.2). The prevalence of 2/4

Table 5.1. A Musical and Dramatic Outline of the Conclusion of Act 1, Scene 3 of *Of Thee I Sing* (vocal score, No. 3)

Subdivision	Motif	Tempo, Meter	Cast	Action	Comments
Introduction: instrumental fanfare		*Andante pomposo*, 2/4			
1	A	*Allegretto*, 2/4	Chairman (Fulton), committee	The officials judging the beauty contest announce that a winner has been chosen	Brief vocal solo built on motif A, with music repeated by the ensemble, followed by a quick transition
2	B	*Comodo*, 3/4	Fulton, ensemble	The chairman introduces Diana Devereaux; the ensemble sings of her beauty	Waltz: Chairman speaks as the orchestra plays a 16-bar tune based on motif B, then the ensemble sings it, then another brief transition
3	C	*Allegro non troppo*, 2/4	Ensemble	The committee extols Diana's physical attributes	This is a more extended, formally irregular passage, unified by recurrences of motif C; subdivision 4 follows directly
4	A	[same]	Chairman, assistants	The press is called in	Very like subdivision 1; moves directly into subdivision 5

5	D	[same]	Wintergreen, ensemble	Wintergreen refuses to marry Diana; general consternation	Brief vocal solo, then ensemble music repeats Wintergreen's motif (D); no cadence
[recitative]			Wintergreen	"I love someone else! Mary Turner"	
6	A, varied	A *tempo*, 2/4, then 3/4, then 2/4	Committee, Diana, Wintergreen	Anger over Wintergreen's choice and obstinacy	Complex and formally irregular passage, unified by motif A; subdivision 7 follows directly
7	C	A *tempo*, 2/4, then *Slowly*, 4/4	Diana, ensemble	Diana threatens court action, asks what Wintergreen sees in Mary Turner	8-bar restatement of C material, then 6 bars of song-like new material, with ensemble echoing Diana at the end; no cadence
[recitative]			Wintergreen, Diana, ensemble	"Corn muffins"	Directly recalls Wintergreen's recitative preceding subdivision 6
8	E	*Allegretto*, 2/2	Wintergreen solo, then with ensemble and Diana	Wintergreen extols the joy of (Mary's) cooking; committee agrees, but not the girls or Diana	16-bar tune based on motif E is sung, then repeated with two lines of accompanying counterpoint; subdivision 9 follows directly
9	D	*Allegro*, 2/4	Ensemble	In praise of Mary, muffins, and marriage	Extended presentation of motif D; music is similar to subdivision 5; cadence at end

Example 5.3. *Of Thee I Sing*, No. 3, mm. 1–16 of the vocal line

meter serves as another unifying factor. The importance of vocal ensembles in moving the action forward through music is evident, while the alternation of ensemble singing with various solo voices assures diversity of texture and engenders an ongoing dramatic tension of its own.

The subdivisions themselves typically are organized around their dominating motifs through the processes of presentation, repetition, variation, and small-scale development. Gershwin's modus operandi may be illustrated by the vocal line that opens subdivision 1 (see ex. 5.3). The first eight measures introduce motif A with four successive presentations, all identical in pitch but each with a distinguishing rhythmic detail. The following eight measures subject the motif to transposition, variation, and extension, ending with a half cadence on the fifth of the D-major scale.

The second half of subdivision 1 repeats this material, with new words sung by the male chorus and with a varied ending to effect a cadence to D. (The cadence is almost immediately subverted by a C-natural in the bass that initiates a modulation to G major, the key of subdivision 2.) The repetition has the effect of creating a little two-part form for subdivision 1, an organizational strategy seen again in subdivisions 2 and 8; but the basic techniques Gershwin employs in subdivision 1 to create a musical unit from a concise motif are in evidence throughout the number.

The repetition, variation, and development of previously introduced motifs function as organizational strategies on a larger scale to bind the subdivisions into a larger, coherent musical number. When motif A first recurs in subdivision 4, the vocal line begins in a manner exactly parallel to that in subdivision 1, but the line is transposed a half step down and provided with a new accompaniment. (The ending measures are altered as well, to set up Wintergreen's abrupt entrance and subdivision 5.) When motif A recurs again in subdivision 6, it starts with three repeated pitches instead of two, and is subjected to new rhythmic variations and transpositions when the meter changes to 3/4. Subdivision 6 also introduces some fresh material that contrasts with its dominating motif, a strategy seen in subdivisions 3, 7, and 8 as well.

Within this complex and unconventionally structured musical number, traditional elements appear in unexpected contexts, sometimes with parodic intent. The waltz music of subdivision 2 offers one instance: the graceful, flowery choral setting of "The charming, the gracious, the dutiful Diana Devereaux" sounds suddenly, if appropriately, sentimental, but proves ironic in retrospect, once Diana's self-involved and contentious personality is revealed by subsequent developments.[35] The closest thing to a "big tune" in the entire number is Wintergreen's solo in subdivision 8, but this deliberately understated passage—marked "*simply*" in the score—undermines the conventions of music theater on several levels. This should be the place for a major, self-contained song: the "hero" has his first significant solo opportunity, and not only is he introducing himself musically, but he is elaborating upon his love for the heroine to boot. Why not have a substantial, freestanding, thirty-two-bar "hit" number, in familiar AABA or ABAC form and full of memorable hooks, in this seemingly critical spot? Instead Gershwin enfolds a modest, sixteen-bar, through-composed tune—based on varied repetitions of an unpretentious two-bar motif—within his much larger musical structure. In the context of this larger structure, Wintergreen's solo becomes just one notable feature among many.

Of course, anything more elaborate at this point would have clashed with Ira's appropriately homey lyrics about pies, blintzes, and, above all, corn muffins. With their music and lyrics for subdivision 8, the Gershwins succeeded efficiently in deflating the (admittedly unimpressive) hero, the hero's (admittedly ridiculous) rationale for falling in love, and an entire complex of Broadway traditions. Wintergreen's solo arguably is deflated even further during its repetition, as the original tune is nearly buried in the added counterpoint with which Gershwin surrounds it.

The use of recitative is another element that evokes tradition, even if the tradition is more that of operetta or opera than of the typical Broadway musical. Gershwin employs recitative in this number to highlight certain

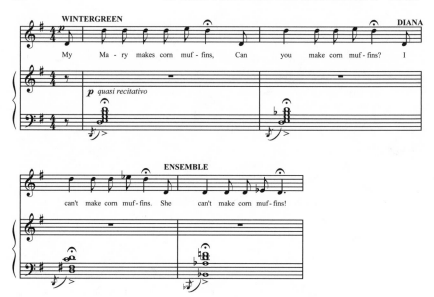

Example 5.4. *Of Thee I Sing*, No. 3, recitative

critical lines in the script without interrupting the flow of music, and what might have been musical dead spots become instead imaginative means to effect transitions.[36] The two recitatives shown in table 5.1 assume a formal significance as well, because of their obvious musical similarities. These similarities emphasize the relationship between Wintergreen's love for Mary (proclaimed in the first recitative) and Mary's corn muffins (the subject of the second recitative). Particularly amusing—and highlighted by the recitative texture—is Gershwin's dramatic alteration of E-natural to an ominous-sounding E-flat when it is revealed that Diana can't make corn muffins (see ex. 5.4).

In terms of its overall structure, it is possible to regard the elaborate number that concludes act 1, scene 3, as a two-part form, bisected by Wintergreen's first, electrifying recitative. From this standpoint, each of the two large sections begins with motif A material and ends with motif D material, incorporates motif C material as well, and includes a distinctive sixteen-bar tune (the waltz in the first section, and Wintergreen's "Some girls can bake a pie" in the second). The first section leads directly into Wintergreen's recitative without a cadence, reflecting the unsettled situation at that point, but the second section does conclude with a cadence as the ensemble sings "Let's all rejoice!" The cadence is to a relatively unexpected chord, however (A major with the added sixth F-sharp), which marks this moment musically and dramatically as only the most provisional of resolutions.

The technique of building an extended musical number out of smaller musical units arranged in coherent, albeit unconventional, patterns is demonstrated on one scale by "Wintergreen for President," on a much larger scale by the concluding number of act 1, scene 3, and on a larger scale yet by the finale to act 1 (no. 8 in the vocal score, and at thirty pages by far the longest single number in it). Gershwin created a substantial portion of this finale by importing into it, virtually as a unit, a large body of music from the conclusion of act 1, scene 3. After Diana interrupts the inauguration and wedding by serving Wintergreen with her summons for breach of promise, the music of subdivisions 5–9 from table 5.1 is heard again, in its original order and with relatively few significant alterations—apart from the provision of (mostly) new lyrics. (Wintergreen's first recitative, between subdivisions 5 and 6 in table 5.1, recurs essentially unchanged in text or music, and his solo "Some girls can bake a pie" is reprised literally.) The entire act 1 finale synthesizes the constructive methods characteristic of *Of Thee I Sing* with the Broadway tradition of employing reprises at the endings of acts. Immediately following the substantial reprise from act 1, scene 3, the finale concludes with a traditional, rousing reprise of the song "Of Thee I Sing" by Wintergreen and the ensemble.

If we review the categories outlined in chapter 3 for understanding the relationship between a given musical number and the plot in a 1920s musical (see table 3.1), the question arises how—or even if—the terms "defining," "action," or "specialty" might be applied to the music from *Of Thee I Sing* outlined in table 5.1. It immediately becomes apparent that the "specialty" category is unsurprisingly irrelevant, but it also follows quickly that any distinction between "defining" and "action" numbers has collapsed in relation to this music, since it is all obviously designed to move the stage action forward while simultaneously defining the characters and their relationships. Simply put: when the music is this essential to the drama, an attempt to determine a category or level of relevance—or importance—for any given number (or part of a number) no longer makes much sense. This observation applies to the entirety of *Of Thee I Sing* as well as it applies to the concluding number of act 1, scene 3.[37]

There are spots in the script for *Of Thee I Sing* that might have invited a musical number of minimal importance to the plot, or even provided the occasion for something like an old-fashioned specialty number, but the Gershwins turned such opportunities around to suit their own purposes and to further the larger interests of the show. For example, the characters of Sam Jenkins and Miss Benson, who serve as assistants first in the Wintergreen campaign and then in the White House, could have been given an audience-pleasing but plot-diluting love duet, to establish them as a secondary couple of the sort found frequently in musical comedies. Instead they begin act 1, scene 4 (the Madison Square Garden scene) by performing "Love Is Sweeping the Country," which defines the spirit of the Wintergreen campaign by presenting love as a national, rather than a personal, preoccupation.

Another instance, and a particularly inspired one, of creative play with a spot that might have allowed for some agreeable but unimportant music and lyrics occurs within the huge act 1 finale, when Wintergreen presents a formal farewell to his bachelor days and "to the girls I used to know."[38] At first Gershwin seems to mock the occasion's inherent insignificance by elaborating it with an excessive quantity of music, allowing Wintergreen a full thirty-two-bar AABA' solo, and then having him repeat the first sixteen measures while a line of counterpoint (with independent text) is added, sung by the ensemble. But Gershwin has further plans for this particular train of musical thought. Mary makes a grand entrance dressed as a bride, and then *she* sings Wintergreen's "bachelor" melody—*Meno mosso*, in a remote key, and with new lyrics ("Is it true, or am I dreaming? Do I go to Heav'n to stay? Never was a girl so happy on her wedding day!")—as if to mock the mockery and lend an unanticipated tenderness to the occasion. Wintergreen and Mary exchange wedding vows, and then both sing the newly dignified tune, the expected final cadence of which is foreclosed by the abrupt entrance of Diana. This entire passage illuminates the way in which Gershwin, sensing a spot where the show's momentum might have flagged, found instead the occasion for inspired parody, effective transformation of mood, and formal ingenuity.

There is one point where the dialogue in *Of Thee I Sing* literally calls for a song (in act 1, scene 4): "Sing 'em the campaign song, Jack! Sing the campaign love song!"[39] Gershwin duly obliges with a self-contained number, but this song is no ordinary plot-stopping specialty piece. It is the crucial

Example 5.5. "Of Thee I Sing," refrain, mm. 1–4

title song of the show, capturing unforgettably the plot's linked themes of politics and love. Ira's lyrics do the job right at the beginning of the refrain; its now celebrated opening phrase "Of thee I sing, baby" encapsulates brilliantly in five words the essential elements of patriotic cliché, amorous sentiment, and incisive parody that drive this musical. George's memorable setting of the phrase juxtaposes a broad, anthemic, stepwise presentation of the patriotic words with a leap down to the intimate "baby," which has the effect of positioning this last word parenthetically (and humorously) apart while also calling special attention to it (see ex. 5.5). It is doubtless the tremendous verbal and musical impact of this phrase that led to the decision to omit the verse that had been written for the song, instead having Wintergreen launch immediately into the refrain once the "campaign love song" has been requested.[40]

The refrain of "Of Thee I Sing" maintains its quality of dualism—nationalistic anthem-cum-love song—throughout. Ira's couplet "Shining star and inspiration, / Worthy of a mighty nation," set to George's sturdy and steady quarter notes, builds effectively to the final assertion, "Of thee I sing," set to longer notes that definitively proclaim a cadence. This is a song that is inherently wedded to its show; yet, with its irresistible and familiarly structured refrain (thirty-two bars, in ABA'C form, and in 4/4 meter), it was also beautifully positioned to be extracted as a popular hit. And much the same could be said of the big showstopper from act 2, "Who Cares?"

"Who Cares?" fulfills two essential functions in *Of Thee I Sing*: it proclaims the strength of the devotion shared by Wintergreen and Mary, and even more significantly it convinces the audience that these two will stand by one another in the face of adversity, regardless of the consequences (i.e., the threat that Wintergreen could be impeached). The song is first presented midway through act 2, scene 1. Sung in unison by the president and the First Lady, it is hurled exuberantly and almost defiantly at reporters who are clamoring to know what Wintergreen intends to do about Diana Devereaux. The

Example 5.6. "Who Cares?" refrain, mm. 1–8

refrain of "Who Cares?" resembles that of "Of Thee I Sing," insofar as it opens with a phrase featuring prominent long notes, as befits a major public pronouncement (see ex. 5.6). And Ira's lyrics for "Who Cares?" once again juxtapose the implicitly political with the explicitly personal: "Who cares what banks fail in Yonkers / Long as you've got a kiss that conquers?"

"Who Cares?" recurs at the conclusion of act 2, scene 1, after the appearance of the French ambassador and the ensuing pressure on Wintergreen to forsake Mary or to resign the presidency—otherwise he will face impeachment. It is here that the song must do its most serious work, by making it seem credible that Wintergreen now feels motivations beyond those of mere political expediency, and that the appeal of corn muffins has for him metamorphosed into an authentic—and reciprocated—love. The refrain is reprised, *Meno mosso con espressione,* with the addition of an expressive and highly chromatic violin obbligato and the substitution of a new couplet for the one previously quoted about bank failures: "We two together can win out; / Just remember to stick your chin out." The strategy here is reminiscent of that employed in the finale of act 1, when Wintergreen's seemingly frivolous "bachelor-farewell" song was transformed into something newly tender and serious upon the appearance of his bride and their formal exchange of vows. The recurrence of "Who Cares?" injects a telling, if momentary, note of sentiment and even pathos into *Of Thee I Sing,* allowing the audience a welcome breathing space in which to feel for the hero and heroine before the tone of comedy resumes at full tilt.[41] The complex harmonic language of the song effectively assists its expressive functions; if it works well with the aggressive initial presentation of the number, it works equally well with the intensely intimate and somewhat fraught atmosphere surrounding the reprise.

"Who Cares?" shares several important characteristics with "Of Thee I Sing," among them an unconventionally structured verse (also an extensive one, which did survive into the Broadway performances), and a thirty-two-bar refrain in ABA'C form. "Who Cares?" also departs from the 2/4 meter that permeates much of the score; in both of its presentations, it is in 2/2 meter.

Of "Prequels" and a Sequel

In surveys of Gershwin's career, *Strike Up the Band* is frequently linked with *Of Thee I Sing* and *Let 'Em Eat Cake* to form a trio of "political operettas." While *Let 'Em Eat Cake* was conceived by Kaufman, Ryskind, and the Gershwins as a sequel to *Of Thee I Sing*, there never was any intentional relationship between either of these shows and the earlier *Strike Up the Band*. Nevertheless, the question arises naturally whether any aspects of *Strike Up the Band* clearly anticipate the distinctive characteristics of *Of Thee I Sing*—especially considering the involvement of Kaufman (as author of the book for the original 1927 version of *Strike Up the Band*) and Ryskind (who revised Kaufman's book in 1929 for the second version of the show, which opened on Broadway early in 1930). Were the two versions of *Strike Up the Band* in some conceptual sense "prequels" to *Of Thee I Sing*?

Reasoning from hindsight has inherent dangers, and naturally one tends to find that for which one is searching. Compounding these problems is the difficulty of getting a reliable handle on *Strike Up the Band* itself, particularly on the unsuccessful original version that never made it to Broadway. Tommy Krasker's 1990 restoration of the show—which has been recorded, and published as a vocal score—does make it possible to offer modest observations with some degree of certainty.[42] *Strike Up the Band* is significant insofar as it presented Gershwin with opportunities to try his hand at musical parody and at composing a few extended musical numbers. With regard to parody, there are operetta-like sections in 2/4 and 6/8 meter, even the waltz makes an appearance, and there is considerable and humorous use of a chorus. But while his work on *Strike Up the Band* may have offered Gershwin some excellent preparation for undertaking *Of Thee I Sing*, there remain essential differences between the two shows, and the overriding one is this: the remarkable unity that exists within and between the book and the score for *Of Thee I Sing* is simply not to be found in *Strike Up the Band*.

In his original libretto for *Strike Up the Band*, Kaufman presented a satire on the motivations for and the conduct of war—certainly darker material than the genially amoral carryings-on of American politicos he and Ryskind depicted in *Of Thee I Sing*. In Ryskind's revision of *Strike Up the Band*, the war turns out to be a dream in the end. Neither libretto, however, presented opportunities to develop love relationships among the characters in a way that had meaningful, causal ties with the plot; apparently the love situations demanded by musical comedy were simply grafted onto the political satire.

Consequently, Gershwin's music for the show (in both versions) included self-contained love songs of a typical Broadway character, music that existed side by side with parodic and less conventionally structured material written around the war theme. Representative of the situation was producer Edgar Selwyn's determination to feature "The Man I Love" in the original version of *Strike Up the Band*. It is difficult to conceive of a song less suited to the subject matter, and presumably the tone, of Kaufman's book. (In the revised version of the show, "The Man I Love" was replaced with "Soon," a haunting and equally bluesy love song that simply perpetuated this dichotomy.)

In *Of Thee I Sing*, of course, Kaufman and Ryskind ingeniously integrated the themes of love and politics, and the Gershwins ingeniously responded with "love" songs such as "Of Thee I Sing" and "Who Cares?" Even when Wintergreen and Mary turn out to be truly in love, the thematic integration remains unbroken. Their devotion directly precipitates a *political* crisis, the ultimate solution to which is found through political means—via the office and person of the suddenly essential Throttlebottom.

Why a sequel to *Of Thee I Sing*? There were no loose threads left dangling as the curtain came down on this show. All major plot complications were resolved; all the principal characters were given a reason to feel acknowledged and satisfied. In addition, the characters in *Of Thee I Sing* lacked—by design—the level of complexity that would have encouraged audience members to identify seriously with them, or to wonder what further adventures might await these characters in a fictional future. The always infallible tool of twenty-twenty hindsight allows us to regard *Let 'Em Eat Cake* as an ill-conceived and ill-fated project from the get-go. Nevertheless, *Let 'Em Eat Cake* boasted a flawless pedigree, carried over from the earlier show: not only Kaufman, Ryskind, and the Gershwins, but Sam H. Harris once again as producer, Kaufman once again as director, and many members of the original cast of *Of Thee I Sing* (including William Gaxton, Victor Moore, and Lois Moran re-creating their roles as Wintergreen, Throttlebottom, and Mary). Surely an ensemble of such talent should have been able to bring forth something worthwhile, even if the inspiration for the project was problematic.

Today those curious about *Let 'Em Eat Cake* may consult the original published libretto[43] and a recording of the restored score.[44] (A piano-vocal score has never been published; a few numbers from the show were published individually.) While occasionally very funny, the book strains with an increasing sense of desperation to force exaggerated humor from sobering contemporary conditions: the deepening economic depression, public discontent and protest, revolutionary rhetoric, international war debts, and the rise of dictatorships. Without characters of any real substance with which to work, Kaufman and Ryskind had to depend on plot to make their satiric points, and the situations in their play become progressively more out-rageous. For example, in act 2 the issues surrounding the payment of war debts are settled by means of a baseball game between representatives of the League of Nations and the members of the U.S. Supreme Court! There is also no compelling love interest that might have leavened the proceedings. Wintergreen and Mary retain their mutual devotion, but this is old news, and nothing is provided in the way of either challenge or counterpoint to this couple.

Gershwin responded to this unpromising book with music that is, of course, thoroughly competent and often much more than that, but the fresh-ness and warmth of the score for *Of Thee I Sing* are lacking.[45] *Let 'Em Eat Cake* allowed for a single love song, a testament to Wintergreen's and Mary's continuing commitment, and this song became the show's best-known number, "Mine." But the occasion for it (in act 1, scene 4) is dramatically static, and while Gershwin enlivens the situation musically by making the song a contrapuntal piece—Wintergreen sings the refrain as a solo, then the ensemble responds with a contrasting "patter," and then it is revealed that the two can be sung simultaneously to winning effect—the composer cannot make the number seem particularly relevant to the plot. In fact, "Mine" functions much like an anachronistic specialty number in the context of *Let 'Em Eat Cake*, and its serenely static quality places it in stark contrast to "Of Thee I Sing" and "Who Cares?" from the earlier show—two love songs that are "moving" in all senses of the word.

The admittedly privileged Broadway audience for *Of Thee I Sing* had obviously been receptive to a good-natured ribbing of the American political system. But by the time *Let 'Em Eat Cake* was having its brief Broadway run during the final months of 1933, this same audience in all likelihood had a grimmer view of the nation and of the world generally, and a new musical inviting them to laugh at grim humor onstage consequently was poised, whether by intent or not, to strike some sour notes. The United States was four years into the Great Depression, with Roosevelt's very new New Deal an unproven promise to the nation, and prominent refugees (among them Arnold Schoenberg and Albert Einstein) were already fleeing to its shores from a Germany now under Hitler's despotic rule. When *Let 'Em Eat Cake* ended with a scene in which the execution of Wintergreen and his cronies is foiled by Mary's introduction of a fashion display (an obvious parody of the scene from *Of Thee I Sing* in which Mary foiled the impeachment of Wintergreen with a pregnancy announcement), we might understand if the audience elected not to care whether these stick-figure characters lived or died—let alone what they might choose to wear.

Let 'Em Eat Cake was obviously out of sync with its time and its audience, and it closed after only ninety performances on Broadway. If *Of Thee I Sing* provides outstanding evidence of what great creative minds can achieve when left to their own devices, *Let 'Em Eat Cake* offers a counterbalance, demonstrating that occasionally even great creative minds might benefit from some benevolent outside interference, to help them differentiate their good ideas from their lesser ones.

The remarkable artistic and commercial success of *Of Thee I Sing*, and its pivotal importance to Gershwin's Broadway career, naturally make one wonder whether the show can be successfully resurrected. While the musical has been revived on and off Broadway over the years, *Of Thee I Sing* has yet to achieve that mythic "canonical" status that seems permanently denied to any Gershwin show save *Porgy and Bess*—an exceptional case, in any event, since it is an opera—or to any pre-*Oklahoma!* musical save (some would argue) *Show Boat*.[46]

If *Of Thee I Sing* is judged to be hopelessly dated, it is paradoxically for the opposite reason that one might judge a 1920s Gershwin show such as *Lady, Be Good!* to be dated. The 1920s shows have librettos that, by design, are too amorphous for today's tastes and practices; *Of Thee I Sing* has a libretto that is fixed—but fixed in a time now long past. A specific political era, and particular attitudes toward politics that typify that era, are beautifully captured in *Of Thee I Sing*. But we live in quite a different political era, marked by substantially different attitudes, and the world evoked by *Of Thee I Sing* may well strike us as both excessively naive and excessively benevolent. Could the application of a 1920s-style freedom to the libretto of *Of Thee I Sing* liberate the show to work better in our time? It is impossible to say, but the question as posed is itself plagued by anachronisms.

It may be noticed that the matter of genre as it applies to *Of Thee I Sing* has been avoided throughout the preceding discussion. References to the show from its own time do not prove conclusive.[47] Given the prominence of extended musical numbers and of choral writing in the score, the appellation "operetta" seems justifiable for *Of Thee I Sing*, especially since Gershwin's employment of patter songs and waltzes often evokes the spirit of operetta in a parodic manner. Calling *Of Thee I Sing* an operetta may, however, distract from what is arguably the most important aspect of this work, namely its sui generis character.

Of Thee I Sing represents an unprecedented achievement in Gershwin's oeuvre and in the history of American musical theater. It is also an achievement that proved not to be duplicable; *Let 'Em Eat Cake* demonstrated that—at least in this instance—lightning was not about to strike twice, and that the distinctive blend and balance of elements that defined the artistry of *Of Thee I Sing* were inimitable. With *Of Thee I Sing*, "Broadway Gershwin" joined "concert hall Gershwin" in the production of sui generis works, and the two would soon join forces (so to speak) to produce an unprecedented, inimitable, and unique "American folk opera" on Broadway.[48]

CHAPTER 6

The Nonpareil

Porgy and Bess *in Catfish Row, on Broadway,* *in America, and throughout the World*

ERSHWIN'S *PORGY AND BESS* EMERGED AS AN EXCEPTIONALLY AM-
bitious, seemingly impractical project, an undertaking that should
by all rights have had little chance of success. George Gershwin as
a full-fledged opera composer? As the composer of an American *folk* opera?
(What's that?) Of an American folk opera mounted on *Broadway*? (What
happened to the Metropolitan Opera, which doubtless would have relished
the opportunity to offer a Gershwin premiere?) And with an *all-black* singing
cast? (That answers the Metropolitan Opera question, but if the Metropolitan
wouldn't provide such performers, how was Gershwin going to find them?)

It is true that the plot, characters, and setting for Gershwin's opera project
had already demonstrated their Broadway stage-worthiness, in the form of
the successful play *Porgy* by Dorothy and DuBose Heyward. The play, which
arrived on Broadway in 1927 and had a substantial run, was based in turn on
DuBose Heyward's popular novel of the same name (published in 1925). On
the other hand, all this previous familiarity could have rendered the material
old news for Broadway denizens, who by the time *Porgy and Bess* opened in
October 1935 may even have started having doubts about Gershwin himself.
The man hadn't had a hit show since *Of Thee I Sing* (his two 1933 shows,
Pardon My English and *Let 'Em Eat Cake,* had both been flops), and his
work had in fact been absent from Broadway for the better part of two years.

Against such odds it seems remarkable that *Porgy and Bess* made it to
Broadway at all. Yet it did, and while achieving only a modest run (124 performances) it occasioned a great quantity of notice and discussion. More remarkably, this proved to be just the beginning of an extraordinary career for

Gershwin's magnum opus; not only has *Porgy and Bess* refused to die, but it has traveled a "long, long road," frequently over rough terrain, to arrive at an unprecedented and unparalleled position among works of music theater. Gershwin's prodigious, protean creation has made its way around the world: into formal opera houses and concert halls and onto less formal musical stages, into movie theaters and onto television screens, and more generally into the milieus of jazz and popular music, to an extent that makes it both unique and uniquely successful. Not only in terms of Gershwin's output, but in terms of music theater considered as a whole, *Porgy and Bess* is *the* sui generis work among all sui generis works.

To create a convincing musical setting for Heyward's tale of "Catfish Row," Gershwin had to cross boundaries of race, ethnicity (the community in question is one of Gullah people, with distinctive characteristics of language and cultural practice), geography (Catfish Row is based on the Cabbage Row district in Charleston, South Carolina), class, and religion.[1] Often too much is made of this. The employment of subjects and settings utterly foreign to the creator's personal experience is a longstanding tradition in opera. Gershwin enthusiastically and assiduously went to work, as always, and while *Porgy and Bess* has encountered objections and even assaults—racial, ethnic, cultural, and specifically musical—from the time of its premiere to the present day, the opera has not simply endured, it has triumphed.

This chapter will seek to elucidate some significant aspects of Gershwin's achievement, concentrating on the why and the how of his creative process in musicalizing Catfish Row and in bringing it to Broadway as an "American folk opera." A thorough history, analysis, and critical treatment of *Porgy and Bess* is clearly beyond the scope of this discussion; fortunately, there is a good deal of worthwhile material on the opera that is readily available to provide fuller coverage, and new scholarship is appearing regularly.[2]

That Gershwin might want to write an opera is not in itself surprising. Such an enterprise was perfectly poised to synthesize the dual sets of skills he had developed and honed, as an experienced composer for both music theater and the concert hall. Indeed, Gershwin apparently discussed the possibility of an opera based on *Porgy* with DuBose Heyward as early as 1926, although the composer felt unprepared to take on the project at that point in his career.[3] And late in 1929 Gershwin was involved in serious discussions with the Metropolitan Opera regarding a work to be based on the S. Ansky play *The Dybbuk*, but this project fell through when the rights to that play proved unavailable.[4] The medium of opera was by definition much more elaborate and demanding than that of traditional musical comedy, but it would also afford Gershwin a level of control over his music that far surpassed anything possible in a typical Broadway situation. The experience he had enjoyed with *Of Thee I Sing* must have sharpened Gershwin's appetite for creative control—even if *Let 'Em Eat Cake* had revealed that control in itself did not provide assurance of a successful outcome.

Assuming full control, Gershwin played a significant role in virtually every aspect of the conception, creation, and initial production of *Porgy and Bess.* He personally selected the subject (*Porgy*), chose his collaborators for the libretto (DuBose Heyward, and eventually Ira Gershwin as well), and established the musical format—grand opera, with recitatives throughout. His preferences proved decisive in the choice of production company (the Theatre Guild, the group responsible for the play *Porgy* and many other successful productions), of conductor (Alexander Smallens), and of vocal coach (Alexander Steinert). He was also extensively involved in the long and complex process of auditioning and selecting the cast, and his choices ranged from classically trained singers (Todd Duncan and Anne Brown, for the title roles) to the members of a song-and-dance duo with roots in vaudeville ([Ford L.] Buck and [John W.] Bubbles, for the roles of Mingo and Sportin' Life, respectively). In some of these decisions he faced opposition from others involved in the project, but Gershwin stood his ground. Early on, Heyward questioned whether sustained recitative rather than spoken dialogue could be effective in the work; Gershwin stuck by recitative and prevailed.[5] Later, when during rehearsals the behavior of John W. Bubbles proved exceptionally trying to the conductor and to other formally trained musicians in the cast, Gershwin staunchly defended the man who came to embody memorably the composer's conception of Catfish Row's skeptical dope dealer.[6]

But what was it about *Porgy* itself that so captivated the composer in the first place? What might have attracted Gershwin so strongly to the story, characters, and setting of *Porgy*? The answers to such questions cannot be known definitively. Nevertheless, an appreciation of the ambitious and impressive opera that Gershwin made from *Porgy* leads to the understanding that the composer saw in Heyward's Catfish Row not a singular community isolated by its "otherness," but a microcosm of the larger human community that included Gershwin himself. From this standpoint, Heyward's fictional neighborhood serves in effect as a crucible in which issues of wide-ranging importance are played out, not least among them the very role of community itself. Conflicts over tradition and religion; the desires, devotion, disputes, and devastation that come in the wake of love; the many varieties of personal aspiration and ambition—all are to be found in Catfish Row. The community offers a provocative mixture of the comic and the tragic, brought to full-blooded life by characters who cannot be reduced simplistically to the "good" and the "bad."[7] Gershwin also may have found it striking that many of the boundaries he had to cross in formulating his own imaginative relationship to Catfish Row—especially the boundaries of race, class, modernity, and geography (and this last category includes, in addition to issues of South versus North, issues of cultural "backwaters" versus "sophisticated" urban settings)—were illuminated by conflicts within the imaginary community itself.

If this line of thought is followed through, one must be struck by the provocative conceptual leap that was required for someone of Gershwin's background to notice these particular aspects of *Porgy*. In fact both the novel and the play strongly encourage a perception of Catfish Row in terms of "otherness," and for a cosmopolitan New Yorker the typical reaction to this fictional Gullah community would probably have been encapsulated by descriptors such as "primitive," "backward," and "exotic." Yet clearly the composer was able to establish for himself a sense of identification and empathy with the characters and life of Catfish Row. Gershwin must also have realized on some level the magnitude of the task he would face in seeking to evoke analogous reactions of identification and empathy from a Broadway theater audience; it represented a truly radical stance to suggest that a small and highly individual community of impoverished black people in Charleston could serve to represent humanity—or at least America (as in "American folk opera")—writ large. Gershwin had an enormous asset in his favor, of course, for bringing such a task to fruition, and this was his distinctive musical genius. Gershwin lavished all of his imagination, stylistic breadth, and technical skill on *Porgy and Bess*, harnessing the strength of his music to make of the operatic Catfish Row a community of unlimited expressive scope and communicative power.

Antecedents

All the major incidents and characters that fundamentally would come to shape *Porgy and Bess* are present in Heyward's novel *Porgy*.[8] There is a Saturday night crap game in Catfish Row that turns ugly when the brutally strong stevedore Crown kills Robbins in a dispute over the dice, leaving the

Figure 6.1. The fatal crap game (publicity still), from the original Theatre Guild production of *Porgy and Bess*, 1935

dead man's deeply religious widow, Serena, to mourn him. Crown's subsequent flight to avoid arrest leaves his woman, Bess, without resources, but she finds shelter and eventually a steady home life with the crippled beggar Porgy. When the members of the community sail to a nearby island to enjoy a picnic, it turns out that Crown has been hiding there, and he lures Bess away temporarily, resolving to return to Catfish Row for her soon so that they both can flee.

The story continues as Bess reunites with Porgy. Shortly thereafter, a terrific hurricane devastates the area, causing the deaths of many fishermen from the row, and leading to the unexpected development that Bess and Porgy become adoptive parents for a newly orphaned baby. Bess expresses to Porgy the conflict between her sensual attraction for Crown—fueled by the alcohol and "happy dust" (cocaine) that has clearly played a role in that relationship[9]—and the "good" life she shares with the crippled man; Porgy decides he must eliminate the conflict by eliminating Crown. When the stevedore returns to Catfish Row for Bess, Porgy murders him. Although the police can secure no hard evidence concerning the murder, the coroner decides to summon Porgy as a "witness" to identify Crown's body, and when Porgy comes back to Catfish Row he finds Bess gone.

Those who know the opera will recognize all these elements. There are significant differences between the novel and the opera, however, and more striking than the many details of plot and character that might be cited are the basic issues of tone and shaping. The novel takes its readers into a community clearly set apart in a separate, special place and time; this is apparent from the first sentence: "Porgy lived in the Golden Age." The entire first paragraph is worthy of quotation, because it captures immediately and effectively the highly individual ambience of Heyward's creation: "Porgy lived in the Golden Age. Not the Golden Age of a remote and legendary past; nor yet the chimerical era treasured by every man past middle life, that never existed except in the heart of youth; but an age when men, not yet old, were boys in an ancient, beautiful city that time had forgotten before it destroyed."[10] In terms of shaping, the novel is episodic—almost a series of vivid vignettes—and the strong linear drive of the opera's plot, decisively centered around the evolving love relationship between Porgy and Bess, is lacking.

The play *Porgy* reshaped the novel into a form to which the opera would adhere closely.[11] (We should remember, however, that Gershwin sensed the dramatic potential of Heyward's material *before* it was made into a play.) Perhaps the most important change was the decision to introduce Bess as a character much earlier in the action, right in the opening crap game scene, and to plant the dramatic motif of Porgy's interest in her even before she comes onstage. This makes the love triangle of Porgy, Bess, and Crown the cynosure of the audience's awareness, whereas in the novel this configuration explicitly emerges considerably later and consequently receives less emphasis. (It is noteworthy that the listing of the cast of characters for the play names the woman at the apex of the triangle as "Crown's Bess.")

The role of the dope dealer Sportin' Life is very much enlarged in the play. In the novel he is kicked out of Catfish Row by shopkeeper and community matriarch Maria before the hurricane, and he is not an explicit factor in Bess's final departure. In the play Sportin' Life is touting to Bess the appeal of an escape to New York with him by the end of the first scene, and it is to this temptation that she finally succumbs in Porgy's absence. (At the conclusion of the novel, Maria tells Porgy that Bess was abducted by a gang of men, who lured her with liquor and dope and carried her away on a river boat to Savannah.)[12] The vastly increased prominence of Sportin' Life in the play serves the function of increasing the dramatic pressure on Porgy and Bess's relationship; now there are three men who actively desire Bess, each for different reasons. But the new importance of Sportin' Life also enhances the role of New York in the story—surely a savvy alteration in adapting Catfish Row for Broadway.[13] The opposition of North to South, which is given only passing attention in the novel, becomes a more significant issue in the play, along with the idea of modernity exerting pressure on the traditional ways and human ties of a small, insular community.

Other modifications from novel to play reinforce the centrality of Bess and Crown, both as individuals and in terms of the relationship each of them bears to the Catfish Row community. In the play, as a consequence of her early entrance, Bess participates in the scene of communal mourning for Robbins following his murder by Crown, and she even comes to lead a group spiritual at the end of the scene—representing her acceptance of, and into, the spiritual life of Catfish Row. For his part, Crown in the play returns to Catfish Row during the hurricane scene. His ability to make his way in the face of such a storm attests to his enormous physical strength and suggests great personal courage. Upon his arrival, Crown's courage immediately finds direct expression—first antisocially, through his mockery of the community's desperate songs and prayers, and then socially, through his willingness to venture into the storm again to try to save the young mother Clara (who has impulsively run outside upon seeing her husband's fishing boat in the river, upside down). All these alterations made for higher and better drama, and it should come as no surprise that they were all retained in the operatic version of the story.

What did not change in the adaptation from novel to play was the former's tone of separateness and "otherness" in presenting Catfish Row. Nothing could make this more apparent than the following extensive stage direction from the printed text of the play, describing the effect of the opening scene:

> As the curtain rises, revealing Catfish Row on a summer evening, the court reëchoes with African laughter and friendly banter in "Gullah," the language of the Charleston Negro, which still retains many African words. The audience understands none of it. Like the laughter and movement, the twanging of a guitar from an upper window, the dancing of an urchin with a loose, shuffling, step, it is a part of the picture of Catfish Row as it really is—an alien scene, a people as little known to most Americans as the people of the Congo.

Gradually, it seems to the audience that they are beginning to understand this foreign language. In reality, the "Gullah" is being tempered to their ears, spoken more distinctly with the African words omitted.[14]

This "alien" aspect of the conception is what Gershwin altered, crucially, in fashioning his opera. The only thread that links the opening of the opera with that of the play is the suggestion of music and dance in the description just quoted. *Porgy and Bess* opens with instrumental music, onstage dancing, and then only the hints of language—but not of "foreign" Gullah or even English, just the universal "language" of scat as couples hum wordlessly to the dance tune. The program may say we're in Jasbo Brown's room in Catfish Row, but the sound environment could just as well be that of a Harlem rent party; the musical style is not remotely "exotic"—not for Gershwin, nor for the bulk of his original Broadway audience. In other words, Gershwin was seeking something quite other than "otherness" in his *Porgy and Bess*.

Music does play an important part in the play *Porgy*, fleshing out suggestions already present in the novel concerning the role of music in the life of Catfish Row. The novel's first community scene, centered upon the crap game that turns deadly, is already provided with a soundtrack of voices "singing drowsily" and of one inhabitant "picking a guitar monotonously, chord after chord, until the dark throbbed like an old wound."[15] Later in the book, the episode of communal mourning for Robbins, the picnic preparations, and the hurricane sequence are all animated with descriptions of music and occasionally with song lyrics; these scenes and others become elaborately musical in the play, with the script providing the texts for many folk songs and spirituals.[16] While the specific and extensive presence of music in both novel and play must certainly have encouraged Gershwin's interest in the material, the composer made a point of not employing any preexisting "folk" music in his own *Porgy and Bess*, and this decision may be seen as a critical aspect of his rejecting self-conscious "otherness."

There is one highly significant characteristic of the opera's sound world that may be traced directly back to Heyward's novel. It involves not music per se, but its absence—what might be termed the "negative" musical space in which the white characters live and act. The impact upon the community of a white man's intrusion into Catfish Row is memorably captured in Heyward's prose: "the court had been full of the many-colored sounds that accompanied its evening life. Now, gradually the noise shrunk, seeming to withdraw into itself. All knew what it meant. A white man had entered. The protective curtain of silence which the negro draws about his life when the Caucasian intrudes hung almost tangibly in the air."[17]

This "protective curtain of silence" also descends upon the play whenever the daily life of Catfish Row is interrupted by the appearance of white people. Such a dramatic portrayal of the racial barrier finds expression in Gershwin's opera through his denial of any music to the white characters. They speak against a backdrop of silence, in conversation with Catfish Row residents who sing responses accompanied by the orchestra.[18] The impact of this procedure is decisive, whether it is perceived as reflecting the total exclusion of the white characters from the world of the blacks or as reflecting the utter inability of the former to enter the world of the latter.

In sum, a reader who comes to the novel *Porgy* knowing Gershwin's opera will find many things familiar, while having a substantially different kind of experience. A reader who comes to the play knowing the opera will find a great deal of the libretto already in place, but might feel—to employ a loaded, yet relevant, analogy—as if a glorious full-color picture had been reduced to black and white. Gershwin's music is not the only thing missing. The exceptional lyrics to numbers such as "Summertime," "My Man's Gone Now," "I Got Plenty o' Nuttin'," "Bess, You Is My Woman," "It Ain't Necessarily So," "There's a Boat Dat's Leavin' Soon for New York," and many others, are also absent from the play's script. With *Porgy and Bess* Gershwin once again played an indispensable role in a creative team characterized by extraordinary synergy; not only was Ira Gershwin at the top of his form as a lyricist, but DuBose Heyward made remarkable contributions as well.[19]

The play *Porgy* proved so readily adaptable into a Gershwin libretto because its material shared significant commonalities with the scripts for Gershwin's previous successful musical comedies. *Porgy and Bess* is an opera, and it is not a comedy despite the presence of comedic details, but it is also a work of music theater designed for Broadway, and it in no way belittles the work to identify the typical Broadway elements that helped to make it viable as such. The most prominent among these elements is the plotting around a love triangle—actually, a love quadrilateral if Sportin' Life is included, as he probably should be. The picnic scene offers opportunities for dancing and physical jests. The genially shady lawyer Frazier represents a black version of a venerable stage archetype, although he is also provided with a benevolent white foil (Archdale) and an extremely malevolent white foil (the detective).

The concept of the exotic "Other" defined the entire Catfish Row community in Gershwin's source material, but in *Porgy and Bess* he turned the concept on its head to render the white characters as the "Others." In adding lyrics to the material, wordplay found a niche in Ira's witty "I Got Plenty o' Nuttin'" and "It Ain't Necessarily So." The former is one of the opera's many splendid examples of a solo "defining" number (Porgy expresses the happiness and security that have come from his now stable relationship with Bess), while the latter is clearly a solo "specialty" number (for Sportin' Life, at the picnic). Or perhaps we should call these solo numbers, and others, "arias," since arias in operas usually serve in effect either as defining or as specialty numbers for the characters performing them. Among the other major defining numbers in *Porgy and Bess* are Sportin' Life's "There's a Boat Dat's Leavin' Soon for New York," and all three duets involving Bess, which articulate the status of her relationships with Porgy ("Bess, You Is My Woman" and "I Wants to Stay Here"—the latter more commonly known as "I Loves You, Porgy") and with Crown ("What You Want wid Bess?"). A list of specialty numbers might include the immortal lullaby "Summertime," Crown's "A Red Headed Woman," and the instrumental specialty "Jasbo Brown Blues," although Gershwin employs all of these in complex contexts that enhance the drama in various ways. There are also many ensemble "action" numbers in the opera, including "Oh, I Can't Sit Down" (sung as the community prepares for the picnic), "Oh, Dere's Somebody Knockin' at de Do'" (sung during the hurricane), and the exquisite lament "Clara, Clara" (sung to commemorate those lost in the hurricane).

It is more important for the purposes of this book to connect *Porgy and Bess* with the traditions of Broadway than to connect it with those of grand opera, especially since most of the recent literature on the work considers it in terms of operatic traditions. Nevertheless, the operatic legitimacy of *Porgy and Bess* was important to Gershwin, and the matter merits some brief consideration here.

While he was hard at work on his opera, the composer made the oft-quoted remark, "If I am successful it will resemble a combination of the drama and romance of *Carmen* and the beauty of *Meistersinger*, if you can imagine that."[20] The remark deserves to be taken seriously. By evoking in a single sentence both one of the most celebrated "number" operas and an elaborate Wagnerian music drama, Gershwin made clear the scope of his ambitions for *Porgy and Bess*, which has the strong individual songs of a number opera and the continuity of a music drama—along with elements of a Broadway musical. *Porgy and Bess* surely possesses "drama and romance," with the love triangle of Porgy, Bess, and Crown suggesting clear analogies to the plot of *Carmen*; Gershwin also drew upon the precedent of Bizet's masterpiece to defend himself against the silly charge of having diluted the impact of his opera with "song hits," asserting that "*Carmen* is almost a collection of hits."[21] As for *Die Meistersinger von Nürnberg*, Gershwin's opera shares with Wagner's an immersion in the life of a community and a consequent abundance of ensemble writing, along with an ambitious role for the orchestra and an array of leitmotifs employed imaginatively and extensively throughout (many of which are given to the orchestra).[22]

There might be an additional, more personal connection for Gershwin with *Meistersinger*. Could the composer have felt a sense of kinship with the character of Wagner's Walther—the possessor of extraordinary, apparently spontaneous musical gifts who is disdained by the establishment "masters" for his lack of traditional formal training? And could *Porgy and Bess* have been seen by Gershwin as his own "prize song," a composition of such compelling beauty and mastery that it wins over the masters as well as the community at large? These are tempting, if utterly unprovable, conjectures.

In discussions of operatic antecedents for *Porgy and Bess*, much is often made of the brief (albeit through-composed) one-act "Opera Ala Afro-American" *Blue Monday* that Gershwin wrote to Buddy DeSylva's lyrics as a special feature for *George White's Scandals of 1922*.[23] I think too much is made of it. *Blue Monday* is, to be sure, Gershwin's only "operatic" effort other than *Porgy and Bess*, and its characters are African Americans—although it was performed, as was intended, in blackface by members of the *Scandals* cast. But an enormous gulf separates Gershwin's two operas in terms of both ambition and aesthetic achievement. This is scarcely surprising, when we consider that *Blue Monday* was thrown together in great haste by a promising but still quite immature composer, while *Porgy and Bess* was a carefully considered and painstakingly executed labor of love by an experienced genius functioning at the height of his powers.

From a dramatic standpoint *Blue Monday* is extremely clumsy, climaxing abruptly with a virtually implausible, scarcely motivated murder and ending with a self-consciously anthemic tribute by the dying hero to his mother. While some of the music is interesting, it is doubtful it would attract much interest today were *Blue Monday* not an early work by Gershwin. The score is notable for harmonic adventurousness, however, with many passages reminiscent of the harmonically adventurous verse in Gershwin's big hit from the *Scandals of 1922*, "I'll Build a Stairway to Paradise." The music of *Blue Monday* tends to sag not so much in its overall shaping or its transitions as in those spots where it settles into brief set pieces, which indicates th Gershwin was capable of some relatively large-scale formal thinkii not yet the consistently outstanding songwriter he was soon to bec

Where Is (and What Is, and Who Lives in) Gershwin's Catfish Row?

Writing in the *New York Times* shortly after the Broadway opening of *Porgy and Bess*, Gershwin unapologetically told readers, "When I began work on the music I decided against the use of original folk material because I wanted the music to be all of one piece."[25] Let us put aside temporarily the question of how this decision squared with the subtitle of "folk opera" for his work, to ponder just what the composer might have meant by "all of one piece." What kind of "piece" was this? Better, *whose* piece was this?

The answer seems to be that it was *Gershwin's* piece—first, foremost, and solely. His refusal to employ borrowed music could be used to buttress charges that Gershwin dared inappropriately to "speak for" African Americans. But I think such charges would be more convincing had Gershwin actually used preexisting folk songs and spirituals in *Porgy and Bess*; in that case the characters singing them might legitimately be regarded as representative of African Americans (or of a particular group of African Americans) and their culture. As it stands, Gershwin the composer did not position himself to speak for a race or a culture in *Porgy and Bess* at all; the work is not an African American work nor is it a Gullah work, and in it Gershwin ultimately is only representing himself. (The opera is an *American* work simply because Gershwin was a consummately American composer; it remains significant that Gershwin did not call *Porgy and Bess* an "African American," let alone a "Charleston" or a "Gullah," opera.) What Gershwin did do was give musical voice to his fictional residents of his fictional Catfish Row community, and through this music express feelings and concerns that spoke to the broadest human community he could envision.[26]

The fact that the musical "voice" heard throughout *Porgy and Bess* is intentionally and indisputably Gershwin's own should free the composer from facile claims of expropriation and exploitation. If nothing else, that voice should be appreciated as a form of creative honesty: Gershwin knew he could not pretend to be a Gullah black person. His ingenuousness may seem remarkable to us, but it is congruent with the generosity and fearlessness that typified what we know of Gershwin's character. In any case the composer's desire to make his opera "all of one piece," and the creative manifestation of this desire in the score of *Porgy and Bess*, paradoxically render the contentious issue of "authenticity" a bogus concern. *Porgy and Bess* is authentic Gershwin, that is all, and all that it was intended to be.

This is not to say that the Catfish Row individuals and community lack characteristic and distinctive features. Indeed, such features are required in a serious opera, where the stereotypical and two-dimensional figures and generalized settings that function effectively in Gershwin's musical comedies could not bear the expressive weight the music would thrust upon them. Heyward's material provided Gershwin with highly individuated characters and ample local color, including Gullah-tinged dialect, to give the drama a realistic basis. Since Heyward's Catfish Row is a working-class community, occupied by inhabitants whose straightforward concerns revolve around the basics of life and livelihood, the story of Porgy and Bess became for Gershwin a "folk tale," out of which he consequently fashioned a "folk opera."[27] Gershwin's great inspiration was to use the material as a springboard for artistic outreach, rather than as an invitation to burrow inward and underline what would seem to be the intrinsic "otherness" of the material. The composer's well-publicized visits to South Carolina were certainly useful in providing some basic understanding of the sources for Heyward's own inspiration,[28] and in stimulating some of Gershwin's own musical conceptions—such as the memorable six-voice prayers that open and close act 2, scene 4.[29] But these visits must also have made Gershwin realize how far his own background and culture lay, not only from those of the Gullah blacks but also from those of Heyward. The assumption of a viewpoint toward the material that was emphatically his own—not that of the Gullahs (utterly impossible to emulate), nor that of Heyward ("otherness")—made a virtue out of necessity on Gershwin's part.

Gershwin's *New York Times* article about *Porgy and Bess* set up a distinction between "opera" and "theater" that the composer claimed to have bridged in his new work. Of course opera is a form of music theater, but Gershwin was writing opera for Broadway and doubtless sought to assure his audience that he was not abandoning the concerns and techniques that had previously earned him success in the theater—simply enhancing them. The opening sequence in *Porgy and Bess* is supremely theatrical, while avoiding anything that remotely suggests traditional opera. (What this opening does bring to mind is the analogously unconventional opening of *Of Thee I Sing*, which so successfully dislodges traditional expectations while preparing the particular and unusual character of the work to follow.) This opening merits detailed attention for the many ways in which it positions the audience within the musical world of *Porgy and Bess*.

The essential inspiration for the manner in which Gershwin's opera begins must in fact be credited to DuBose Heyward. Early in their collaborative process, Heyward wrote to Gershwin: "What I have in mind is to let the scene, as I describe it, merge with the overture, almost in the sense of illustration, giving the added force of sight and sound. I think it would be very effective to have the lights go out during the overture, so that the curtain rises in darkness, then the first scene will begin to come up as the music takes up the theme of jazz from the dance hall piano."[30]

The opening onstage piano music is a literal, uninterrupted continuation of what the orchestra has just been playing in the brief overture (which Gershwin called an introduction), and the curtain does rise on a stage "dark except for Jasbo Brown's room, which can be exposed to view by use of a sliding panel."[31] The solo piano continues for a while as couples dance in Jasbo's room and then begin to sing along in a wordless chant; eventually the piano reverts to its opening motif and the orchestra rejoins it, rounding off this first episode and leading directly into the music that introduces the lullaby "Summertime." Gershwin obviously adopted Heyward's highly effective ideas for setting the scene in *Porgy and Bess*. Questions must be posed, however: Just what kind of scene is Gershwin setting? Where are we, musically, at the opening of this opera?

The music of the introduction is unlike that of either a traditional Broadway overture or a conventional opera overture, which was doubtless deliberate on Gershwin's part. Lasting barely one minute, this scurrying music—"*resoluto* [sic] *e ben marcato*"—focuses attention and sets up expectations, without grounding those expectations anywhere in particular.[32] There isn't even a hint of a big tune or melodic aria to come, only a kind of perpetual sixteenth-note motion against which is played a syncopated chordal motif. A generalized modal feeling, which might be called folklike, is present, but it remains unspecific; the tonality is indefinite as well, with the harmony characterized by chords of stacked fourths, and the absence of anything resembling a cadence. The chordal motif will provide the link to and from the "Jasbo Brown Blues," while the sixteenth-note idea will not recur prominently until we are well into the opening scene, when it will alert us to the entrance of Porgy. Nevertheless, the main function of the introduction is the immediate one of lifting the audience's attention away from the physical environment of the Broadway theater or the opera house, without providing any definite clues regarding a destination.

When the curtain goes up, Jasbo Brown's room is revealed. But where are we, really? The deliberate musical ambiguity of this place has already been mentioned. And who is Jasbo Brown anyway—a character who never speaks or sings, whose only role is to play the onstage piano in this brief episode, and who then vanishes from the opera? This resident of a lower-class Charleston neighborhood in the "recent past" (the 1920s?—at the latest) has obviously managed to acquire a considerable and sophisticated familiarity with jazz piano styles, including ragtime and blues, and it would seem he might even have heard some boogie-woogie! Does Jasbo get around a lot? Or does he, or some Catfish Row neighbor of his, have a phonograph and a terrific, up-to-date record collection?

Of course such questions cannot be taken seriously, because "Jasbo Brown Blues" is not intended to evoke literally the sounds one would have heard in the black enclaves of Charleston at the time. The music is designed to position the audience within a relatively familiar place—with jazz piano, couples dancing, and singers scatting—but without the burden of absolute specificity. What "Jasbo Brown Blues" really sounds like, naturally and inevitably, is Gershwin himself playing in the heat of inspiration, at a party for friends—or perhaps even in a Broadway theater (or even an opera house). Not only was the piano Gershwin's personal instrument, but its sound was closely associated with Gershwin's shows going back to the days of *Lady, Be Good!* and Ohman and Arden. Is the character of Jasbo Brown, then, a symbolic stand-in for the composer himself, establishing Gershwin's personal voice and authority as soon as the curtain rises? In any event, Gershwin is here employing his music to set only a generalized kind of scene.

A further layer of ambiguity and complexity is achieved upon the reentry of the orchestra, as gradually new notes are added to the repeated chordal motif. Eventually the individual chords come each to contain eight different notes of the chromatic scale. Where are we now, amid this explosion of dissonance? Gershwin is subjecting his audience to renewed musical dislocation; these are assuredly not the sounds of black Charleston, nor of any jazz piano venue, nor of any previously known Broadway musical event. If anything, they suggest the most aggressive modernist music then being played in any concert hall at the time.

It should not surprise us that Gershwin employs an unprecedented opening for his unprecedented work. Within the first five minutes of the opera, Gershwin systematically subverts all expectations of what Catfish Row should sound like, without providing any unequivocal indication of what it *does* sound like. Evidently it can sound like many things, but like no single thing in particular; it can encompass many musical styles, without being tied to any one of them. Musically, Catfish Row seems to be almost anywhere or everywhere (in twentieth-century America, at least). Everything that follows in the work bears this out. For Gershwin, Catfish Row embraces the known musical universe, extending stylistically even beyond the broad range he had already explored in his earlier music.

The violent ending of "Jasbo Brown Blues" dissipates, and after "zooming out" from the pianist's room we "zoom in" again to a different, even more intimate, situation as Clara lulls her baby with "Summertime." (The cinematic terminology seems particularly apt for describing the opening sequence of *Porgy and Bess*, and it is worth remembering that the director of the first production, Rouben Mamoulian, had established himself as an innovative film director prior to undertaking Gershwin's opera.) The famous opening lyrics to "Summertime," as the first words heard in the opera, accord well with Gershwin's strategy of avoiding the highly specific. If the South is evoked with the mention of cotton, and the phrase "fish are jumpin'" references the life of Catfish Row itself, "yo' daddy's rich" jumps abruptly far from the realities facing Clara and her child—at least from the vantage point of a Broadway audience—and places the lullaby in the realm of wishes. The enormous and enduring popularity of "Summertime" as a song independent of the opera attests to its virtually universal appeal; like the scene of a mother rocking her child, the song seems to inspire empathy in almost everyone.

Gershwin takes advantage of the opportunity afforded by "Summertime" to shift his stylistic focus yet again. The lullaby is an obvious example of one of Gershwin's composed "folk songs"; its unpretentious sixteen-bar structure with balanced phrases, a clear ABAC form, and a diatonic melody line built from a six-note scale creates a remarkable contrast with all that has come before. And yet there is a vague, persistent feeling of unease about the song, as the chromaticism so characteristic of "Jasbo Brown Blues" continues to permeate the orchestral accompaniment. Musically, as in other respects, it is impossible to fix "Summertime" in a single, simple place. For that matter, one could search the entire rich score of *Porgy and Bess* in vain for examples that would encourage the reduction of Gershwin's music to any single, simple stylistic descriptor.

It is significant that the first song heard in the opera stands at a certain distance from the hard realities of life in Catfish Row—realities of poverty, human brutality, destructive storms, and the dangerous lure of alcohol and cocaine, factors that will soon become evident and that will play essential roles in the drama's unfolding. The significance is twofold. "Summertime" attests to the universality of human longing for an existence where "the livin' is easy" (especially when it isn't). But as it becomes increasingly obvious that the dreamworld of "Summertime" bears no relationship whatsoever to the onstage experience of the opera's main characters, the foundation is estab-lished for the departures from Catfish Row of both Porgy and Bess (along with Sportin' Life), which bring the work to its conclusion. The crippled beggar and his woman each leave a Catfish Row that no longer holds any promise for them, and their desire to escape is completely understandable. Even with its ending, then, Porgy and Bess reaches outward.

The juxtaposition and coexistence of diverse stylistic elements, a compo-sitional strategy that emerges so clearly in the opera's opening sequence, is in evidence throughout the opera. The four occurrences of "Summertime," and considerations of the contexts in which these take place, serve well to illus-trate. It has already been established that, when first heard, "Summertime" creates a strong contrast with the music that precedes it. The passages that immediately follow "Summertime" introduce the crap game and its players, and unsurprisingly bring another stylistic shift to the fore: this spiky, rhyth-mically disjunct, and markedly dissonant music jars in every possible way with that of the song—just as the gruff, contentious, all-male environment of the crap game creates a stark juxtaposition with the unruffled, empathetic, mother-and-child ambience of the lullaby. Yet these two "worlds" coexist in Catfish Row (as their equivalents do in the world at large) and, to make the point, Gershwin shortly thereafter sets "Summertime" in startling but effec-tive counterpoint to the musicalized shouts of the crap game players. Then Clara's husband, Jake, offers a contrasting "answer song" to "Summertime" in the form of "A Woman Is a Sometime Thing," the bluesy inflections of which stand in opposition both to the lullaby and to its sentiments, while sug-gesting at least a surface kinship to the music of "Jasbo Brown Blues."

The next appearance of "Summertime" is in the hurricane scene that concludes act 2. Here the song functions as a momentary respite of imposed calm in the midst of the storm's swirling chromatic chaos; the touching fra-gility of the lullaby in this context underlines how ultimately helpless fami-lies are against nature's fury. By the end of the scene, the fate of Jake and his crew has been mercilessly revealed by the sight of his upturned boat, and Clara has run out impulsively toward her own similar fate in the hurricane, leaving her baby with neither Daddy nor Mammy "standin' by."

"Summertime" recurs for the last time in the opening scene of act 3, sung by Bess to the baby that she and Porgy have effectively adopted, and by now one is probably anticipating an unfortunate aftermath of some kind in the wake of this ironically ill-omened song. The music associated with the crap game follows, but it portends violence and death rather than harmless play in light of the murder by Crown in act 1. And as if inevitably, this music in act 3 proves to accompany the murder of Crown himself by Porgy. Gershwin's employment of stylistic juxtapositions to create drama and form both on a localized and on a large scale demonstrates exceptional resourcefulness, while the juxtapositions themselves help emphasize the broadness and diversity of the sound world the composer devised for *Porgy and Bess*.

If Gershwin's music locates his opera in an expansive sound environment without fixed geographical roots, the question then naturally arises: who lives in this "place"? Gershwin's approach in creating music for his major characters to sing was evidently informed by the same strategy he employed for setting the scene; the writing for his two protagonists in particular reveals an exceptionally wide stylistic range. He could have elected, of course, to keep his characters tied to individually defined, discrete musical styles, and to achieve diversity via contrasts among these styles. Such an approach might have been easier, and would certainly have kept everyone onstage "in character" musically, in a traditional way. Gershwin typically chose to do something much riskier, to achieve results that are much more compelling.

Gershwin could rely on the set and the costumes, and on the skills of his cast, to provide the illusion that there were characters onstage possessing firm local and individual identities. With his music these characters could give voice to the broadest scope of human feelings, encompassing an unrestricted expanse of stylistic possibilities. Through the act of singing they may transcend the circumstances and limitations of Catfish Row, or of any specific environment, to become simply representatives of the human community. Physically Porgy is portrayed as a poor, crippled beggar; musically he is revealed to have the soul of an artist and a remarkable capacity for creative expression. To assert that a black man in Porgy's situation merits—even requires—the most sophisticated, wide-ranging, and exquisite music a composer can devise, and to imply in consequence that such a character may

Figure 6.2. Todd Duncan as Porgy: publicity still from the
original production of *Porgy and Bess*, 1935

serve as a representative for any or all of us, surely seems a provocative, if not
radical, position for Gershwin to have assumed, aesthetically or otherwise.
But Gershwin was apparently unconcerned about challenging the assump-
tions and presumptions a Broadway theatergoer might have brought to his
American folk opera. His lack of concern was daring for his time, and it remains inspiring today.

Some musical examples from act 2, scene 1, will help to focus the issue
of "who is Porgy?" Porgy sings three major numbers in this substantial scene:
two solos, the "banjo song" "I Got Plenty o' Nuttin'," and the dramatic "Buzzard Song"; and "Bess, You Is My Woman," which begins as a solo and be-

comes a duet with Bess.[33] Placing the opening vocal passages of these three selections side by side proves to be revealing (see ex. 6.1).

The diversity of style among the three excerpts is immediately obvious. Superficially they appear as if they could be music from completely different operas—certainly music for completely different characters. The straightforward diatonic, "popular" style of the "banjo song," with its boom-chick accompaniment, seems worlds removed from the tense, chromatic language of the "Buzzard Song" and its compressed vocal line, while the diatonically based but blues-inflected "Bess, You Is My Woman," with its operatic vocal range and expressive leaps, sets forth a complex style lacking ready commonalities with either of the others. The gamut of musical expression that Gershwin wishes to accord Porgy—especially considering the fact that these three numbers are all heard within a single scene—is striking indeed.

Each of the three selections serves a highly individual dramatic function, and from this standpoint their marked differences are surely appropriate. It is worth noting that Porgy is given no fully realized solo songs in act 1; his newly expansive expressivity in the first scene of act 2 reflects the influence of his recently established relationship with Bess.[34] The first big solo, "I Got Plenty o' Nuttin'," represents in effect the musical certification of his newfound happiness, and its air of unpretentious joviality is thoroughly convincing for the purpose. His next number, the "Buzzard Song," suggests the vulnerability of Porgy's hold on happiness, as he superstitiously reacts to the omen of a large vulture flying over Catfish Row. The dissonant chords in the accompaniment reflect the tension of the moment, and the constrained vocal line is the embodiment of Porgy's fearful but focused concentration as he attempts to drive the buzzard away. Finally, with "Bess, You Is My Woman" Gershwin must convey musically the depth of Porgy's feelings for Bess (and of hers for him). The presence of rich, sensuous harmony in the accompaniment and of long, flowing phrases in the vocal line confirms both ardor and commitment.

There is a potentially significant problem with Gershwin's methodology, however. Amid such expressive diversity, what happens to consistency of character? Does the music work in any way to tie together the various stylistic strands present in these three numbers so it seems dramatically plausible that the same character is singing all of them? In fact Gershwin does provide connective aspects, but they are subtle, and one must look past the opening passages of the three numbers to appreciate them.

It has already been established that the music of *Porgy and Bess* does not lend itself to strict categorization, and this observation applies to many facets

Example 6.1. Porgy's solos from act 2, scene 1

of the selections under consideration. While "I Got Plenty o' Nuttin'" is the joyous testimony of one who "Got my gal, got my Lawd, got my song," it is simultaneously a clever critique of materialism; this second part of the song's agenda is already apparent in the wordplay on "plenty" and "nuttin'" in its opening lines (see ex. 6.1), the familiarity of which do not obscure their incisive wittiness. As the ensuing lyrics elaborate Porgy's intelligence along with his happiness, the music rapidly expands its harmonic horizons, arriving by the tenth measure at a C-sharp major triad a tritone away from the song's tonic chord. Ultimately no "banjo song" before or since has been anything like "I Got Plenty o' Nuttin'." Even if Gershwin's number starts out by evoking folk traditions in a general way, with an atmosphere of deceptive simplicity, the verbal and musical character and sophistication of the whole link it in the deepest sense only to the other material in Gershwin's opera.

The "Buzzard Song" analogously cannot be defined solely by its opening measures. An arresting passage in the middle section of the song drastically alters the rhythmic and harmonic landscape (see ex. 6.2). Porgy here regains his balance, forcefully addressing "trouble" and the buzzard with

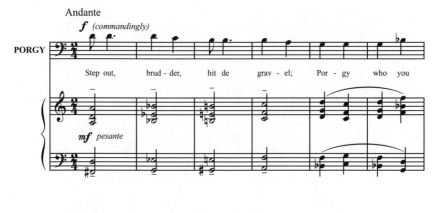

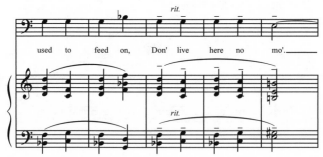

Example 6.2. "Buzzard Song," excerpt

the news that they no longer have a home with him since Bess has brought
love into his life. The steady quarter-note rhythms and the triads and open
fourths and fifths in the accompaniment create a strongly contrasting feeling
at this point; the musical style is temporarily more congruent with that of
the simpler music that opens "I Got Plenty o' Nuttin'." At the same time,
the narrow compass of Porgy's vocal line maintains continuity with the preceding material of the "Buzzard Song."

The complex musical style that characterizes "Bess, You Is My Woman"
comprises remarkably diverse elements. While any of these elements individually—diatonic progressions, chromatic embellishments, blue notes,
modulations to distant keys—may be found readily elsewhere in the opera,
their composite impact in "Bess, You Is My Woman" creates a number that
sounds distinctive and set apart. This is as it should be. The duet presents the
one time in the opera when we see and hear Porgy and Bess by themselves,

Figure 6.3. Anne Brown as Bess: publicity still from the
original production of *Porgy and Bess*, 1935

together in their love, completely happy and untroubled. They are transfig-
ured in this moment, a state reflected by the unanticipated ending of the
duet in the remote key of F-sharp major, a key prominent nowhere else in the
opera.

A brief look at the opening of two other numbers will demonstrate how
Gershwin projects both complexities and consistencies within the character
of Bess. It might be said that her complexities *are* her consistencies. Bess is a
woman torn between her sympathetic love for Porgy (and the concomitant
desire to live "decent" with the crippled man) and her intense, physically
based love for Crown (which is linked to the excitement of an alcohol- and

Example 6.3. Bess's solos from act 2

cocaine-fueled lifestyle outside the norms of Catfish Row). The opening passages of "What You Want wid Bess?" from act 2, scene 2, and "I Wants to Stay
Here" from act 2, scene 3, both portray Bess's conflicted character, but each
does so in a distinctive manner appropriate to the particular situation (see
ex. 6.3).

"What You Want wid Bess?" is a duet between Bess and Crown during
the picnic scene, following his interruption of her attempted return to the

boat leaving for Catfish Row. Bess's agitated condition is represented by the jagged, syncopated vocal line and by harsh cross relations—between voice and accompaniment (A-natural in the voice against A-sharp in the orchestra), and within the accompaniment itself. On the surface, Bess is seeking to convince Crown that he no longer should find her desirable, but the music reveals that internally Bess is not so certain that this is what *she* wants; the aggressive, swerving movements of the accompaniment suggest sensuous dance (arguably even striptease) rather than denial. This is an outstanding instance of astute character portrayal on Gershwin's part.

In "I Wants to Stay Here," Bess directly articulates her conflict to Porgy. Her greater ease and comfort with Porgy find expression in the flowing lyricism of her vocal line, but the constant shifts of direction in that line—first soaring upward, then falling back down—betray her wavering emotional condition. Meanwhile the chromatic ornamentation in the accompaniment (see the left-hand part for the piano in ex. 6.3) creates passing cross relations with the voice, like gentler cousins to the harmonic clashes in "What You Want wid Bess?" The relationship between melody and bass line in "I Wants to Stay Here" is often a dissonant one, emphasizing further the instability of the situation at this point, both within Bess herself and between Bess and Porgy.

The subject of musical characterization in *Porgy and Bess* is too broad and rich to receive comprehensive treatment here. It should be emphasized, however, that Gershwin was careful to accord even his minor characters memorable individuation through his music. Whether it is a question of the unpretentious but unforgettable "street cries" of the Strawberry Woman, the Crab Man, and the Honey Man, or of Maria's hilarious, rhythmically spoken dressing-down of Sportin' Life ("I hates yo' struttin' style" in act 2, scene 1— is this the first rap number to be heard on the American musical stage, and performed by a woman yet?), it seems to have been Gershwin's intention to breathe the fullest life possible into every character and every moment of his opera.

Even in the group numbers sung by the Catfish Row community, Gershwin avoids the pitfall of generic "folksiness." "Oh, I Can't Sit Down," heard as the residents of the row depart for their picnic, begins as an utterly straightforward diatonic tune, but at the approach to the cadence toward the end of the first main section (on the words "I's gwine to *town*") the phrase is unexpectedly prolonged, with striking chromatic writing in the vocal lines. "Oh, I Can't Sit Down" is thus emblematic of the approach to style that typifies the entire opera and that reflects the intricacies of its characters and situations. In *Porgy and Bess* little, if anything, remains pure or simple: not the individuals nor their actions, and certainly not the style of the music depicting them.

This observation extends to the variety of musical forms employed for the individual numbers in *Porgy and Bess*. The straightforward strophic structure of songs such as "Summertime" or "Clara, Clara" may be suggestive of folk song. "There's a Boat Dat's Leavin' Soon for New York" is appropriately modeled on the AABA format typical of Broadway show tunes. "Bess, You Is My Woman" (a duet) and "Oh, Bess, Oh Where's My Bess?" (a trio) clearly reflect operatic antecedents in the extent and complexity of their structures. But even the simpler numbers cannot be reduced to formulas. When "Summertime" is presented for the first time, a women's chorus joins Clara for the second strophe ("One of these mornin's . . ."), adding sophisticated chromatic counterpoint. In "There's a Boat Dat's Leavin' Soon for New York," the bridge (B) section is elongated well past any point that would be characteristic for a musical comedy song—it lasts twenty-three measures— and the final A section (itself fourteen measures in length) concludes with a sustained high B-flat for Sportin' Life that can only be called operatic.

Perhaps the most extraordinary fusion of Broadway and operatic influences is manifested in Serena's great song, or aria, of lamentation, "My Man's Gone Now." Its vocal range and the chromaticism of its middle section and of its wailing melismas place this number firmly in operatic territory, yet the underlying form of "My Man's Gone Now" is clearly the venerable old Broadway AABA—a form that, in Gershwin's hands at least, proved to be almost infinitely flexible and versatile. The mingling of musical styles, forms, and categories in Gershwin's opera is reflected even by the index of major numbers in the vocal score, an index tellingly labeled "Index of Songs, Arias and Themes."

Gershwin did not condescend to Catfish Row. The music he provided for his imaginary community and its individuals is characterized overall by a breadth of expression that encompassed the full range of styles and forms familiar to the composer—and then some. It is scarcely surprising that Gershwin's only remaining means for differentiating the white characters in his opera was to have them not sing at all; he had no distinctive music left for them! Of course the potential for expression that was thereby denied to the whites "speaks" volumes; their exclusion from the sonic world of Catfish Row is indicative of a cultural impoverishment much more profound than the economic disadvantage that afflicts the black community. Gershwin surely achieved his desired "sensational dramatic effect" by giving the white characters only spoken lines, but it should also be understood that this dramatic virtue was at least in part the outcome of sheer musical necessity.[35]

In Lieu of Summary

Attempting to summarize Gershwin's achievement in *Porgy and Bess* is as daunting a task as attempting a comprehensive treatment of the work. Like much of the finest American music, *Porgy and Bess* eludes summary as effectively as it eludes categorization, overflowing or popping abruptly out of any boxes into which one might hope to confine it. If from a purely factual standpoint the opera stands as both the summation and the grand finale of Gershwin's career on Broadway, this was by no means the composer's stated intent. Who can say what further wonders Gershwin might have revealed to theatergoers had he lived even a few years longer?

From another standpoint, however, it is difficult to conceive just how Gershwin might have gone beyond *Porgy and Bess*. The work is so rich, consisting virtually of one musical and dramatic high point after another, that it can seem as if Gershwin was determined to pour every last ounce of himself into this single opus. The opera has much compelling music that has received little attention in the preceding discussion—for example, the instrumental fugue that accompanies the fight between Crown and Robbins in the first scene (and that recurs in act 3, scene 1, to accompany the fight between Porgy and Crown), or the six-part vocal prayers in the hurricane scene, which create a counterpoint free of any specific metrical framework. A fatalist might wonder whether Gershwin knew, on some mysterious level, that he had little time left, given the stupendous creative investment he made in this score.

In any event, Gershwin's *Porgy and Bess* stands as a special, monumental, and ultimately unclassifiable achievement in a brilliant and unclassifiable career. Apart from its intrinsic artistic merits, the opera also offers, to those twenty-first-century listeners and theatergoers who wish to accept it, a temporary refuge from our contemporary morass of identity politics, disputes about diversity, and claims of victimization by one group or another. *Porgy and Bess* has the temerity—or the simple humanity—to propose that there are issues that unite and that should concern us all, irrespective of race, place, religion, ethnicity, class, or culture: issues such as the ill-treatment of one individual or community by another, the impact of substance abuse upon individuals and communities, and the struggles of both individuals and communities for livelihood, self-respect, and love. I would argue that a rejection of this proposition can result in much greater problems than merely a diminished capacity to appreciate Gershwin's opera.

CHAPTER 7

An Unintended Hollywood Coda

WITH *PORGY AND BESS* GERSHWIN LEFT TO BROADWAY—AND to the opera house—a magnificent final legacy. Yet when the composer departed New York for Hollywood to work on films in August 1936, it was surely without any intention of bidding more than a temporary farewell to the live musical stage. By most accounts Gershwin was unhappy as an artist and restless personally in Hollywood.[1] Given the level of control he had come to exert over productions bearing his name on Broadway during the 1930s, the limited influence accorded a composer in the Hollywood movie industry must have come as a most unpleasant surprise and letdown.

Certainly the movie studios enjoyed gracing the ads, marquees, and sheet music for their musicals with the prestige of "name" composers—Berlin, Kern, Porter, Rodgers, and Gershwin. But composers and lyricists were hired simply to provide songs, and on occasion some incidental music, for movies and were then expected to get gracefully (and gratefully, for they were offered good money for their services) out of the way. Film composers generally had little or no influence upon which of their songs were used and which were discarded, or upon the specific contexts provided for their musical efforts in the films. Hands other than those of the composers provided arrangements and orchestrations for Hollywood movies, as was also typical for Broadway musicals, but in films these other hands also exercised control over the opening title music and the underscoring and were able ultimately to slice, dice, augment, and diminish the composers' efforts in numerous ways.

The result is that a film such as *Shall We Dance*, while having a Gershwin score, is not at all a "Gershwin movie" in the sense that *Of Thee I Sing* is unquestionably a "Gershwin show." In terms of the role of the composer, and the relationships the music establishes with the script and with the entire finished product, *Shall We Dance* may be seen as something more like a return to the early 1920s *Lady, Be Good!* type of model for a musical. Perhaps it seemed a retrogression of that sort to Gershwin as well. In any case, those coming with a knowledge and appreciation of Gershwin's Broadway output may well find his late films most enjoyable in that 1920s frame of mind. Granted, this point of view utterly fails to take into account the specifically cinematic virtues and aesthetics of these (and other) film musicals. Such considerations open up an entirely different window, however, and pose issues for a different book. From the Broadway perspective of the present volume, the late Gershwin movies seem simply an inadvertent coda to a great but unfinished body of work.

In late 1936 and early 1937, Gershwin completed the scores for two movies, *Shall We Dance* and *A Damsel in Distress*, and he had only begun work on a third (*The Goldwyn Follies*) when his fatal illness overtook him. According to Howard Pollack, the filming of *A Damsel in Distress* did not commence until shortly after Gershwin's death.[2] This leaves *Shall We Dance* as the only one of the three films for which Gershwin was a presence during the production process, and the only one he lived to see as a finished movie. Consequently it is *Shall We Dance* that will receive attention here, even though the composer apparently was none too happy with the completed project.[3]

Gershwin initially must have been pleased by the opportunity to reunite and to work with Fred Astaire in Hollywood. When George and Ira first arrived in the movie capital, however, there was not so much as the beginnings of a script for what was to become *Shall We Dance*, and the two had to undertake work on songs with precious little to go on, other than the fact that the film was to be a Fred Astaire and Ginger Rogers vehicle.[4] It consequently comes as no surprise that, of the eight songs the Gershwins wrote for the film, two ended up unused ("Hi-Ho!" and "Wake Up, Brother, and Dance"), and only two others ended up illuminating plot and character to an extent that would bear comparison with the brothers' most effective "defining" Broadway numbers: "(I've Got) Beginner's Luck" and "They Can't Take That Away from Me."[5] The remaining songs—"Slap That Bass," "They

Figure 7.1. George and Ira Gershwin with Hermes Pan (dance director), Fred Astaire, Mark Sandrich (director), Ginger Rogers, and Nat Shilkret (music director, right) on the set of *Shall We Dance*, 1936

All Laughed," "Let's Call the Whole Thing Off," and "Shall We Dance?"—function in the movie essentially as brilliant "specialty" numbers, showcasing the singing and especially the dancing of Astaire and Rogers. It is true that the two protagonists come together at last during the final selection ("Shall We Dance?"), which turns it into an "action" number. But their reunion occurs during an instrumental treatment of the song, there is nothing in the song's lyric that is particular to this situation in the plot, and any large-scale production number would have served at this point.

These comments should in no wise be construed as a commentary on the quality of Gershwin's score itself. The score is of a high quality and includes some instrumental material along with the songs—in particular, the delightful and piquant "action" number "Walking the Dog" (also called "Promenade"), which is prominent in the film not least because of its unusual

chamber ensemble orchestration, provided by Gershwin himself.[6] Nevertheless the interrelationships between songs and script for the most part remain
loose, at times even careless, and one could be forgiven for feeling that the
quality of the film, considered as a totality, does not measure up to the potential Gershwin provided with his score.

On the other hand, it could be argued that *Shall We Dance* possesses
its own kind of artistic integrity. If the employment of the music suggests an
approach characteristic of the 1920s musical, this is congruent with many
other aspects of the film that are equally suggestive of that model. *Shall We
Dance* is obviously a movie built around its two star performers. The plot
is little more than an excuse to provide Astaire and Rogers with ample opportunities to dance, and the score was composed with that exigency clearly
in mind. The script is replete with amusing wordplay and opportunities for
physical humor. As always, love is the motivating factor: the Astaire character
has fallen in love (at first sight, one presumes) with the Rogers character from
seeing pictures of her, but of course a love triangle emerges to run interference with the two dancers' inevitable final coupling. A similarity to the plot
of *Oh, Kay!* may be discerned in the continuing confusion over the two protagonists' marital status (are they or aren't they married to each other?) in
Shall We Dance. While there are no shady lawyers, officers of the law, or
politicians in *Shall We Dance*, the idea of the exotic "Other" receives a nod
insofar as the Astaire character (a very American Peter P. Peters) has assumed
an identity as the "Russian" ballet star Petrov—complete with phony accent.
Arguably, ballet dancer/contortionist Harriet Hoctor, introduced only in
the concluding dance number as a kind of exaggerated foil to the unpreten-
tiously graceful Ginger Rogers, functions here like an exotic "Other" as well.

The two defining songs in the movie, "(I've Got) Beginner's Luck" and
"They Can't Take That Away from Me," serve complementary functions.
Both are sung by Astaire, without dancing. The former serves to convince the
Rogers character (and the movie audience) that he is truly in love with her,
while the latter provides evidence to her (and to the movie audience) of the
permanence of his affection, and evidence to him (and to the movie audience) of her reciprocation—by way of her tearful reaction.

The four specialty numbers fit into the plot framework with varying degrees of relevance and effectiveness. Since both the Astaire and the Rogers
characters are professional dancers, their dancing is ipso facto appropriate.
A subtext is provided by Petrov's interest in synthesizing ballet with tap and
other modern popular elements, a synthesis that presumably is facilitated

when he dances with Rogers, who portrays the popular American star Linda Keene. Petrov's affinity with vernacular dance styles is demonstrated by the first number in the movie, "Slap That Bass," as it develops into an elaborate solo dance for Astaire. While "Slap That Bass," an extroverted "rhythm" tune, fulfills no direct plot function whatsoever and could easily be replaced by any upbeat song in a similar style, it does provide the first full expression of a dance personality for the Astaire character. Presumably it also enhances anticipation for the duets that the audience knows must follow.

"They All Laughed" is set up as a specialty number within the plot itself, first for Rogers as Linda Keene is invited to perform a song before an audience, and then for Rogers with Astaire as he joins her "by popular demand" to dance to the band's continuation of the song. The dancers' compatibility is convincingly established by this number, but again there is nothing about the song per se—however clever it might be—that corresponds to the particular personalities or to the plot situation in the movie at this juncture.[7] Analogous observations could be made about the remaining two specialties, "Let's Call the Whole Thing Off" and "Shall We Dance?" A particularly striking example of irrelevant, if musically pleasing, song placement is provided by the ending strain of "They All Laughed" that concludes the film, appended as a coda to "Shall We Dance?" When the Astaire and Rogers characters sing "They all said we'd never get together, / They laughed at us and how," the two seem to be singing about a different movie entirely. Indeed, nobody has laughed at these characters during *Shall We Dance*, and a major source of humor and confusion throughout the film has been the erroneous public belief that the two are in fact married, a belief that is shown to inspire almost universal public enthusiasm.

The ballet-versus-vernacular or "high art"–versus–"low art" subtext of *Shall We Dance* is noted by Pollack as something that must have resonated with Gershwin.[8] This aspect of the film is treated concisely but provocatively by Gerald Mast, who finds *Shall We Dance* to be a high point among the Astaire-Rogers movies, and is discussed exhaustively and brilliantly by John Mueller, who nevertheless finds the film a low point in the series.[9] Whatever one's final judgment either about its subtext or about *Shall We Dance* as a whole, I don't think the movie should or can be regarded as a representative aesthetic "statement" on Gershwin's part. The music functions in a manner too oblique for this, a reflection of the limited control the composer was able to exercise over the project.

The Music for *Shall We Dance*

The Gershwin songs from *Shall We Dance* have received a good deal of critical attention, along with the other songs he completed in the year before his death, doubtless because of their unintended status representing Gershwin's musical "testament."[10] As a group, these late songs exhibit the stylistic diversity and seemingly effortless mastery that was characteristic of Gershwin's mature output. The question naturally arises to what extent the formal innovations so apparent in the songs for *Of Thee I Sing* and *Porgy and Bess* operated, or could operate, as an influence upon Gershwin's compositional approach in the significantly more restricted arena of film music. The answer is that a marked flexibility in the shaping of both phrase structure and overall song structure is a prominent aspect in at least some of the late songs. Among those written for *Shall We Dance*, it is tellingly ironic that the two not used in the film, "Hi-Ho!" and "Wake Up, Brother, and Dance," display this formal flexibility most obviously; both are ambitious, unusually long songs with atypical phrase structures, and "Hi-Ho!" exhibits an overall design of striking originality and complexity. While the six songs that do appear in *Shall We Dance* are of more traditional proportions, "(I've Got) Beginner's Luck" demonstrates that, at this final stage in his career, Gershwin could innovate in the direction of compactness as well as expansion: the song's AA′BA″ refrain is only twenty-eight measures long instead of the usual thirty-two, due to the fact that the first two A phrases are each six-measure units.

The outstanding quality of Gershwin's last songs was captured memorably by Ira, when he remarked, "What was wonderful to me was that after writing "the Great American Opera" George wrote some of the best hits he ever did in his life. He met the boys at their own game. He went back to his first love and did that better than ever before."[11] One could choose any song from *Shall We Dance* to illustrate the wealth of melodic, harmonic, rhythmic, and formal resources at Gershwin's command as he composed what were to be his final works. As an example, let us briefly consider the refrain of the title song, which demonstrates how much imagination the composer could bring to his handling of an outwardly conventional thirty-two-bar ABA′C structure.

"Shall We Dance?" obviously belongs to the basic category of Gershwin's "rhythm" songs. Its marriage of syncopation and harmonic restlessness evokes a lineage going back to "Fascinating Rhythm" from *Lady, Be Good!* while the specific rhythm of the refrain's opening motif clearly recalls the analogous motif in the famous "I Got Rhythm" from *Girl Crazy* (see ex.

Example 7.1. "Shall We Dance?" refrain, mm. 1–8

7.1).[12] But "Shall We Dance?" establishes a tone quite different from that of "Fascinating Rhythm" or "I Got Rhythm," or indeed any other of Gershwin's celebrated rhythm numbers—including "Slap That Bass" from *Shall We Dance.*

The distinctive character of "Shall We Dance?" is established right from the opening of the refrain, with its insistence on the dissonant major seventh as the melody note over the tonic F in the bass.[13] A complex harmonic relationship between melody and bass line, in which traditional consonance is the exception rather than the rule, typifies the entire refrain, which features an overall harmonic vocabulary consisting almost exclusively of seventh and ninth chords. Coupled with the breathless two-measure vocal phrases that commence obsessively off the beat, the harmonic language engenders an atmosphere of unease, even anxiety, as opposed to the playful taunting of "Fascinating Rhythm" or the overflowing joyfulness of "I Got Rhythm."

Contributing to the edgy atmosphere that permeates the refrain of "Shall We Dance?" is the tendency of the melody either to dwell on repeated notes or to move by leaps. This is true even of the ending phrase, which proceeds

Example 7.2. "Shall We Dance?" refrain, last four measures

from the fifth scale degree up to a blue seventh and concludes with a rather
startling leap down to repeated tonic notes from the sixth degree of the scale
(see ex. 7.2). Although this is the only vocal phrase in the entire refrain that
commences on a downbeat and ends on the tonic, these potentially stabi-
lizing gestures are undercut not only by the angular shape of the melody but
by the underlying harmony as well—which creates a strikingly unconventional cadence.

Ira Gershwin described this "distinctive tune" as possessing "an overtone
of moody and urgent solicitude,"[14] and this overtone is certainly reflected
at points in his lyrics for it—not just in the reference to "moping" (see ex.
7.1), but later in the refrain as well: "Shall we give in to despair, / Or shall
we dance with never a care?" and "Life is short; we're growing older, / Don't
you be an also-ran." It would be very satisfying if the placement of "Shall We
Dance?" in the movie took advantage of the song's sophistication and complexity, but this isn't really the case. It is true that, while the Astaire character
is singing this number in a show-within-the-movie, he believes that he has
lost his love forever and has arranged to dance with an ensemble of masked
replicas of Linda Keene in lieu of the real thing. (The real Linda sneaks into
the dance as it is in progress, and the requisite happy ending is provided.) But
neither "Petrov" nor the situation have an emotional heft fully worthy of this
unusual and somewhat troubled song.

In Gershwin's Broadway musicals of the 1920s, one rarely feels a sense of
disconnect in tone between song and show akin to that just described. But
Gershwin and the Broadway musical grew to maturity together. The composer came to Hollywood in 1936 a seasoned, sophisticated showman and
a fully developed artist, and he found the movie musical still at a relatively

early stage of evolution—a stage unable to take maximum advantage of what he had to offer. This is the major reason why the films that mark the end of Gershwin's career seem to represent a less than satisfying coda to his oeuvre.

A Few Words on Gershwin's Many Legacies

Gershwin's long-term impact on American and world musical culture has been so extensive and profound that any attempt to summarize it succinctly is doomed to inadequacy. It is tempting to quip: if you wish a monument, just open your ears. On Broadway, in the opera house, in the concert hall, in cabarets and other pop music venues, in all types of jazz venues, and of course on recording formats ranging from 78 rpm discs to digital files, Gershwin and his influence are everywhere to be heard. This book will conclude with a brief consideration of two of Gershwin's many legacies: his place in the specific history of the Broadway musical, and his contribution to a rapprochement between the "cultivated" and the "vernacular" aspects of American musical culture.[15]

Gershwin was an essential and virtually continual presence on Broadway from 1924 into the early 1930s. With shows like *Lady, Be Good!* and *Oh, Kay!* he, probably more than any other composer, helped establish the format and musical tone of the characteristic 1920s Broadway musical comedy. When Kern's *Show Boat* redefined and enlarged what was possible for the musical in terms of subject matter and artistic integrity, Gershwin proceeded to add further chapters to this line of development—first with *Of Thee I Sing* and then, in an extraordinary leap, with *Porgy and Bess*.

The descriptor "Broadway opera" has been applied to works by others that have come after *Porgy and Bess*, such as Weill's *Street Scene*, Bernstein's *Candide*, Loesser's *The Most Happy Fella*, and Sondheim's *Sweeney Todd*. Still, it is safe to say that no work so categorized has had remotely the global impact of Gershwin's masterpiece, not just in opera houses, but in terms of the music's wide diffusion into the repertoires of musicians performing in all conceivable styles and genres. In this respect it may be said that *Porgy and Bess*—as Gershwin's last "cultivated" work—followed in the footsteps of his very first work written for the concert hall, *Rhapsody in Blue*. And this brings us neatly around to Gershwin's contribution in blurring, perhaps even collapsing, the distinction between American "art music" and American "popular music."

Certainly the perception of a schism, serendipitous or otherwise, between "high" and "low" elements in American culture has permeated the con-

Figure 7.2. The last known photograph of George Gershwin, RKO convention, June 1937

sciousness and influenced the work of many American artists, and this perception has also dominated many a discussion of American music. Gershwin himself was unquestionably aware of it. He was always concerned about the reception of his concert works by prominent musicians who operated primarily or exclusively in the classical sphere. On the other hand, he was anxious to reassure the Hollywood moguls that even after *Porgy and Bess* he was thoroughly capable of, and interested in, writing hits.[16] Although Gershwin might seem to have established an archetypical model for the American composer who can move freely and successfully between the cultivated and the vernacular, two uncomfortable facts shadow this hypothesis. The first is that, from his time to ours, considerations of Gershwin's career and achievements have been couched in terms of the schism itself, which points to the probability that perception of the schism remains pervasively in place, despite the composer's efforts at least to diminish its influence. The second is that the "model" of Gershwin remains unique in American music. There had been nobody like him before, and there has been nobody truly like him since.

This last assertion will naturally be deemed contentious by some readers, who may regard it as the wishful thinking of an unabashed Gershwin fan. Surely there have been others who have followed significantly in Gershwin's path? In the context of Broadway, the most obvious candidate would be someone like Leonard Bernstein, an American composer who also made essential contributions to both cultivated and vernacular genres. An examination of Bernstein's long and complex career, or even of his problematic relationship to Gershwin's legacy, is beyond the scope of this discussion. A few observations may be made, however, to suggest the fundamental differences between Bernstein and Gershwin.

In "An Appreciation" of Gershwin written in 1973, Bernstein remarks of Gershwin that he "came from the wrong side of the tracks, grew up in the ambience of Tin Pan Alley, song-plugging, and musical near-illiteracy. His short life was one steady push to cross the tracks."[17] The schism defines everything in this passage; above all, these statements reflect the viewpoint of one who must have conceived of himself as born on, and living on, the "right" side of the tracks—as Bernstein unquestionably did. Bernstein's viewpoint reveals a fundamental dichotomy that separates him from Gershwin as an individual and as a creative figure, but underlying the dichotomy is a deep irony.

As we now know, Bernstein was dead wrong about Gershwin's early training and "musical near-illiteracy." Gershwin certainly had the stuff to pursue training and a career as a concert pianist, or to undertake a conservatory education, had he so desired. For reasons both practical and personal, Gershwin *chose* Tin Pan Alley and Broadway over further systematic training in classical music or any other advanced education, a choice that would have been unthinkable for the college-age Bernstein (who went to Harvard). But it must immediately be added that, for Gershwin, making this choice never implied the *aesthetic* choice of one kind of music over another. As a composer, he never seriously evinced a divided allegiance. For this reason it is ultimately erroneous to speak of a rapprochement between cultivated and vernacular in Gershwin's art; his music tells us in the clearest possible way that, while the schism might be our perception, it is not his aesthetic reality. And it could not be more obvious, either from Bernstein's writing on Gershwin or from Bernstein's own creative career, that the schism was very much a reality for the brilliant but conflicted creator of *West Side Story*.

The efforts of Bernstein and others to bridge the gap—or the abyss—that separates "classical" from "popular" in American culture must command our admiration. Yet Gershwin set a singular benchmark in this area, and it is simply because he never believed in the validity of the schism to begin with. His oeuvre doesn't offer any healing of cultural wounds, for the simple reason that it proceeds from no fundamental position of illness or imbalance whatsoever. There is a terrific feeling of healthiness to Gershwin's art—a healthiness in relation to aesthetic, cultural, racial, and any number of other perplexing matters—that may strike us as naive. But this is our problem. The composer of "The Man I Love," the slow movement of the Concerto in F, and "My Man's Gone Now" surely understood longing, profound contemplation, and grief, while the composer of *Rhapsody in Blue*, "Who Cares?" and "I Got Plenty o' Nuttin'" reveals to us that true happiness is a complex emotion compounded of diverse elements. Gershwin's music, nearly always accessible, is almost never simple. The composer's ability to express complex states of mind and feeling in immediately compelling ways accounts both for the wide appeal of his music and for the all too frequent underestimation of the breadth and depth of his achievement.

We can never measure what was lost when Gershwin died at thirty-eight, and to this day it is painful to contemplate. But the compensation is what we do have, and the value of that is immeasurable. George Gershwin, the Broadway master, remains a man for the world, and for the ages.

Principal Works by George Gershwin

Stage Works

Unless otherwise noted, all works are Broadway musicals for which Gershwin provided all the music.

1919 *La-La-Lucille!*
1919 *Morris Gest's Midnight Whirl*
1920 *George White's Scandals of 1920*
1921 *George White's Scandals of 1921*
1922 *George White's Scandals of 1922*
1922 *Our Nell* [music by Gershwin and William Daly]
1923 *The Rainbow* (London)
1923 *George White's Scandals of 1923*
1924 *Sweet Little Devil*
1924 *George White's Scandals of 1924*
1924 *Primrose* (London)
1924 *Lady, Be Good!*
1925 *Tell Me More*
1925 *Tip-Toes*
1925 *Song of the Flame* [music by Gershwin and Herbert Stothart]
1926 *Oh, Kay!*
1927 *Strike Up the Band* (first version, closed in Philadelphia)
1927 *Funny Face*
1928 *Rosalie* [music by Gershwin and Sigmund Romberg]
1928 *Treasure Girl*
1929 *Show Girl*
1930 *Strike Up the Band* (revised version)
1930 *Girl Crazy*
1931 *Of Thee I Sing*

1933   *Pardon My English*
1933   *Let 'Em Eat Cake*
1935   *Porgy and Bess*

Film Musicals

1931   *Delicious*
1937   *Shall We Dance*
1937   *A Damsel in Distress*
1938   *The Goldwyn Follies*

Major Instrumental Works

1924   *Rhapsody in Blue*
1925   Concerto in F, for piano and orchestra
1926   Preludes [3], for piano
1928   *An American in Paris*
1932   *Second Rhapsody*, for orchestra with piano
1932   *Cuban Overture*
1932   *George Gershwin's Song-book* (with solo piano arrangements)
1934   *Variations on "I Got Rhythm"* (for piano and orchestra)
1936   Suite from *Porgy and Bess* (later renamed *Catfish Row* by Ira Gershwin)

A thorough listing of Gershwin's compositions, including many details about the stage works, may be found in Robert Kimball and Alfred Simon, *The Gershwins* (New York, 1973).

Notes

CHAPTER 1. In Lieu of Biography

1. See Gregory R. Suriano, ed., *Gershwin in His Time: A Biographical Scrapbook, 1919–1937* (New York, 1998). Among Gershwin's published articles, the only major one that does not appear in Suriano's *Scrapbook* is "Fifty Years of American Music," published in *American Hebrew* (November 22, 1929). This particular article may be found in *The George Gershwin Reader,* edited by Robert Wyatt and John Andrew Johnson (New York, 2004), pp. 114–19.

2. As of this writing, another major book on Gershwin from scholar Richard Crawford is eagerly anticipated. It seems possible that the early years of the twenty-first century will mark an auspicious beginning for a new era in Gershwin scholarship and criticism.

3. Both of Gershwin's parents came from St. Petersburg, Russia; they were married in New York in 1895. The opening pages of Howard Pollack's biography present substantial background on Gershwin's parents and their families; see Howard Pollack, *George Gershwin: His Life and Work* (Berkeley, 2006). Pollack also addresses thoroughly the issue of the impact Gershwin's Russian-Jewish background had upon the composer's personal beliefs (pp. 11–12) and upon his music (pp. 42–47).

4. See Isaac Goldberg, *George Gershwin: A Study in American Music,* supplemented by Edith Garson (New York, 1958; orig. published, without the supplement, in 1931), p. 81, which quotes Gershwin: "Kern was the first composer who made me conscious that most popular music was of inferior quality and that musical-comedy music was made of better material."

5. Ibid., p. 54 and p. 58, respectively.

6. Ibid., p. 56.

7. Rouben Mamoulian, in Merle Armitage, ed., *George Gershwin* (New York, 1938; republished, with a new introduction by Edward Jablonski, in 1995), pp. 53–54.

8. Ira Gershwin, in ibid., pp. 16–17.

9. Goldberg, *Gershwin,* p. 273.

10. Robert Kimball and Alfred Simon, *The Gershwins* (New York, 1973), offers generous selections from Gershwin's correspondence.

11. Among Gershwin's most important teachers were Charles Hambitzer, a well-rounded musician who taught piano, who appreciated his student's exceptional talent early on, and whose premature death in 1918 (probably at age thirty-seven, although sources differ regarding the exact year of Hambitzer's birth) put an arbitrary end to Gershwin's regular study of piano performance; Edward Kilenyi, a gifted teacher of music theory and orchestration with whom Gershwin studied over a period of several years into the 1920s; and Joseph Schillinger, to whom Gershwin was drawn in the 1930s because of the attention being attracted by Schillinger's new approach to the teaching of composition.

12. Ira Gershwin, in Armitage, *Gershwin*, p. 18.

13. See Suriano, *Gershwin in His Time*, p. 77.

14. This excerpt is from Heyward's 1935 article "Porgy and Bess Return on Wings of Song," first published in *Stage Magazine* and reprinted in Armitage, *Gershwin*, p. 35.

15. The remark was made during a 1974 television interview; see *Gershwin Remembered*, a collection of sources and reminiscences edited by Edward Jablonski (London, 1992), p. 82.

16. See Kimball and Simon, *The Gershwins*, pp. 70–71, 152, 169, and 202 for examples of these. There are also many relevant photos in Edward Jablonski and Lawrence D. Stewart, *The Gershwin Years: George and Ira* (New York, 1996; republication, with new discography and updated bibliography, of *The Gershwin Years*, first published in 1958 and revised in 1973). These include examples that document George as a horseman, as a fisherman, and as a golf enthusiast.

17. Armitage, *Gershwin*, p. 5.

18. The article, originally from *Theatre Magazine*, is reprinted in Suriano, *Gershwin in His Time*, pp. 47–49; this quotation is on pp. 48–49.

19. S. N. Behrman, *People in a Diary: A Memoir* (Boston, 1972), p. 256.

20. Ira Gershwin, in Armitage, *Gershwin*, p. 16.

21. Astaire is quoted in Kimball and Simon, *The Gershwins*, p. 45. The original source is Fred Astaire's autobiography *Steps in Time* (New York, 1959), pp. 134–35.

22. Goldberg, *Gershwin*, p. 247.

23. Swift is quoted in Kimball and Simon, *The Gershwins*, p. 66.

24. The cover (of the July 20, 1925, issue) is reproduced in Kimball and Simon, *The Gershwins*, p. 50.

25. The quotation, from the issue of November 29, 1925, may be found in Jablonski's *Gershwin Remembered*, p. 174. It may also be found (without citation of source) in Kimball and Simon, *The Gershwins*, p. 52.

26. For a thorough account of the composer's background and training, classical and otherwise, see Susan Ethel Neimoyer's doctoral dissertation, "*Rhapsody in Blue*: A Culmination of George Gershwin's Early Musical Education" (University of Washington, 2003).

27. Goldberg, *Gershwin*, p. 178.

28. The remark/comment/joke about the "book(s) on musical form (or structure)" has been propagated through generations of Gershwin literature; for prominent instances, see Jablonski and Stewart, *The Gershwin Years: George and Ira*, p. 99; Kim-

ball and Simon, *The Gershwins*, p. 52; and Jablonski, *Gershwin Remembered*, p. 174. A long time passed before appropriate doubt began to be cast on Gershwin's seriousness about it. In his *Gershwin: A Biography* (New York, 1987), Edward Jablonski called the remark "a tongue-in-cheek comment," but then added, "While an exaggeration, it reflects Gershwin's self-consciousness about his lack of a conservatory training" (p. 98). William G. Hyland's *George Gershwin: A New Biography* (Westport, CT, 2003) seems to get it just about right; first echoing Jablonski's "tongue-in-cheek" characterization, he goes on to cite Gershwin's documented attendance at concerts and studies with Kilenyi as indications that the young composer in 1925 needed no initiation into the mysteries of the classical concerto (p. 92).

29. The article, "Rhapsody in Catfish Row," originally published in the October 20, 1935, issue of the *New York Times*, is reprinted in Armitage, *Gershwin*, pp. 72–77.

30. See the article "Jazz Is the Voice of the American Soul" (originally in *Theatre Magazine*, March 1927), in Suriano, *Gershwin in His Time*, p. 49.

31. See Jablonski and Stewart, *The Gershwin Years: George and Ira*, p. 218 and p. 220; this book also reproduces (in black and white) a watercolor by Gershwin depicting the interior of his cottage on the island (p. 219) and a painting by his cousin Henry Botkin showing the exterior of the cottage (p. 218).

32. See Armitage, *Gershwin*, p. 39. Heyward's "Porgy and Bess Return on Wings of Song" first appeared in *Stage Magazine* in October 1935, the month of the opera's New York premiere, and is reprinted in Armitage, *Gershwin*, pp. 34–42.

CHAPTER 2. **In Search of Gershwin's Style**

1. In Suriano's *Gershwin in His Time*, see "Our New National Anthem" (pp. 27–28), "Does Jazz Belong to Art?" (pp. 37–39), "Mr. Gershwin Replies to Mr. Kramer" (pp. 40–41), "Jazz Is the Voice of the American Soul" (pp. 47–49), "The Composer in the Machine Age" (pp. 82–84), and "The Relation of Jazz to American Music" (p. 97).

2. In a newspaper article published a few days before the premiere of his Concerto in F, Gershwin referred to the "American blues" atmosphere of the second movement; see Jablonski and Stewart, *The Gershwin Years: George and Ira*, p. 105. An article by Hyman Sandow in *Musical America* about Gershwin's forthcoming *An American in Paris* quoted the composer's description of a "blues" episode that forms the central section of the work; this article is reprinted in Suriano, *Gershwin in His Time*, with the relevant quotation on p. 58.

3. According to Ira Gershwin, the music that became the refrain of "The Man I Love" was originally sketched by George in April 1924, two months following the premiere of the *Rhapsody*. This information comes from Ira's extensive notes on the song, originally published in his *Lyrics on Several Occasions* (New York, 1959), and reprinted in *The Complete Lyrics of Ira Gershwin*, edited by Robert Kimball (New York, 1993), pp. 54–55. "The Man I Love" was originally intended for *Lady, Be Good!* but was dropped from the production before the show reached New York; the same fate befell the song during rehearsals for *Rosalie* late in 1927, while its inclusion earlier that year in *Strike Up the Band* did little to enhance the reputation of the song—or the show—since this production closed during out-of-town tryouts. One might say that "The Man I Love" had Broadway aspirations but, failing its auditions, never achieved a true Broadway pedi-

gree. Nevertheless, the song was published in late 1924 (along with songs that actually did make it to Broadway in *Lady, Be Good!*) and over a period of several years won a considerable popular following independent of any Broadway associations. In 1928 there were a number of hit recordings of the song—by Marion Harris, Sophie Tucker, and Paul Whiteman, among others.

4. The motif is first heard in measure 19 of the *Rhapsody*, two measures preceding rehearsal number 3 in all the standard editions (copyright 1924).

5. See Geoffrey Block, "The Melody (and the Words) Linger On: American Musical Comedies of the 1920s and 1930s," in *The Cambridge Companion to the Musical*, edited by William A. Everett and Paul R. Laird (Cambridge, 2002), p. 87.

6. According to Ira Gershwin, George considered this tune "Brahmsian"; see Kimball, *Complete Lyrics*, p. 275; Oscar Levant confirms this in his *A Smattering of Ignorance* (New York, 1940), p. 191.

7. According to Walter Rimler, a sketch for a tune that eventually became "Love Walked In" is found in one of Gershwin's notebooks that can be dated back to 1931, but this affects not at all the characterization of this music as a product of Gershwin's full maturity. See Rimler's remarkable *A Gershwin Companion: A Critical Inventory and Discography, 1916–1984* (Ann Arbor, MI, 1991), p. 371.

8. See Kimball, *Complete Lyrics*, p. xiv.

9. It is worth noting the chapter on Gershwin in Alec Wilder's highly regarded *American Popular Song: The Great Innovators, 1900–1950* (New York, 1972); Wilder calls attention frequently to songs he admires that do not conform to the expected "Gershwin style." For instance, he writes of the 1936 song "By Strauss": "It's another of those songs no one, unless told, would ever dream was by Gershwin," and then adds "I have come to realize that these are the songs of his I like the best" (p. 155, in the 1975 paperback edition).

10. In fact the first of Gershwin's "idiosyncratic musical characteristics" cited by Block in "The Melody (and the Words)" is a penchant for pentatonic melodies, a tendency noted by many other commentators. Many Gershwin songs do demonstrate this tendency, but there isn't a trace of pentatonicism in either "The Man I Love" or "Love Walked In."

11. See Kimball, *Complete Lyrics*, p. 54.

12. George Gershwin, as quoted by S. N. Behrman in *People in a Diary*.

13. It is perhaps a minor weakness in the music that it in no way accommodates this striking event; the final A section is musically identical to the second A section, which has no parallel passage in its lyrics. Later in his career, George might have been inspired to effect a small change at this point. On the other hand, later on Ira might have avoided writing the immediately succeeding line, "And so, all else above," which so obviously inverts typical word order to achieve a rhyme with the following (concluding) line: "I'm waiting for the man I love."

14. For other detailed analyses of "The Man I Love" as a composition, see Wilfrid Mellers, *Music in a New Found Land* (New York, 1964), pp. 388–90, and Deena Rosenberg, *Fascinating Rhythm: The Collaboration of George and Ira Gershwin* (New York, 1991), pp. 64–70. My reading of the song has similarities to those of Mellers and Rosenberg, but the overall context for my analysis here is quite different.

15. The presence of D-natural in the bridge section of the refrain does not affect this

observation, since the bridge moves clearly to C minor and therefore the D-natural is heard as the second degree of the C-minor scale.

16. Two examples of how Gershwin could play creatively and effectively with the juxtaposition of blue notes and diatonic scale tones are "Kickin' the Clouds Away" from *Tell Me More!*, a show from the period of his early maturity (1925), and the late song "Slap That Bass" from the film *Shall We Dance* (1937). Many more instances of this particular type of stylistic virtuosity could be cited.

17. This is the theme at rehearsal number 57 in the published score, introduced by two trumpets, *Allegro*. The characterization of this as a "Charleston" originated with the program notes written by Deems Taylor for the premiere of *An American in Paris* in December 1928. Taylor's notes are reprinted complete in Goldberg, *Gershwin*, pp. 232–37.

18. See especially the line played by the cellos and the first and second horns beginning two measures following rehearsal number 58. I am indebted to Ryan Banagale for pointing this passage out to me; see his master's thesis, "An American in Chinatown: Asian Representation in the Music of George Gershwin" (University of Washington, 2004), pp. 57–58.

19. See Jablonski and Stewart, *The Gershwin Years: George and Ira*, pp. 64–65.

20. See "Mr. Gershwin Replies to Mr. Kramer" (originally published in the October 1926 issue of *Singing*), in Suriano, *Gershwin in His Time*, p. 40.

21. As an indication, see Handy's description of his 1903 encounter with a Mississippi singer/guitarist in *Father of the Blues: An Autobiography* (New York, 1941), p. 78.

22. Gershwin is quoted in Goldberg, *Gershwin*, p. 81.

23. Goldberg specifically cites "They Didn't Believe Me" as a song that greatly impressed the young Gershwin; see ibid., pp. 80–81. Later on, discussing the songs from *La-La-Lucille!*, Gershwin's first biographer baldly states, "'From Now On' is Jerome Kern"; see p. 106.

24. The basic organizational strategy underlying "They Didn't Believe Me"—that of employing two-measure units that regularly alternate shorter and longer note values—is one that served both Kern and Gershwin effectively in other songs as well. Two famous Kern examples are "Till the Clouds Roll By" (from *Oh Boy!*, 1917) and "Look for the Silver Lining" (from *Sally*, 1920); two Gershwin examples of this period, both from *George White's Scandals of 1920*, are "My Lady" and "Idle Dreams."

25. "They Didn't Believe Me" seems to be proceeding along the lines of an ABAB' or ABAC model until partway through the second A section, from which point elements of both the A and B sections are employed with remarkable fluidity to create an unexpected, albeit coherent and completely satisfying, ending.

26. Rimler, *Gershwin Companion*, p. 10, notes this resemblance, although his characterization of the dotted motif as "the central idea" of Kern's "Whip-poor-will" is debatable.

27. "Whip-poor-will" had been intended originally for a show called *Zip Goes a Million*, which closed out of town. See Lee Davis, *Bolton and Wodehouse and Kern: The Men Who Made Musical Comedy* (New York, 1993), pp. 214, 218–20, and 235.

28. The fact that "From Now On" was copyrighted on May 5, 1919, while "Whip-poor-will" was not copyrighted until December 27 of that year, would seem to tip the balance in Gershwin's favor. But the Kern show *Zip Goes a Million* had opened in Mas-

sachusetts nearly three weeks prior to the copyright date for "Whip-poor-will" (see Davis, *Bolton and Wodehouse and Kern*, p. 424), so the song was evidently completed and in use on the stage before it was copyrighted, and again we are left in a realm of uncertainty. I am deeply grateful to Judy Tsou for locating the copyright information on these two songs.

29. It is interesting that Gershwin made piano rolls of his own "From Now On" and of Kern's "Whip-poor-will" (in 1919 and 1921, respectively). As realized by Artis Wodehouse on the CD *George Gershwin: The Piano Rolls, Volume Two* (Nonesuch Records 79370-2, originally released in 1995), the two songs are heard in virtually identical tempos that underline the resemblances between them.

30. The closest Gershwin came to writing a song like "Can't Help Lovin' Dat Man" was probably "Clap Yo' Hands," a song one can assume Kern knew, since it was introduced in the hit show *Oh, Kay!* in 1926, the year before the premiere of *Show Boat.* "Clap Yo' Hands" presents a cornucopia of blue notes, syncopation, and repeated note patterns; most significantly, like "Can't Help Lovin' Dat Man," its dramatic function is to serve as an emblematically "black" number (it is introduced in the script as a "Mammy song"), and Gershwin may well have written it with the intent of self-conscious exaggeration. I extend my gratitude to Geoffrey Block for pointing out the dramatic context of "Clap Yo' Hands."

31. Berlin is quoted by Edward Jablonski in *Gershwin Remembered*, p. 89.

32. The *Song-book* was first published in 1932 (New York); see p. x in this original edition.

33. A relevant document here is the popular recording made by the Paul Whiteman Orchestra in 1922 of the Gershwin song "I'll Build a Stairway to Paradise"; the recording was a direct offshoot of Whiteman's participation in *George White's Scandals of 1922*, for which Gershwin provided all the music. This is probably the first recording by an artist with long-term connections to Gershwin that effectively demonstrates an idiomatic "Gershwin style" of performance; it is particularly impressive as an illustration of how a large ensemble can convey Gershwin's desired staccato, brittle rhythms. Whiteman's affinity for Gershwin's Broadway music laid the groundwork for both the commissioning and the compositional impetus of *Rhapsody in Blue*—a work inescapably linked to the Whiteman ensemble, with which Gershwin provided definitive performances.

34. These recordings may be heard on compact disc, in excellent restorations, on Pearl GEM 0193 (*The Ultimate George Gershwin*, vol. 2, issued in 2003).

35. *George Gershwin's Song-book*, p. x. (See note 32.)

36. The recording, titled *For George and Ira*, was reissued on compact disc in 1996 (Audiophile ACD-116); pianists Alfred Simon and Jack Easton accompanied Frances Gershwin on these performances.

37. Jablonski and Stewart, discussing *Lady, Be Good!*, write: "The character of the songs, particularly musically, was pointed up by the presence in the pit of the duo-piano team of Phil Ohman and Victor Arden. Their weaving in and out of the orchestrations endowed the interpretations with an authentic Gershwinesque flavor." See Jablonski and Stewart, *The Gershwin Years: George and Ira*, p. 99.

38. Woollcott's review appeared in the issue of December 29, 1925, and is reprinted in Suriano, *Gershwin in His Time*, pp. 35–36.

39. Oscar Levant attests to Gershwin's study of Stravinsky's *Les noces* (1923), an

exemplary instance of modernist keyboard writing; the work employs four pianos and a large ensemble of percussion instruments, in addition to a chorus and soloists. See Levant, *Smattering*, p. 190.

40. Frances Gershwin herself was evidently an admirer of the distinctive performances of Maureen McGovern, which may be heard on *Naughty Baby: Maureen McGovern Sings Gershwin* (compact disc CBS MK 44995, recorded in 1988; for Frances Gershwin's comments, see the CD insert, pp. 8 and 10). But some contemporary performers continue to seek a traditional feeling of "authenticity" in their performances; a good example of this approach may be heard on the compact disc *He Loves and She Loves: Gershwin Songs and Duets*, performed by Judy Kaye and William Sharp with Steven Blier at the piano (Koch 3-7028-2, recorded in 1990).

CHAPTER 3. In Search of the Gershwin Musical, Featuring *Lady, Be Good!*

1. That great exception to all generalizations about the 1920s musical, *Show Boat*, actually proves the rule. The genius of *Show Boat* lies in this: by presenting the story of a traveling theatrical troupe over an expanse of decades, the show may freely incorporate all kinds of music theater traditions, styles, and influences without appearing to depart significantly from its ongoing plot. A good overview of the diverse music theater scene of the 1920s may be found in Ethan Mordden's *Make Believe: The Broadway Musical in the 1920s* (New York, 1997).

2. Gershwin voiced his praise of *Show Boat* on the Rudy Vallée *Fleischmann Hour* radio program of November 10, 1932; it may be heard on the CD *Gershwin Performs Gershwin: Rare Recordings, 1931–1935* (MusicMasters 5062-2-C, released 1991), track 15. (Vallée, incidentally, was quick to agree with him.) Mordden finesses the entire issue of genre in relation to *Show Boat*: "in the end, *Show Boat* is neither musical comedy nor operetta; nor is it a blend of the two. . . . This is a rich entertainment. Only an operetta would have wanted to field so much story, but only a musical comedy could have had such fun in telling it" (Mordden, *Make Believe*, p. 216). In terms of categorizing *Of Thee I Sing*, the sheet music for the title song, shown in Suriano, *Gershwin in His Time*, p. 89, calls the show a "musical comedy," while the complete vocal score (New York, 1932) presents, according to its cover, the music of "the Pulitzer Prize operetta." Gershwin himself apparently described the work as a "musical comedy" (quoted in Kimball and Simon, *The Gershwins*, p. 146), while his first biographer, Isaac Goldberg, dubbed it "American operetta" (Suriano, *Gershwin in His Time*, p. 86).

3. According to Mordden, Stark Young is the author of this review (Mordden, *Make Believe*, p. 32).

4. The column adjacent to the review of *Lady, Be Good!* in the December 2, 1924, issue of the *New York Times* contains an account (also unsigned) of the *Music Box Revue* that reflects the same priorities, limiting discussion of Irving Berlin's music to a couple of sentences within a six-paragraph article. It is significant that these two shows were approached in a directly analogous manner, despite the fact that one was a self-proclaimed revue and the other a musical comedy with a book.

5. See Suriano, *Gershwin in His Time*, pp. 21–22. The author of the review is Frank Vreeland.

6. For examples, see Kimball and Simon, *The Gershwins*, p. 43, and Suriano, *Gershwin in His Time*, p. 22. The Suriano example shows a London publication demonstrating that, by the time *Lady, Be Good!* crossed the Atlantic (in 1926), the show had become so closely associated with the Astaires that their names were featured prominently, along with a picture of the siblings dancing.

7. This page is reproduced in *The Songs of George and Ira Gershwin: A Centennial Celebration*, vol. 1 (Miami, 1998), p. 11.

8. To cite just one well-known and highly regarded instance of this tendency, a collection of essays by the celebrated musicologist Richard Taruskin bears the title *Text and Act: Essays on Music and Performance* (New York, 1995).

9. Richard Crawford, *America's Musical Life: A History* (New York, 2001), pp. ix and x.

10. See Ethan Mordden, *Coming Up Roses: The Broadway Musical in the 1950s* (New York, 1998), p. 96 (footnote).

11. It could also be claimed that the successful "new Gershwin musicals" *My One and Only* (1983) and *Crazy for You* (1992) offered prototypes for this approach toward creating a show, insofar as the chief attraction of these musicals was the expansive repertoire of Gershwin songs they featured. These two Gershwin fests were supported by newly written books. The films *An American in Paris* (1951) and *Funny Face* (1957, with a script different from the book of the 1927 Gershwin show) might in turn be cited as precedents for the "new" Gershwin shows.

12. The Gershwin brothers had previously fashioned the score for a 1921 show, *A Dangerous Maid*, but it closed out of town. The only selection in the Broadway score for *Lady, Be Good!* that was not solely the work of George and Ira Gershwin was "Swiss Miss," for which Arthur Jackson is credited as colyricist with Ira. The reason for this anomaly helps illuminate once again the performer-centered nature of this show: Fred and Adele Astaire needed a crowd-rousing "11 o'clock number," and for this purpose Ira was asked to revise the lyrics of a preexisting specialty number that George had written with Jackson. (See the notes by Deena Rosenberg in the booklet accompanying the 1992 restoration of *Lady, Be Good!* on Elektra Nonesuch CD 79308-2, p. 29.) When *Lady, Be Good!* opened in London in 1926, three new songs were added— among them the enduring "I'd Rather Charleston," which represented an obvious effort to keep the show both fresh and current—and for these George turned to lyricists other than Ira.

13. In his autobiography, Fred Astaire wrote "I was convinced that the new sound of Ohman and Arden's two pianos . . . had a lot to do with the over-all success of *Lady, Be Good!*" See Astaire's *Steps in Time*, p. 129.

14. Mordden, *Make Believe*, p. 31.

15. Astaire made a recording of this song in 1926, with Gershwin at the piano, and his tap dancing breaks may be heard on it. It has been reissued on the CD *The Ultimate George Gershwin*, vol. 2.

16. For his *Scandals of 1922*, George White even offered Gershwin the opportunity to write an extended dramatic number, the "one-act opera" *Blue Monday*. Although it was unsuccessful with the public, was withdrawn after the opening night on Broadway, and is not an accomplished work aesthetically, *Blue Monday* did force the young composer to experiment with the musical delineation of character and incident over a long

and uninterrupted span of time, and this novel experience proved invaluable to his development.

17. Fortunately, much of *Primrose* was recorded by members of the original cast shortly after its opening, and the CD reissue of this material on *The Ultimate George Gershwin*, vol. 1 (Pearl GEM 0113, issued in 2001) enables listeners to hear this very British Gershwin score performed in the appropriate style.

18. Desmond Carter later provided lyrics for two new songs in the London production of *Lady, Be Good!*, including "I'd Rather Charleston."

19. These recordings are all conveniently collected on *The Ultimate George Gershwin*, vol. 2.

20. Elektra Nonesuch 79308-2, issued in 1992.

21. Ira Gershwin, letter to Lou and Emily Paley, in Kimball and Simon, *The Gershwins*, p. 40.

22. Astaire, *Steps in Time*, p. 126.

23. Ibid., pp. 126–27 and 128.

24. Rosenberg, *Fascinating Rhythm*, pp. 80–81.

25. Ibid., pp. 78 and 80.

26. Kay Swift, liner notes for CBS Records CD MK 42240, a reissue of a 1977 recording (*Rhapsody in Blue* and other works by Gershwin, conducted by Michael Tilson Thomas), p. 7.

27. Rosenberg, *Fascinating Rhythm*, p. 81.

28. Tommy Krasker, "A Wonderful Party: *Lady, Be Good!*" essay in the booklet accompanying Krasker's recorded restoration of the musical (Nonesuch 79308-2), p. 16.

29. Mordden, *Make Believe*, p. 32.

30. Krasker, "A Wonderful Party," pp. 15 and 16.

31. Ibid., p. 18.

32. See note 12 above.

33. Behrman, *People in a Diary*, p. 247.

34. Astaire, *Steps in Time*, p. 55.

35. Woollcott's review appeared in the *New York World*, November 23, 1927, and is reprinted in Suriano, *Gershwin in His Time*, p. 50.

36. Astaire, *Steps in Time*, pp. 127 and 128.

37. Rosenberg, *Fascinating Rhythm*, p. 107.

38. Mordden, *Make Believe*, p. 30.

39. Goldberg, *Gershwin*, pp. 264–65.

40. For a summary history of "The Man I Love," see note 3 for chap. 2.

41. The source for this discussion is the libretto for *Lady, Be Good!* "corrected to Dec. 6, 1924 by William Ritter, Stage Manager" in the general collection of the Music Division of the Library of Congress. (It should be noted that the synopsis by Evan Ross that appears in the booklet accompanying the 1992 Nonesuch recording, pp. 31–32, differs in certain respects from this libretto.)

42. Ibid., act 1, p. 2 and p. 19, respectively.

43. Ibid., act 1, p. 17 and p. 30, respectively. The lyrics for *Lady, Be Good!* are reprinted in the booklet accompanying the 1992 Nonesuch recording.

44. Rosenberg attributes this phrase to female impersonator Bert Savoy (Rosenberg, *Fascinating Rhythm*, pp. 98–99).

45. Perhaps the book's most shameless touch of illogic occurs shortly before the end of act 1. When Susie agrees to Watkins's scheme, he hands her a "little red book" that is supposed to tell her everything she will need to know to impersonate a Mexican widow (libretto, act 1, p. 48).

46. Ibid., act 2, pp. 42–44.

47. Significantly, the book does not even refer to him as "Jeff" for this act 2 "speciality" [*sic*], but as "Cliff Edwards" (ibid., act 2, p. 50). Edwards's voice will still be familiar to many as that of Jiminy Cricket in the famous Walt Disney movie *Pinocchio* (1940).

48. These categories have been established solely for the purposes of this book, and in any case should not be viewed as hard and fast, even in reference to *Lady, Be Good!* Certainly there are numbers, here and in other Gershwin shows, that straddle these categories and are consequently more or less problematic to typecast.

49. In the Nonesuch recording of Tommy Krasker's restoration, Susie sings a brief reprise of "Hang On to Me" as part of the act 1 finale, following the "wedding bells" ensemble and prior to the recurrence of "Oh, Lady Be Good!" This material is not present in the libretto of December 6, 1924.

50. The libretto does not specify whether "Fascinating Rhythm" is to be sung as well as danced at the conclusion of act 1, providing only the direction "Work dance up to big climax" (libretto, act 1, p. 49). In the Nonesuch restoration, the full ensemble sings the complete refrain of "Fascinating Rhythm" to end the act. Considering especially the parallel this creates with the end of act 2, it seems a convincing decision; indeed, it is difficult to imagine an act 1 finale for a 1920s musical comedy that would fail to include singing at its climax.

51. The libretto describes Edwards's "speciality" as follows: "He sings three or four numbers, one of which is 'Little Jazz Bird'" (libretto, act 2, p. 50). The lyrics for "Little Jazz Bird" (only) follow. Presumably the other numbers had no specified relationship to anything else in *Lady, Be Good!* and, subject only to Edwards's pleasure, may well have varied over the run of the show or even among successive performances. Edwards had a string of hit records immediately preceding and throughout the run of *Lady, Be Good!* (including a version of "Hard-Hearted Hannah" in 1924); some of these were performances of Gershwin songs ("Fascinating Rhythm" and "Oh, Lady Be Good!" as well as "Somebody Loves Me," from *George White's Scandals of 1924*—all hits for Edwards in 1925), but many were not. It stands to reason that the audiences for *Lady, Be Good!* heard some selections by composers other than Gershwin during Edwards's specialty number.

52. In the Nonesuch recording, Jack introduces the finale by singing a reprise of "Oh, Lady Be Good!" This material is not present in the libretto of December 6, 1924.

53. As Deena Rosenberg points out, this expression of the sibling bond doubtless had deep resonance for the Gershwin brothers as well as for the Astaires. See Rosenberg, *Fascinating Rhythm*, p. 86.

54. Libretto, act 1, p. 42. In the published sheet music, this substitution is not present, and the number becomes in effect an all-purpose song of romantic longing. In the Nonesuch restoration, "Oh, Lady, Be Good!" opens with a verse tailored to the plot situation, but this material is nowhere present in the libretto of December 6, 1924.

55. This is quoted in Kimball and Simon, *The Gershwins*, p. 43.

56. Libretto, act 1, p. 49. This remark refers to the fact that Jeff's initial performance of "Fascinating Rhythm" also interrupts a sibling quarrel (libretto, act 1, pp. 29–30).

57. Ibid., act 1, p. 48.

58. Another clever feature of the libretto involves its instructions for the placement of the two pianos used in the score. As the long party scene at Jo Vanderwater's estate begins (act 1, scene 3), the pianos are present on the stage but they are "masked from view by hedges, same constructed so they can be moved in finale revealing pianos" (ibid., act 1, p. 13). The audience doubtless assumed that the piano music heard during the party was coming from the pit, and was appropriately surprised by the "discovery of pianos" onstage (ibid., act 1, p. 46), presenting the occasion for Ohman and Arden's "piano speciality." (The libretto represents the duo piano music as commencing the act 1 finale, but the specialty number is listed separately in table 3.1 to distinguish it from the ensuing music, which accompanies stage action.)

59. Rosenberg, *Fascinating Rhythm*, p. 87, points out the unmistakable kinship of mm. 7–8 to the opening phrase of W. C. Handy's "St. Louis Blues." Unless this represents a kind of in-joke on Gershwin's part, it is unclear what the significance of the "quotation" might be in this context. Since both Handy and Gershwin were employing rather common melodic formulas in the respective measures of their songs, it could be questioned whether Gershwin's "quote" of Handy was intentional.

60. In the printed score, the blue note figure in m. 8 of the refrain (on "Forever and a day") does not recur in either of the subsequent A sections—which are otherwise literal repetitions of the opening music. In the libretto of December 6, 1924, however, the lyrics "For ever [sic] and a day" recur at the close of the refrain, along with two additional lines ("We'll make December May / That's all I have to say") that are not found at all in the published music (libretto, act 1, pp. 9–10). In their 1926 recording of "Hang On to Me," Fred and Adele Astaire conclude their performance by singing "Forever and a day" and the two additional lines, all to the music of m. 8. (This recording was reissued on the CD *The Ultimate George Gershwin*, vol. 2.)

61. An effective analysis of the music and lyrics of "Fascinating Rhythm" may be found in Rosenberg, *Fascinating Rhythm*, pp. 92–96. Also see Allen Forte's astute and accessible discussion in his *Listening to Classic American Popular Songs* (New Haven, CT, 2001), pp. 28–37.

62. The lyrics appear here as printed in Kimball, *Complete Lyrics*, p. 48.

63. This is not counting *Rosalie*, Gershwin's collaboration with Sigmund Romberg, which opened on Broadway in January 1928 and achieved a run of 335 performances. For the purposes of this book, a "Gershwin musical" is a show whose musical score is exclusively the work of Gershwin.

64. Lawrence's performance of "Someone to Watch Over Me" was apparently compelling enough to withstand the song's relocation, during the pre-Broadway run of *Oh, Kay!* in Philadelphia, to a position in the show where it made little sense. Originally placed early in act 1, prior to Kay's hoped for but unexpected reunion with Jimmy Winter, the song was moved to act 2, with the result that Kay now seemed to be anticipating in song a reunion that had already occurred. See the notes by Tommy Krasker in the booklet accompanying his recorded restoration of *Oh, Kay!* (Nonesuch 79361-2, issued in 1995), p. 22. Gershwin himself made a contribution to the distinctive flavor of "Someone to Watch Over Me" by providing Lawrence with a "strange-looking" doll to

hold while singing it; see Kimball and Simon, *The Gershwins*, p. 75. This prop may well have given the number just the tinge of playfulness necessary to prevent it from totally disrupting the mood of the show.

65. These numbers can all be heard on Krasker's Nonesuch recording.

66. The refrain of "Fidgety Feet" incorporates some distinctive formal nuances into its ABAC pattern. In the second A, the last four measures are positioned a minor third higher than in the first A section, creating in effect an ABA'C form. And the B as well as the C section make reference to the characteristic A motif.

67. Krasker characterizes *Girl Crazy* as "a vehicle with its roots in vaudeville: a show built around personalities, some of whom varied their routines from week to week." See the booklet accompanying his 1990 restoration of the score on Nonesuch 9 79250-2, p. 42.

68. A succinct history of the genesis of *Girl Crazy* is offered in Miles Kreuger's essay "Some Words about *Girl Crazy*," ibid., pp. 15–24.

69. An early version of the book in the general collection of the Music Division of the Library of Congress, dated July 28, 1930 (less than three months before the Broadway opening of *Girl Crazy* on October 14), includes an extensive role for "Chesty Perkins" (the Bert Lahr character) and presents Kate Fothergill (the part eventually given to Ethel Merman) as a minor role. "Chesty" became Gieber Goldfarb in the Broadway script (played by comedian Willie Howard). The part of "June West," Chesty's love interest in the version of July 28, 1930, seems to have been removed completely from the book en route to Broadway.

70. Kimball and Simon memorably quip that "*Girl Crazy* was about as Western as West End Avenue" (*The Gershwins*, p. 125).

71. In fact the script of July 28, 1930, calls for the Ginger Rogers character to enter riding "on a bronco" (act 1, p. 4).

72. Accounts differ concerning the exact personnel of the band. My source here is Richard M. Sudhalter's essay in the booklet accompanying the Nonesuch recording of *Girl Crazy*, p. 53. According to Sudhalter, Goodman left the band during the Broadway run of the show and was replaced by Jimmy Dorsey (p. 55). Miles Kreuger states baldly: "With Robert Russell Bennett's orchestrations, the Nichols group captured the vivacious spirit of the Gershwin tunes in a fashion that shrieked NOW! NOW! NOW!" ("Some Words about *Girl Crazy*," p. 22).

73. It is noteworthy that the July 28, 1930, script for *Girl Crazy* calls for a "Number: 'Someone to Watch Over Me' type" at precisely the point in the story where "But Not for Me" would eventually be used in the Broadway show. See the script, act 2, p. 5.

74. The verses Ira Gershwin provided for "Bidin' My Time" contain clever references to recently popular songs, such as "Tip Toe through the Tulips," "Singin' in the Rain," and "Cryin' for the Carolines," and George's music incorporates some appropriate motivic responses to these references. Such references were another obvious way for *Girl Crazy* to say "now" to its audiences.

CHAPTER 4. Entr'acte

1. Some recent examples of such writing include chapters 5, 7, 9, and 10 of Steven E. Gilbert's *The Music of Gershwin* (New Haven, CT, 1995), which offers a

sophisticated analytical approach; my own essay, "Musings on 'Nice Gershwin Tunes,' Form, and Harmony in the Concert Music of Gershwin" in *The Gershwin Style: New Looks at the Music of George Gershwin*, edited by Wayne Schneider, pp. 95–110 (New York, 1999); and the considerable quantity of material about the concert music in Pollack, *Gershwin*. See also the provocative evaluation of Gershwin in Joseph Horowitz's *Classical Music in America: A History of Its Rise and Fall* (New York, 2005), pp. 463–72.

2. See Carol Oja, *Making Music Modern: New York in the 1920s* (New York, 2000), pp. 320–23.

3. See Goldberg, *Gershwin*, p. 139.

4. It is possible to regard the "Charleston" episode of *An American in Paris* as something like a specialty number, insofar as its occurrence is quite unexpected and its thematic material is confined to a discrete section of the work. All other major themes of *An American in Paris* are restated in the final section. However, the "Charleston" episode is itself a substantial passage, exceeding sixty measures in length and incorporating several subsections and two repetitions of its main theme, so any analogy with the trumpet tune at rehearsal number 9 in *Rhapsody in Blue* would necessarily be very imprecise.

5. Gershwin employed the phrase "metropolitan madness" in describing *Rhapsody in Blue*, but it seems at least equally apt for characterizing the Paris portrayed in his later composition. See Goldberg, *Gershwin*, p. 139.

6. Any reader who doubts this statement would be well directed to chapter 5 of E. M. Forster's *Howards End*, in which a brilliant exegesis of the dramatic implications of Beethoven's Fifth Symphony is itself employed by the author to illuminate the character of Helen.

CHAPTER 5. Something Completely Different

1. A piano reduction of the overture appears in the published piano-vocal score of *Of Thee I Sing* (New York, 1932), which is the source for all musical information and examples in this chapter.

2. From the *New York Times* of May 3, 1932, quoted in Wayne Joseph Schneider, "George Gershwin's Political Operettas *Of Thee I Sing* (1931) and *Let 'Em Eat Cake* (1933), and Their Role in Gershwin's Musical and Emotional Maturing" (PhD diss., Cornell University, 1985), p. 203.

3. See Pollack, *Gershwin*, p. 513.

4. This is quoted in Kimball and Simon, *The Gershwins*, p. 146. A source for the remark is not given, but presumably it predates the creation of *Porgy and Bess*.

5. A virtually complete recording of the score for *Of Thee I Sing*—and a very fine one—may be found in the two-CD set that pairs this work with its sequel *Let 'Em Eat Cake* (CBS M2K 42522, released in 1987). The recording, conducted by Michael Tilson Thomas, is the fruit of revivals of both musicals produced in 1987 at the Brooklyn Academy of Music.

6. It is true that the two versions of Gershwin's *Strike Up the Band* offered a precedent for politically satirical music theater, but *Of Thee I Sing* is a different and a much more unified, singular, and self-assured creation. *Of Thee I Sing* also differs significantly from its sequel, *Let 'Em Eat Cake*; the relationships among all of Gershwin's political musicals will receive some attention later in this chapter.

7. The most thorough account of the genesis of *Of Thee I Sing* may be found in Schneider, "Gershwin's Political Operettas," pp. 166–77.

8. From the *New York Herald Tribune* of April 10, 1932, as quoted in ibid., p. 197.

9. The April 1932 date is confirmed both in ibid., p. 206, note 111, and in Pollack, *Gershwin*, p. 513. The best modern edition of the libretto may be found in *Kaufman & Co.: Broadway Comedies*, published by the Library of America (New York, 2004), pp. 369–468, which also reprints the original foreword by critic George Jean Nathan on pp. 900–901—in which Nathan claims that, with *Of Thee I Sing*, "American musical comedy enters at length upon a new, original and independent lease of life." This modern edition, edited by Laurence Maslon, is the source for all information about and quotations from the libretto in this chapter.

10. Schneider, "Gershwin's Political Operettas," p. 206, note 111.

11. *Of Thee I Sing* was in fact the third complete piano-vocal score of a Gershwin musical to appear, following close upon the publication of *Strike Up the Band* (revised version) and *Girl Crazy*.

12. *Kaufman & Co.*, pp. 378–79.

13. Ibid., p. 382.

14. Ibid., p. 394.

15. Ibid., p. 457.

16. Ibid., p. 467.

17. Ethan Mordden, *Sing for Your Supper: The Broadway Musical in the 1930s* (New York, 2005), p. 2.

18. Ibid., pp. 155–59.

19. Pollack, *Gershwin*, p. 504.

20. See Schneider, "Gershwin's Political Operettas," pp. 166–69. A curious footnote to the history of *Of Thee I Sing* lies in a plagiarism suit brought by writer Walter Lowenfels, who claimed that the show borrowed extensively from his own preexisting script for *U.S.A. with Music*. The suit was unsuccessful. For details, see ibid., pp. 206–13, or Pollack, *Gershwin*, pp. 513–14.

21. Among the pictures projected on a screen during the election night scene (act 1, scene 5) is one of "An Unidentified Man"; a parenthetical direction in the script indicates that he "looks suspiciously like the vice-presidential candidate." See *Kaufman & Co.*, p. 412.

22. Ibid., p. 444.

23. Two examples of this from *Of Thee I Sing*: the chairman of the committee that is choosing the winner of the Atlantic City beauty contest in act 1, scene 3, announces that "The committee will now state its reasons—with music!" (ibid., p. 395); and Wintergreen admires his own performance of "Who Cares?" in act 2, scene 1, asking "Did you hear that F sharp I gave them?" (ibid., p. 434).

24. Gerald Mast, *Can't Help Singin': The American Musical on Stage and Screen* (Woodstock, NY, 1987), p. 77.

25. Ibid., pp. 80–82.

26. See Schneider, "Gershwin's Political Operettas," p. 195, on the opening-night review by Brooks Atkinson in the *New York Times* (which is quoted at length); see Rosenberg, *Fascinating Rhythm*, p. 205, for a recent affirmation of the scope of Gershwin's contribution.

27. Stanley Green, *Broadway Musicals of the 30s* (reprint of *Ring Bells! Sing Songs! Broadway Musicals of the Thirties*, originally published in New Rochelle, NY, 1971), p. 41.

28. Pollack, *Gershwin*, p. 500. Philip Furia, in his *Ira Gershwin: The Art of the Lyricist* (New York, 1996), p. 91, states that George's music preceded the lyrics for only two numbers in *Of Thee I Sing*, namely the title song and "Love Is Sweeping the Country," but he doesn't directly cite a source for this information.

29. A perfect and well-known example from an instrumental work is the single-bar opening motif of *An American in Paris*. Its open-ended nature made it suitable for employment in an extended piece. Combined with its 2/4 meter and its French associations, it was also irresistible to Gershwin for employment in *Of Thee I Sing* to accompany the arrival of the French ambassador. And so there arose another quotation to grace the score of the new musical.

30. Schneider, "Gershwin's Political Operettas," pp. 221–24, finds in "Wintergreen for President" a "modified sonata form"; despite my admiration for Schneider's work, I find this notion far-fetched.

31. It is indicative of how uncommon 2/4 meter became, in the age of the foxtrot and afterward, that the ever-popular "Swanee" was eventually reprinted in 2/2 time, and it appears as such in some modern collections (such as *The Great Songs of George Gershwin*, Secaucus, NJ, n.d., pp. 63–65).

32. The reader may well wonder how much functional difference there is between 2/4 and 2/2 meter; obviously anything written in the former could be just as easily written in the latter simply by doubling all the note values. However, the written combination of 2/4 meter with sixteenth-note values (as in "Wintergreen for President") or even thirty-second-note values (as in the first part of the Atlantic City scene, the portions identified in the libretto as "The Dimple on My Knee" and "Because, Because") can suggest a comic urgency to the performers that might not be conveyed visually were the passages to be rewritten in 2/2.

33. Comparisons between *Of Thee I Sing* and the Gilbert and Sullivan operettas have been made frequently, beginning with some of the first commentators on the Gershwin work. An effective summary of the early critical material relevant to this issue is given by Schneider, "Gershwin's Political Operettas," pp. 189–92, who sensibly concludes that while *Of Thee I Sing* "struck stylistic nerves reminiscent of the Gilbert & Sullivan English operetta school," nevertheless "the unrelenting satiric tone of the book and the jazzy style of [Gershwin's] music sounded strains distinctly American."

34. For a thorough analysis of the number, and indeed of the entire score and of much else related to *Of Thee I Sing* and to Gershwin's other political musicals, see Schneider, "Gershwin's Political Operettas." It is a pity that Schneider has never condensed his thesis and published it as a book, for it remains the best source of information on these works in every respect.

35. Further instances of employing the waltz for parodic effect occur in act 2, scene 3, which presents two waltzes virtually back to back: the deliberately excessive pathos of Diana's "Jilted" is counterpoised by the deliberately excessive exuberance of Mary's Viennese dance, "I'm About to Be a Mother" (described in the libretto as "such a gay song"; see *Kaufman & Co.*, p. 453).

36. In addition to the two recitatives shown in table 5.1, there are brief passages

of recitative within two of the subdivisions (in 6, a recitative for Wintergreen, just preceding the change to 3/4 meter; in 8, a recitative for Diana, just preceding the repetition of Wintergreen's tune). These brief passages also simultaneously highlight text and create musical transitions. An analogous technique, found at points in the extended number under discussion and elsewhere in the score, is the occasional placement of spoken text over ongoing music.

37. It might be argued that the opening number of act 2 ("Hello, Good Morning"), in which the White House secretaries exchange bromides, produces an effect of deliberate triviality. But this is precisely the point: the number plays an essential role in establishing that absolutely nothing of any importance goes on in the Wintergreen administration.

38. Ira Gershwin, in his *Lyrics on Several Occasions*, p. 307, states that Wintergreen's solo at this point, "Here's a Kiss for Cinderella," is "a takeoff on the bachelor-farewell type of song, best exemplified by John Golden and Ivan Caryll's 'Goodbye, Girls, I'm Through' ([from] *Chin-Chin*, 1914)." Presumably the original audience for *Of Thee I Sing* would have recognized the parodic intent of this music and its lyrics.

39. *Kaufman & Co.*, p. 408.

40. See the note in the vocal score, p. 66; nevertheless, the verse appears in the score (pp. 66–67), and its lyrics are printed with those of the refrain in Ira Gershwin's *Lyrics on Several Occasions*, p. 351, and in the libretto in *Kaufman & Co.*, p. 408. The verse is not without interest, especially from a musical standpoint. Beginning in E-flat major, it modulates to G major, which eventually becomes the dominant of the refrain's C major. The vocal line of the verse begins, however, with four measures of a single repeated pitch—obviously no match for the stunning opening of the refrain.

41. Is there just the slightest hint here that love actually conquers all? Not for George S. Kaufman, who thought that the show was all about "kidding love," but composer Gershwin apparently felt otherwise, telling Kaufman that "when John P. Wintergreen faces impeachment to stand by the girl he married, that's championing love—and the audience knows it." The conversation is quoted in Jablonski and Stewart, *The Gershwin Years: George and Ira*, pp. 171–72; see also Rosenberg, *Fascinating Rhythm*, p. 238, and Pollack, *Gershwin*, p. 504.

42. Krasker's work sought to restore the original (1927) version, although both the recording and the score offer an appendix of numbers that were created for the second version of *Strike Up the Band*. The recording is a 2-CD set, Elektra Nonesuch 79273-2, released in 1991; the score, "an undertaking of the Leonore S. Gershwin—Library of Congress Recording and Publication Project," bears no publication date (but the critical notes at the back of the score are dated March 1995). While the score represents a remarkable achievement in many respects, and the recording is delightful, this restoration necessitated a considerable amount of conjecture; in his critical notes to the score, Steven D. Bowen admits that "the exact form of the show was lost, probably forever" (p. i). Bowen's notes, along with the material in the booklet accompanying the recording, are enlightening for anyone who seeks to understand the many complexities involved in an attempt to restore *Strike Up the Band*. It is unfortunate that a complete recording of the restored 1930 score that apparently formed part of this same large project (see Krasker's notes in the booklet accompanying the recording, p. 20) has never appeared.

43. *Let 'Em Eat Cake, a Sequel to "Of Thee I Sing," a Musical Play by George S. Kaufman and Morrie Ryskind: Lyrics by Ira Gershwin, Illustrated by Donald McKay* (New York, 1933). This libretto was published as a book by Alfred A. Knopf, the publisher previously of the libretto for *Of Thee I Sing.*

44. The restored score can be heard in the 2-CD set CBS M2K 42522, paired with *Of Thee I Sing* (released in 1987); see note 5 above for this chapter.

45. This fact is unfortunately underlined in the 1987 recording of *Let 'Em Eat Cake*, in which the response to the libretto's concluding call for an unspecified "reprise" (*Let 'Em Eat Cake* libretto, p. 241) is an ensemble rendition of "Of Thee I Sing." The listener who knows the earlier show is forcibly reminded of what is missing from the sequel.

46. Pollack gives a thorough account of the various noteworthy *Of Thee I Sing* revivals (*Gershwin*, pp. 515–18).

47. See chapter 3, note 2.

48. All of Gershwin's major instrumental works for the concert hall are sui generis creations in terms of his output (and, in some cases, arguably in broader terms as well): *Rhapsody in Blue*, the Concerto in F (Gershwin's only concerto), *An American in Paris* (his only tone poem), the *Second Rhapsody* (utterly unlike *Rhapsody in Blue* in structure and character), the *Cuban Overture* (featuring a distinctive grouping of percussion instruments), and *Variations on "I Got Rhythm"* (his only set of variations, and the only concert work based on one of his songs).

CHAPTER 6. The Nonpareil

1. Heyward himself had obstacles to overcome in portraying Catfish Row convincingly, as he was a white man of aristocratic descent. But Heyward was also a native of Charleston who had worked among the city's black residents and whose mother took an active interest in Gullah culture, and consequently he had a much less daunting task than Gershwin. See the afterword by James M. Hutchisson in the Banner Book edition of Heyward's *Porgy* (Jackson, MS, 2001).

2. The best and most thorough published treatment of *Porgy and Bess* is in chapters 31–34 of Pollack, *Gershwin*. Pollack analyzes the work dramatically and musically, extensively discusses the first production and its reception, covers its many revivals, and treats the 1959 movie, concert performances, and recordings; this is exhaustive and insightful scholarship. Hollis Alpert's *The Life and Times of "Porgy and Bess": The Story of an American Classic* (New York, 1990) is an experienced journalist's account focusing on the opera's production history. This is the only published book to date that deals exclusively with *Porgy and Bess* and, while offering much valuable information, it lacks scholarly documentation, so the reader ultimately must trust Alpert's authority. Published articles on *Porgy and Bess*, ranging from the scholarly to the anecdotal, are far too numerous to list here. Among unpublished doctoral dissertations, two should be mentioned, however: John Andrew Johnson's massive study "Gershwin's 'American Folk Opera': The Genesis, Style, and Reputation of 'Porgy and Bess' (1935)" (Harvard University, 1996), and Gwynne Kuhner Brown's "Problems of Race and Genre in the Critical Reception of *Porgy and Bess*" (University of Washington, 2006), in which Brown offers particularly astute coverage of the reception of Gershwin's work by African American writers and performers.

3. See Jablonski and Stewart, *The Gershwin Years: George and Ira*, pp. 112–15.

4. The most thorough account of Gershwin's abandoned *Dybbuk* project is in Pollack, *Gershwin*, pp. 461–63.

5. See the letter of November 12, 1933, to Gershwin from Heyward, reprinted in Wyatt and Johnson, *George Gershwin Reader*, p. 204.

6. See Pollack, *Gershwin*, p. 600. Gershwin's commitment to Bubbles was such that he personally taught the gifted but musically illiterate performer his part by rote. (See also Jablonski and Stewart, *The Gershwin Years: George and Ira*, p. 227.)

7. In his article "Rhapsody in Catfish Row," first published in the *New York Times* of October 20, 1935, and reprinted in Suriano, *Gershwin in His Time*, pp. 112–14, Gershwin wrote that "when I chose *Porgy and Bess*, a tale of Charleston Negroes, for a subject, I made sure that it would enable me to write light as well as serious music and that it would enable me to include humor as well as tragedy" (Suriano, p. 112).

8. A fine modern edition of the novel has been published under the auspices of the University Press of Mississippi (2001). All succeeding references to the novel will be to this edition.

9. "Happy dust" is identified as cocaine on p. 79 of Heyward, *Porgy*.

10. Ibid., p. 16.

11. A modern edition of the play is not readily available at the time of this writing. I used the text as published in *Famous American Plays of the 1920s*, selected and introduced by Kenneth MacGowan (New York, 1959; new Dell edition, 1967), pp. 207–307.

12. Heyward, *Porgy* (novel), p. 157.

13. In the novel, Sportin' Life is given a background as (he claims) a waiter in a New York hotel, but this remains a relatively minor detail (ibid., p. 50).

14. Text as in *Famous American Plays of the 1920s*, p. 210.

15. Heyward, *Porgy* (novel), p. 21.

16. A collection of music sung in the play *Porgy* was published in 1928 in New York: *Spiritual Songs from the Theatre Guild Production of Porgy, a Folk Play by DuBose and Dorothy Heyward*, arranged and edited by George Shackley.

17. Heyward, *Porgy* (novel), p. 51.

18. It would be more exact to say that the white characters are provided in the score with musical rhythms and contours, but no specific pitches. Such notation may be the result more of practical necessity than anything else on Gershwin's part, since these passages are always placed in rapid alternation with accompanied sung material by the black characters. The composer is quoted in Jablonski and Stewart, *The Gershwin Years: George and Ira*, as follows: "I am trying to get a sensational dramatic effect. I hope to accomplish this by having the few whites in the production speak their lines while the Negroes, in answering, will sing" (p. 222). In practice the white characters' parts tend to be performed quite freely in an everyday speech–like manner.

19. Ira Gershwin wrote the lyrics for "Oh, I Can't Sit Down," "I Ain't Got No Shame," "It Ain't Necessarily So," "Oh, Hev'nly Father" (the six-voice prayer), "A Red Headed Woman," "There's a Boat Dat's Leavin' Soon for New York," and "Oh, Bess, Oh Where's My Bess?" and collaborated with DuBose Heyward in fashioning the lyrics for "I Got Plenty o' Nuttin'," "Bess, You Is My Woman," and "I Wants to Stay Here." DuBose Heyward wrote all the remaining lyrics himself. No less an authority than Stephen Sondheim deemed Heyward's lyrics for *Porgy and Bess*, which include those for "Summer-

time" and "My Man's Gone Now," the "best lyrics ever written, I think, for the musical stage." See Pollack, *Gershwin*, p. 576.

20. See Jablonski and Stewart, *The Gershwin Years: George and Ira*, p. 222, where the source of the remark is identified as a "news release of July 7, 1934."

21. Gershwin, "Rhapsody in Catfish Row," in Suriano, *Gershwin in His Time*, p. 113.

22. Oscar Levant states that Gershwin "referred constantly" to the Wagner work "as a guide to the plotting of the choral parts and for general precepts in vocal writing" (Levant, *Smattering*, p. 190).

23. The opera is sometimes called *Blue Monday Blues*, although this is more properly the title of one of the songs in the work.

24. For those wishing to explore *Blue Monday*, a published vocal score is available (Secaucus, NJ, 1976 and 1993) and commercial recordings have been made.

25. "Rhapsody in Catfish Row," in Suriano, *Gershwin in His Time*, p. 112.

26. It is true that there are passages in "Rhapsody in Catfish Row" where Gershwin appears to be simultaneously speaking for and stereotyping African Americans, as when he refers to "the drama, the humor, the superstition, the religious fervor, the dancing, and the irrepressible high spirits of the race" (ibid.). He may have intended only to defend the suitability of Heyward's material for operatic treatment, but this doesn't lessen the problematic nature of such passages for twenty-first-century readers. While it cannot be known how Gershwin's contemporaries received this article, we should remember that Gershwin was not a professional prose writer, ethnomusicologist, or aesthetician; as a professional composer he expressed his ideas, feelings, and insights primarily through his music.

27. For "folk tale," see "Rhapsody in Catfish Row" (ibid.).

28. See "On Folly Island" in chapter 1 for a brief discussion of the most famous of these visits.

29. Heyward's description of the experience that inspired Gershwin's six-voice prayer sequences may be found in his article "Porgy and Bess Return on Wings of Song" (originally published in *Stage Magazine*, October, 1935); see Armitage, *Gershwin*, p. 40.

30. See Kimball and Simon, *The Gershwins*, p. 173, which gives a date of November 12, 1933, for Heyward's letter.

31. The stage direction is from the published vocal score of *Porgy and Bess* (New York, 1935), p. 4. This score is the source for all musical descriptions and examples to follow.

32. Ibid., p. 1. (The orchestral manuscript provides the proper spelling: *risoluto*.)

33. The "Buzzard Song" is often omitted from *Porgy and Bess*, a practice that dates back to the first production, when concerns about the opera's overall length and about preserving Todd Duncan's voice for frequent performances resulted in extensive cuts. (See Jablonski and Stewart, *The Gershwin Years: George and Ira*, p. 229.) I am incorporating the "Buzzard Song" into this discussion because it enhances understanding of the scope and complexity of Gershwin's musical vision for Porgy, and also simply because I think it is a fine piece that merits inclusion in any performance of the opera.

34. This is not to say that Porgy lacks a musical personality prior to act 2, scene 1. In the first scene of act 1, he sings the brief but poignant, arioso-like "They Pass By Singin'," and later the recitative "Oh Little Stars" (which anticipates melodic and harmonic features of "I Got Plenty o' Nuttin'") as an incantation over the dice during the crap game.

But neither of these assumes the form of a finished song; their inclusion in the "Index of Songs, Arias and Themes" in the vocal score points rather to the presence in them of important themes heard later in the opera. Porgy also participates significantly in the community songs of act 1, scene 2, but the only solo number in this scene is quite properly given to the bereaved widow Serena.

35. See note 18 for this chapter.

CHAPTER 7. An Unintended Hollywood Coda

1. For a good brief overview of this last period in the composer's life, see Kimball and Simon, *The Gershwins*, pp. 199–200.

2. Pollack, *Gershwin*, p. 677.

3. See Gershwin's letter to Isaac Goldberg (May 12, 1937), quoted in Jablonski and Stewart, *The Gershwin Years: George and Ira*, p. 281. In this letter Gershwin rather uncharacteristically complains even about the singing of Fred Astaire and Ginger Rogers in the movie—perhaps an indication of how out of sorts he was feeling about his Hollywood experience.

4. Goldberg, *Gershwin*, p. 342.

5. Ironically, it is these two "defining" numbers to which Gershwin might have been referring when he lamented to Isaac Goldberg, in the May 12 letter, that in *Shall We Dance* "They literally throw one or two songs away without any kind of a plug." This is Howard Pollack's interpretation; see Pollack, *Gershwin*, p. 675. John Mueller, in his *Astaire Dancing: The Musical Films* (New York, 1985), also ties Gershwin's complaint directly to "They Can't Take That Away from Me" (p. 123, note 8).

6. See Goldberg, *Gershwin*, p. 343, and Jablonski and Stewart, *The Gershwin Years: George and Ira*, p. 281. It is unknown to what extent the filmmakers did or did not encourage and enjoy Gershwin's involvement, atypical for a Hollywood songwriter, in at least some of the instrumental music for *Shall We Dance*.

7. John Mueller astutely points out (*Astaire Dancing*, pp. 122–23) that the immediately ensuing events in the movie seem completely to ignore the new compatibility between the protagonists that is established so well by "They All Laughed."

8. Pollack, *Gershwin*, p. 671.

9. Mast, *Can't Help Singin'*, pp. 158–59; Mueller, *Astaire Dancing*, pp. 115–25. Overall, Mueller is uncharacteristically dyspeptic about *Shall We Dance*, but he accords it the same remarkably thorough and penetrating treatment he gives to all of Astaire's musical films.

10. For discussions of Gershwin's last songs, see Steven E. Gilbert's "Nice Work: Thoughts and Observations on Gershwin's Last Songs," in Schneider, *The Gershwin Style*, pp. 67–94, and chapter 8 of Rosenberg's *Fascinating Rhythm*.

11. Ira Gershwin (1941), quoted in Rosenberg, *Fascinating Rhythm*, p. 352.

12. For a discussion of "Fascinating Rhythm," see chapter 3 in this book.

13. Gershwin characteristically prepares both the rhythmic motif that opens the refrain and the importance of the pitch E in the verse to "Shall We Dance?" (which, fortunately, is sung in the film). The melody of the verse begins with a rhythm identical to that which starts the refrain, while E minor temporarily emerges as an unexpected and emphasized key in the latter part of the verse.

14. Ira Gershwin, *Lyrics on Several Occasions*, p. 287.

15. The terms "cultivated" and "vernacular" are those of the late American music scholar H. Wiley Hitchcock; see any edition of his *Music in the United States: A Historical Introduction* (the most recent is the fourth edition, Upper Saddle River, NJ, 2000).

16. See Goldberg, *Gershwin*, p. 342.

17. Bernstein's brief essay is included as prefatory matter in Charles Schwartz's *Gershwin: His Life and Music* (Indianapolis, 1973). It should be noted that the tone of this essay, which by and large reflects a highly positive view of Gershwin on Bernstein's part, differs in significant ways from that of an earlier and frequently quoted Bernstein article, "Why Don't You Run Upstairs and Write a Nice Gershwin Tune?" which first appeared in *Atlantic Monthly* 195 (April 1955), pp. 39–42.

Credits

Photographs

Cover: Courtesy of the Ira and Leonore Gershwin Trusts.

Figures 1.1, 1.2, 1.4, 2.1, 2.2, 3.2, 4.1, 4.2, 5.1, 7.1, 7.2: Courtesy of the Ira and Leonore Gershwin Trusts.

Figure 1.3: Reprinted through the courtesy of the Editors of TIME Magazine, © 2008 TIME Inc.

Figure 3.1: Museum of the City of New York, Theater Collection.

Figures 5.2, 5.3, 5.4, 6.1, 6.2, 6.3: Photos: Vandamm Studio. Museum of the City of New York, Theater Collection.

Musical Examples

"Bess, You Is My Woman Now": Words by Ira Gershwin and DuBose Heyward. Music by George Gershwin. In *The Great Songs of George Gershwin*. Secaucus, NJ: Warner Bros. Publications, n.d.

"Buzzard Song": Words by Ira Gershwin and DuBose Heyward. Music by George Gershwin. In *Porgy and Bess*. New York: Gershwin Publishing Corporation/Chappell & Co., 1935.

"Everybody Step": Words and Music by Irving Berlin. In *Irving Berlin Anthology*. Milwaukee: Hal Leonard, 1994.

"Fascinating Rhythm": Words by Ira Gershwin. Music by George Gershwin. In *The Great Songs of George Gershwin*. Secaucus, NJ: Warner Bros. Publications, n.d.

"Finaletto Scene IV Act I" [No. 3]: Words by Ira Gershwin. Music by George Gershwin. In *Of Thee I Sing*. New York: New World Music, 1932.

"From Now On": Words by Arthur J. Jackson and B. G. DeSylva. Music by George Gershwin. In *Rediscovered Gershwin*. Miami: Warner Bros. Publications, 1991.

"Hang On to Me": Words by Ira Gershwin. Music by George Gershwin. In *Gershwin on Broadway (from 1919 to 1933)*. Secaucus, NJ: Warner Bros. Publications, 1987.

"I Got Plenty o' Nuttin'": Words by Ira Gershwin and DuBose Heyward. Music by George Gershwin. In *The Great Songs of George Gershwin*. Secaucus, NJ: Warner Bros. Publications, n.d.

"I Loves You, Porgy": Words by Ira Gershwin and DuBose Heyward. Music by George Gershwin. In *Porgy and Bess*. New York: Gershwin Publishing Corporation/Chappell & Co., 1935.

"Love Walked In": Words by Ira Gershwin. Music by George Gershwin. In *The Great Songs of George Gershwin*. Secaucus, NJ: Warner Bros. Publications, n.d.

"The Man I Love": Words by Ira Gershwin. Music by George Gershwin. In *The Great Songs of George Gershwin*. Secaucus, NJ: Warner Bros. Publications, n.d.

"Of Thee I Sing": Words by Ira Gershwin. Music by George Gershwin. In *Of Thee I Sing*. New York: New World Music, 1932.

Rhapsody in Blue, by George Gershwin. In *The Complete Gershwin Keyboard Works*. Miami: Warner Bros. Publications, 1996.

"Shall We Dance?": Words by Ira Gershwin. Music by George Gershwin. In *The Songs of George and Ira Gershwin: A Centennial Celebration*, vol. 2. Miami: Warner Bros. Publications, 1998.

"They Didn't Believe Me": Words by Herbert Reynolds. Music by Jerome Kern. In *Jerome Kern Collection*. Milwaukee: Hal Leonard, n.d.

"What You Want wid Bess?": Words by Ira Gershwin and DuBose Heyward. Music by George Gershwin. In *Porgy and Bess*. New York: Gershwin Publishing Corporation/ Chappell & Co., 1935.

"Whip-Poor-Will": Words by Bud DeSylva. Music by Jerome Kern. In *Jerome Kern Collection*. Milwaukee: Hal Leonard, n.d.

"Who Cares?": Words by Ira Gershwin. Music by George Gershwin. In *Of Thee I Sing*. New York: New World Music, 1932.

"Wintergreen for President": Words by Ira Gershwin. Music by George Gershwin. In *Of Thee I Sing*. New York: New World Music, 1932.

General Index

Page numbers in italic type refer to photographs.

Index of Gershwin's Works